KU-511-105

PREVIOUS CONVICTIONS

Assignments from Here and There

A.A. GILL

Weidenfeld & Nicolson
LONDON

First published in Great Britain in 2006
by Weidenfeld & Nicolson

1 3 5 7 9 10 8 6 4 2

A CIP catalogue record for this book
is available from the British Library.

ISBN-13 978 0 297 85162 2
ISBN-10 0 297 85162 4

Typeset by Deltatype Ltd,
Birkenhead, Merseyside

Printed in Great Britain by
Clays Ltd, St Ives plc

Weidenfeld & Nicolson

The Orion Published Group Ltd
Orion House
5 Upper Saint Martin's Lane
London, WC2H 9EA

The Orion Publishing Group's policy is to use papers that are natural, renewable and recyclable products and made from wood grown in sustainable forests. The logging and manufacturing processes are expected to conform to the environmental regulations of the country of origin.

www.orionbooks.co.uk

For my sister Chloe, and Violet –
Cyril Connolly's granddaughter

Writing is solitary. Journalism is a gang activity. The joy of being a hack is that there is a back room of people far cleverer, more experienced and adept than I working to make me look clever, experienced and adept. If on occasion I fail to do so, naturally it's their fault. So I should begin by thanking some editors, all of whom have their fingerprints on this book: Robin Morgan, Steph Clark, Deirdre Fernand, Cathy Galvin, Lucas Hollweg, Helen Hawkins, Dylan Jones, Tiffany Darke, John Witherow, Alex Bilmes, Graydon Carter, Dana Brown, Anthea Lucas, Pat Nurse, Alan Samson, Alex Bulford and Lucinda McNeile. Also, the photographers I travel with whose contribution is always more than pictures: Matthew Donaldson, Peter Marlow, Tom Stoddart, Harriet Logan, Gigi Cohen and Tom Craig. I also want to thank my brightly stoical amanuensis Michelle Klepper, and agents Ed Victor and Grainne Fox; Diane von Furstenberg for designing the endpaper; Jeremy Clarkson for the double act. And, as ever and ever, my Nicola.

A.A. Gill

New York and Tirana, 2006

CONTENTS

FOREWORD

With the morning e-mail came the proof for the cover of this book, the picture you're holding now. I stared at it with that intense, freeform, aimless scrutiny that is specific and unique to authors regarding their books, as if they were the guts of some auspicious soothsaying chicken. Nobody judges a book by its cover as mercilessly or rigorously as the author. You may have noticed that it's a big picture of me. It seems to convey something of the contents, which are mostly my opinions. So all things considered, I was quietly pleased with it, and I sat and wallowed in that peculiar, authorial cocktail of airy vanity and earthly doubt, when a voice from beyond the office door shouted – with the merest glint of restrained irritation – that I needed to go out and get some cash for the cleaner right now. So I saved my face and trudged down to the cash machine at the garage.

On the way back, as I invariably do, I stopped to look in the window of a second-hand bookshop. There was a nice copy of *The Jungle Book*, a first edition on thin paper with the original illustrations by Kipling's father, and I thought I might get it. Beside it, another book caught my eye. There was something familiar. Something familiar and something wrong, like when the sergeant whispers, 'It's quiet, sir . . . far too quiet.'

The book was called *Previous Convictions*. It took a moment to catch up. Anyway, it did; it arrived all at once with a thud. I was looking at my book – already in a second-hand bookshop – except it wasn't my book because it didn't have a big picture of me on it.

It was a book with the same title as my book. And anyone who has ever written a book will know that finding a title is by far and away the hardest, most intellectually arduous, gut-wrenching, nerve-fraying and tear-jerking part of authorship. A title can make a book, raise it above the sum of its content; or it can damn it, be the dead weight that draws brilliant prose down to unread obscurity. Brevity is so much harder than loquacity. I don't know a writer who wouldn't swap half a dozen chapters for a winning title.

There is a necromancy about titles, they are a dark art. When writers meet at literary festivals, in green rooms and in the queue at Oddbins, what they ask each other nonchalantly, as if they were just being nice, is, 'What's it called?' Not, what's it about? What's its view? Is writing it like gestating the kraken? And they'll suck on the new title like a borrowed barley sugar.

There is no pain in the literary world as masochistically, self-despisingly painful as title envy. All authors have a secret list, a buried hoard of sure-fire, brilliant, memorable, posterity-guaranteeing titles – if only they could come up with the small inconvenience of a book to act as a plinth.

Only so many good-as-gold titles are allotted to a person of letters in an average lifetime, and *Previous Convictions* is one of mine. Or at least I thought it was mine. I stared at the usurping doppelgänger book and things got weirder. They couldn't have been any weirder if I'd been wearing Dorothy's red shoes. Not only had the past come to steal my title, but it was also for a collection of journalism. What are the odds on that? Not only was it a collection of journalism, but it was journalism from the *Sunday Times*; and not only was it from the *Sunday Times*, but from a critic on the *Sunday Times*. All of that was as naught on the international scale of weirdness, coincidence and serendipity, because the author was my father-in-law. Or would have been my father-in-law, briefly, if he'd lived to see me marry his daughter. Hand on my heart, I had never seen this book before.

So I called my editor. And after a long pause, he said, in a measured tone, like a consultant trying to make the best of an X-ray with a shadow the size of a grapefruit on it, 'Well, it isn't necessarily a terminal problem. Not necessarily. I remember several years back there were three books published simultaneously all called *Wish You Were Here*. I seem to remember they did OK.' Well they may have done. *Wish You Were Here* is a terrible title. The three of them probably huddled together for comfort. The stark fact is I can't plagiarise Cyril Connolly. 'No, well, if you say so. But we do need a title pretty sharpish. Have you seen the cover? Nice picture of you.'

It was desperate. I was desperate and press-ganged titles like a mad recruiting sergeant. Pathic, gimpy little things that couldn't run away fast enough. A roll-call of bumpkin puns and wide-boy glibs: *Brought to Book*; *The Naked Eye*; *Written Off*; *As If*. I rather fancied *As If* for ten minutes. *Sunday Best*; *Nothing Personal*; *Critical Mass*; *Looking Daggers*; *Wit Sunday*. Hopeless, all of them. In the first serious scuffle on the tables of Waterstone's or on Amazon's bloody field, they'd have collapsed and played dead. They all sounded remaindered.

So I did two things. I went and bought Cyril Connolly's book and *The Jungle Book*, which is a very nice edition, and also a very good title. Kipling is very good on titles. A thousand coolies on a thousand typewriters could tap away for a century before coming up with *Just So*. The second thing I did was I called Cressida Connolly, who, for an exciting, youthful moment, had been the first Mrs Gill, and I told her the story. And she laughed. And when I finished, she said, 'But you simply must use the title.' No I couldn't. 'You have to. It's a very, very good title, and it's perfect, and we should keep it in the family.' Really? 'Really.' Really, really? 'Really, really, really.'

There is no suspense at the end of this anecdote. You are holding the book. You already know how it begins, if not how it ends. So *Previous Convictions*, like the name of a ship, has been transferred from one barque to another. It carried Connolly's collection of paper souls and now it carries mine. But I am only the captain for a season. If any other Connollys or Gills want a name for a sheaf of thoughts and opinions, they're welcome to this one. We are, between us, an extended-titled family.

I read the original *Previous Convictions* and rediscovered what a supremely great critic Connolly was. The writing is precise and elegant, but never effete or pedantic. Rather muscly and exuberant, it fizzes and sings with enthusiasm. All memorable, worthwhile criticism grows out of enthusiasm. It can never be the schoolmaster's dry marginalia or the collector's pursed lip and raised brow; only if you love something can you be transported when it's done beautifully, and infuriated when it's made badly. Great criticism is cerebral *and* emotional. But it is the head that is the passenger and reads the map, and the heart that has the wheel.

Here

GLASTONBURY

What is it with hippies and fire? You only have to spark up a Zippo and four of them will come and stare contentedly into the flame. At Glastonbury they light up everywhere. In the field in front of the main stage while some deathless bit of old pop flotsam is offering his timeless classic in the middle of 300,000 swaying, wigged-out happy campers, you'll trip over a little family of hippies, cross-legged in front of an improvised bonfire, watching the salamanders and phoenixes in the flames with their third eyes. I saw a bloke stroll down one of the festival's makeshift ley-lines and just put a match to a pile of rubbish. It wasn't so much an act of pyromania as the offering of a small prayer, the elemental, Promethean act of spiritual bollocks. In the age of nuclear fission and quantum physics, plasma screens and 3G cells, hippies can still look into a fire and see the meaning of life and the answer to everything.

So there I am, you see, seven sentences in, and I've started already with the hippy baiting. You just can't help it; to know them is to mock them. What's amazing is that they've lasted so long. At the bottom of the child-line of bullied pop trends, hippies are now in their third generation. Born in the mid-sixties into a blizzard of mockery, they've suffered, for forty years, the ridicule of almost everyone. They've tried rebranding as yippies, travellers, crusties, hairies, the tribe, the clan, eco-warriors, alternative health practitioners and outreach coordinating social workers. But we all know they're just the same old hippies in a new shapeless jersey.

And credit where credit's due, what other useful fad or fashion has lasted as long? No one says, 'Oh, you sad old teddy boy.' Your mods, rockers, suedeheads, soul boys, new romantics, Goths, punks and Bay City Rollerettes are now just embarrassing photographs and a ridiculous pair of shoes at the back of the wardrobe. Only hippies have transcended the natural lifespan of their music and knitwear.

And if you sit down and think about them without sniggering, there's a lot of hippy shit you quite like. Flower power became the green movement, and you quite like that. The don't-work-just-feel-the-vibe-and-roll-a-spliff thing has its points, and as a weekend mini-break you'd rather make love than war. And you wouldn't mind fathering a lot of blond kids from a number of surprisingly attractive and non-judgemental free-spirited women who can bake. Actually, when you get right down to it, there's a bit of you that would like to live in a tepee. Yes, there is. With some mates and Liv Tyler in August. It would be a laugh and you quite fancy having a go on those Celtic drums. (Obviously, you don't want the Hoover-bag hair, the scabies, the compost sleeping bag, a mate called Bracken and a lurcher called Stephen.)

Perhaps we all need to get in touch with our inner hippies. Which is partially why I decided, finally, that it was time to go to Glastonbury. It's funny, Glastonbury. It's a secret password. Whisper it to grey men in offices, your accountant, your MEP, a hedge-fund analyst, and it's likely a look of beatific remembrance will pass like a cloud over the sun and they'll say, 'Yes, I went once, years ago.' Glastonbury is a secret medieval heresy that's remembered with hidden joy. 'I was once a free-love hippy, Mott the Hoople acolyte and hand-painted chillum maker,' is probably not what you want to hear from the merchant banker handling your corporate takeover. Actually, medieval heresy is the decorative theme of Glastonbury, which, by the way, means 'place of woad', or more exactly 'place of the woad people'. Inside, the huge curtain wall of the temporary, self-governing state of Glastonbury is a reprise of the thirteenth century, or at least the *Jabberwocky* version of it, while outside the Black Death of progress tears up the earth and eats people. Getting into Glastonbury is about as easy as the Black Prince found getting into Calais.

Having made the decision to find my inner hippy at Glastonbury, I had to make a decision as to what sort of hippy I was looking for. Was it Swampy? Or Donovan? Or was it the Marquis of Bath? Over the years there's been quite a variety of hippies. You could, if you so wished, hold a Eurovision Hippy Contest or a Hippy Olympics. I like to think of Glastonbury as Hippy Crufts, a walled, heretic, medieval Hippy Crufts. That just about gets the flavour.

I have an advantage in shopping for an inner hippy because this is my second go. I was there at the start. I'm a child of the sixties, albeit at school in rural Hertfordshire, which wasn't exactly Woodstock or the Prague Spring or even Eel Pie Island. But we had the music and the hair and a bit of Red Leb and I know where my nascent, born-again hippy lurks. He's a cross between Malcolm McDowell and William Blake with a dash of Jethro Tull. This is really the crux. I'm fifty this year. Glastonbury is the last act of my forties. Glastonbury is unfinished business now that I'm closer to an undertaker than I am to boarding-school.

When I was a hippy first time round we used to say, never trust anyone over thirty (with shrill, clipped, upper-middle-class accents). Now I'm over fifty I'd add, never sleep in a tent over thirty. I'll do Glastonbury but I'll do Glastonbury Soft, Glastonbury Lite, which is why I'm sitting above the twenty-mile traffic jam in a Winnebago. Not for me the stews and refugee camps of windy canvas, the dank sleeping bag; a Winnebago is the way to go. You see, a mobile home is a great luxury, the stars' accessory, the private box on nature unless – and this is a big unless – it actually is your home, in which case it's trailer trash. Ours appears to be the main residence of the man who's driving it. It has the mildly weird feeling of trying to hold a dinner party in a peculiarly strange man's bedsit with him in the inglenook saying, 'Don't mind me.'

I'm travelling with my girlfriend. This will be the last year I'm able to say girlfriend without sounding utterly Alan Clark. I'm also taking Matthew, my personal photographer, another little luxury you can give yourself after forty-five (going to Books and sticking the things in the albums is such a bore) and Alice BB, who's a dear and here because when I told her I was going, she became so overexcited I thought she just might rip off all her clothes and do floral finger-painting on her body. So I said she was welcome to tag along, as it was a sort of hippyish thing to say. She is still improbably buoyant, staring out of the window, squeaking like a spaniel going shooting.

Getting in to Glastonbury is like crossing a particularly fraught border: there are thousands of policemen – or pigs as I suppose I must go back to calling them, hundreds of cones and signs and labels, a Kafkaesque amount of paperwork and when you see the security fence marching across the country it's a reminder that the price of freedom, to be a bit of an anarchist and a fire-worshipper, is a lot of razor wire and a bulk discount from Group Four.

We finally park in the private, behind-stage, Bands and VIPs field, which is like a pilot for a Channel 4 sitcom: *Celebrity Trailer Trash*. Over there is Kate Moss, the pin-up sprite, the Bardot of postmodern Notting Hippydom. I go and find the press tent to get more passes and paperwork, and bump into Roland White, a man whose hidden hippy has probably been sold for medical research. He does my television column when I'm not there. I'm only introducing Roland as a walk-on here because he made one very clever observation and I don't want him to think I'm stealing it. 'Have you seen the tented village yet?' he asked. 'Well, when you do, you'll notice it's become a tented suburb. Well, a number of suburbs. It's rather John Betjeman; there are people laying out gardens and putting up carriage lamps.'

Inside the press tent the latest news is that no one's managed to make it over the wall but security guards with dogs have apprehended ten people and they're all Liverpudlian (the liggers, not the dogs). It's like the punch line to a joke, isn't it? ' . . . And they were all Scousers.' The tickets are now £100 each so naturally, in a right-on, hippyish way, we're all for people breaking in over the wire. But on the other hand we're jolly pleased when they get caught. There's a lot of nostalgia about Glastonbury: people who've been here every year since they did it without microphones say they miss the gangs of Hell's Angels, the drug-dealers' turf wars, the endemic thievery, the adulteration and overdoses, which just shows you can be nostalgic about anything.

The truth is that this alternative weekend nirvana all comes down to plumbing and waste management. There are armies of kids who've been given tickets in exchange for picking up rubbish, of which there is an extraordinary amount. But it's bogs that are really the central leitmotif of Glastonbury. It's all about one thing: colonic endurance. Can you go the full three days without going? Because the very thought is so nauseous, so utterly medieval, it makes a colostomy bag sound like a civilised option. There are plenty of loos laid out like back-to-back miners' cottages. You can see the rows of feet in the morning, the whole-earth pasty-shoe next to the Nike Airs, next to Doc Martens. That's the thing that's rarely mentioned about hippies – they've managed to achieve completely unisexual footwear but, my darling, the smell.

By the third morning it's, well, it's half a million turds and all the trimmings. There are horror stories of dropped stashes, of tripping and slipping, of horrible, horrible rectal explosions. But for me the most poignant, the most grisly, is the girl who told me she'd been putting off the call of nature for as long as sphincterally possible and until she was so comprehensively stoned and drunk she could face the drop. So at 2 am she gingerly made her way to the pitch-black amenities block. Opening the door, she dropped her pants and with the tense precision of a Romanian gymnast, lowered her posterior over the open sewer. Something cold and clammy squidged between the cheeks of her buttocks and in a sudden dark, repulsive flash of third-eye insight she realised she was squatting on the point turtle's head of the last occupant's offering, which itself was the high peak of a mountain of shit that had risen like the devil's soufflé from the bowl. She said her scream woke at least 4,000 people.

Glastonbury is all about plumbing, 100,000 sloppy bladders. I came across my goddaughter, Florence, a gamine French girl with the most beguiling look and syrupy accent. She's an art student and therefore penniless, so she was here on a green ticket, her job to stop men peeing in the little river that runs through the site. In years past it has become so urically toxic that it's cleared out all the animal and vegetable life for a couple of miles downstream. It's also so pharmaceutically complex that frogs have been found copulating with mushrooms, and sheep lying on their backs baaing 'Green, Green Grass of Home' in three-part harmony.

I asked Florence how it was going. 'It's going a lot. Zer are many, many very drunk boys and zey don't listen. I say, "No, no, put it away, you must not pee-pee, it will damage zee nature." But it is too late, and I am 'aving to jump.'

On that first night we walked out into the humming darkness and stood at the crossroads in an improvised street along a hedge under a stunted hawthorn. A cold moon gave everything the silvered look of an old photograph. Thousands of people walked past in the dark. As Alice said, it was like those films of city streets where all the car lights make long red-and-white streamers. Every single person who passed us was off their face. Not just a little tipsy, not a bit mellow, but utterly slaughtered, mullered, wrecked, legless, shit-faced, arseholed, fucked – deeply, deeply irretrievably fucked. They were like sleepwalking commuters. Faces would leer out of the dark, glassy-eyed, beatific. Occasionally the very undone would stand and rock before being taken up again by the stream of alternative humanity.

What made it all the more weird was that I was utterly, utterly straight. I was so chemical-free you could have tattooed the Soil Association logo on my forehead. I have been straight since the Falklands, since before most of these kids could eat with a fork. It was a straightening feeling to know that I was the only person within a city mile who could, as the label says, safely operate heavy machinery.

But an even weirder thing happened and I still can't really explain it. I never take notes. I trust my memory to edit out what's not needed, and in a decade of reporting it's never let me down until Glastonbury. As if in sympathy, as if by osmosis, it pressed the delete button and I have forgotten pretty much everything that happened. I can't remember coherently, even less chronologically. I've looked at Matthew's photographs and unarguably I'm in them. There I am in a pixie hat and a harlequin velvet coat. Where the fuck did they come from? It jogs only static. My memories of Glastonbury are like putting your head in the sea and staring at the bottom. It's another medium, another world.

'You must remember free hugs,' said Alice. 'That big man who was giving away free hugs, he gave you lots; and the banana shaman, the man dressed in a black bin-liner with a banana skin.' No, but I do remember the girl standing in front of her crudded boyfriend, grooming him like an ape, delicately picking coke-bogies out of his nose and eating them. And I remember standing at seven in the morning in the middle of tented suburbia, as the chill and full bladders woke the weekend hippies far too early, and the transcendent look of pain and nausea on their faces as they poked their heads out of their tents to confront a bright good morning. It was like a slap. I stood and watched it happen over and over again like open auditions for a silent movie. And I remember the lost boy in the middle of the night, fucked and buggered, stopping one in three to ask: 'D'you know where my tent is?' What's it look like? 'It's green.' Right, and is it near anything? 'Yeah, yeah. [Excited] It's next to another tent, a blue one.' Sorry, can't help you, mate.

And I remember buying Florence a fairy ball gown so she could go to a late-night costume party that looked like an Otto Dix painting. And I remember the T-shirt stalls 'Dead Women Don't Say No' and 'I am Spartacus' – I so wanted one of those. I wanted one that said, 'I am the Eggman', and I wanted to give Matthew one that said, 'I am the Walrus'. And I remember the Welsh 'Te A Tost' stall where the bloke said, 'What you want is a feast, see? That's two rounds with my Auntie Wendy's marmalade and a cup of tea.' And that's exactly what I did want. And it was a feast.

And I remember the nude wanker. Occasional nudity is respected at Glastonbury. It is the original flavour and spirit of non-violent alternative protest, where hippies came from. Where would your flower power happening be without some flaxen-haired, clear-eyed child of the morning getting her tits out and flicking peace signs at the world? This one wasn't exactly from central casting.

In front of the un-amplified folk gazebo where real, head-shaking, lonely mandolin-pluckers and finger-in-ear, off-key whingers attracted a crowd of two or three delicate souls so hammered and wrung-out that their heads had been turned into iPods, there was a lady who had been so carried away by a folk combo that she'd taken all her clothes off. Nothing wrong with that. She'd been so transported by the music she was moved to give herself a bit of a wank. Not a gentle, feel-good fingering, but the complete, top-of-the-range, brace-yourself-Doris, blurred-wrist seeing to. No, maybe not too much wrong with that either. But there's an over-twenty-one age limit and it's Glastonbury. The half-dozen pigs walk round with blinkers on doing community relations funny-hat-wearing. Lord Lucan jacking up with Osama Bin Laden would have difficulty getting arrested here, but the trouble was that this wasn't some buff, fit, pert hippy chick with flowers in her hair and plaited pubes. It was an old, fat, hideous, meat-faced nutter bagwoman and something had to be done on purely aesthetic grounds. She was putting the folk off their protest songs, and they were complaining.

Two large security guards spent a lot of time animatedly shouting into their walkie talkies before gingerly approaching the frotting troll with rubber gloves and a blanket, the old trout desperately trying to finish off the full Meg Ryan while at the same time telling Securicor to fuck themselves, like what she was doing. And they danced around her trying to grab her wrists without getting the finger. I watched with bated breath on tenterhooks. Would they? Will they? And then one of them did. Gave me the punch line. 'Oh, please, love. Come quietly.' Yes!

And I can remember the alternative health field, with every variety of absurd astral chakra voodoo hokum known to people under forty who've never been really ill. There were lots of circles for noddy-humming away cancer or drumming for a better back and world peace. But what I remember most was a bloke in the door of one tent doing utterly perfect yoga sun salutes. He must have been about my age and as supple as pollard willow. He drew an admiring crowd, they'd all tried a bit of yoga and they knew how difficult it is to link your fingers on the soles of your outstretched feet from a sitting position. But all I could think of was that in the time he'd learnt to do this, Tony Blair had gone from being in a band called Ugly Rumours to being Prime Minister, J.K. Rowling had become a billionaire and most of the blokes he was at school with had got careers, bought houses, had wives and kids, built things, made stuff, taken an interest. And in all that time he'd mastered the sun salute. I looked at him and I thought, there but for the grace of God, if I hadn't fortuitously lost my inner hippy.

And, finally, what I remember is the tepee field. In hippy terms this is the dock at St Tropez. Living in a tepee makes you traveller mega A-list royalty. This is having it all, in that it's having hardly anything. The rest of us are just here rubbernecking in avaricious awe. The tepee field really does look like a glimpse into another world: hippy Jerusalem. And the dwellers go about their blessed daily chores with the sort of casual insouciance that comes from having been stared at a lot. The difference between these and the mega-yachts of the South of France is that these aren't hideous. These are the essential accessories of the wilfully modest. There are a few ethnic blankets, a log or two, black pots hanging over state-of-the-art fires, a brace of shaggy, blond children in thirteenth-century jerkins and jellybean sandals, a couple of lurchers, a Merlin staff, and a tom-tom finishes off the look that makes the rest of us want to burn our central islands with breakfast bar and trash the Range Rover.

We know in our hearts that our Philippe Starck is stupid bollocks, the espresso machine and *sorbetière* dust and ashes in our mouths, the weight and vast amount of our stuff is a rock about our necks. It's vacuous, unnecessary petty snobbery, a terrible indictment of our insecurity, our earthbound, hoarding dullness. We look at these soaring tents and the fragility of devoting our precious existence to things with plugs and keys. What do you give the man who has everything? A tepee and the opportunity to have nothing but his life back and some self-worth and maybe a dose of goodness and bravery. Bravery and goodness and nits. Bravery, goodness, nits and bad breath. Bravery, goodness, nits, bad breath and cold water with bits in, a bird with organic wilderness body hair and a shit in a shrub.

The tepee field was where I finally faced my inner hippy and found that he was wanting. He was wanting under-floor heating and dinner at the Wolseley. So that was Glastonbury as far as I can remember. I have this feeling it was a life-changing event. My life has a no-returns policy but I got a credit note. The girlfriend loved it; Matthew the snapper, I think, loved it; Alice BB adored it and for Florence the goddaughter it was just another weekend in that gilded time of your life. I have a picture of her in her dressing-up frock on my desk.

You will have noticed that I haven't mentioned the music. Well, it was there, it's the reason for Glastonbury but it's really not the point. And that's another good thing about the Winnebago. You can watch it on the telly.

I asked Nick Mason of Pink Floyd what he thought of Glastonbury. 'Well, it's like the English hajj, it's going to Mecca.' And I reckon that's pretty spot-on. Glastonbury's a secular pilgrimage. Music and getting off our tits are the only things we all still believe in. Did you ever play there, I asked? 'No, I don't think we did.' Have you ever been? 'Good grief, no,' he replied with a look of mild horror. This is a man who really, honestly, doesn't know how many cars he owns to the nearest ten.

BRITAIN

Britain is possibly the only place in the world where a blind man could join in a discussion on the countryside. Britain, and in particular the English part, is a country that exists on a parallel geography of words over the map of counties, villages and dales. This is a descriptive literary notion – there's Hardy country and Brontë country; Austen, Gaskell, Thackeray and Chaucer country; Wordsworth, Coleridge, Betjeman, Marvell and Larkin all have little patches of country. There's Jilly Cooper country, James Herriot country and Melvyn Bragg country. There's also the metaphysical country of Blake and Tolkien, the Wesley, Wodehouse and Harry Potter countries.

Britain is a series of overlapping views, each as fixed and unchanging as the real places they took their life from are fugitive and changeable. This exhibition* also examines landscape as a reflection of the British character: the homely, reserved south; the imported romance and wilderness of the north; and the industrial and manufacturing landscapes of the Midlands. The landscape fades away but the image remains and, for many Britons, their countryside is primarily a descriptive place that they may never have visited and that nobody could possibly visit except page by page.

Whereas France and Italy are gastronomic landscapes and America is a journey, Britain is a country that is best seen by

* 'A picture of Britain', Tate Britain, 2005

drawing the curtains, opening a book and never leaving the room. This makes Britons' relationship with the real mud both deeply emotional and bizarrely disengaged at the same time. Their literary landscapes montage together and become a received image of their land, a rural place that is a collectively shared virtual nation. For instance, witness last year's huge countryside debate and rallies. The concept and purpose of the country were being publicly questioned for the first time since the enclosures, and it struck a deep chord, particularly among the urban population, who have always had the most lushly romantic vision of the country and the least access to it. It's in urban drawing-rooms that most of these rural pictures will have ended up.

Pervasive and seductive pictures of Britain, whether the watercolours of the Holland school, the woolly damp of Victorian north Wales, the rustic fat sheep of primitive pub signs or tourist-board calendars, are always illustrations of a wordy place. They evoke half-remembered stanzas, scenes from set books and Sunday TV adaptations.

The British have a utilitarian relationship with the pictures of their country. Whereas most European artists create images of symbolic landscapes to contain myths, saints and the metaphors of inner turmoil, Britons demand realistic pictures of an imagined place. The overriding sense of an English landscape painting is of a calm and pleasant land; even when the elements of natural energy – waterfalls, precipices and storm clouds – are present, they are all kept at a safe distance. It is as if we see the country through the window or from a train.

The British Isles in art are a safe and beautiful place that is both natural and ordered, aesthetically displayed and artlessly rustic. The technical realism and emotional understatement of the British landscape tradition are far more intellectually appealing than the *Sturm und Drang* or hysterical religiosity of much European landscape painting. It also suits the English reserve. We like this remembered place of equilibrium and quiet voices, of lyric poetry and rural plots. It catches the throat and pricks the eye; it is the brochure advertising a Bupa-private patriotism. And most Britons like it far more than the real thing. It's good to be reminded that the corner of a foreign field that is for ever England is actually paper and ink.

It's got him and it's slowly, capriciously losing him, rubbing him out so that in the end all that will be left is the whine of dementia and a hieroglyph that looks like him. It has a bleak trendiness, Alzheimer's: old Ronnie Reagan had it, Iris Murdoch's has been turned into a book and a film, no doubt somewhere there's the T-shirt.

I know how it works. I've seen it before. We've all seen it before, some grandparent, husband, friend, father. It begins with a misplaced word – so easy to lose a word, we all do it. But as it goes on, language escapes, there's a hole in the vocabulary, memories slip away or take on new significance. So much of the familiar furniture of life vanishes or is rearranged, but there's a growing confusion and often panic. At this point someone – a spouse, a child, a friend – has to make the choice to go to a doctor to confirm what they already secretly know. That's the big decision, because there's a world of difference between dementia and dottiness. Eccentric is an anecdote; Alzheimer's is a sentence. Or, as my dad puts it, 'You know I've got that terrible illness, what's its name?'

I've been trying to remember my first memory of him and, you know, I can't – he's always been there. But one keeps coming back. I must have been about eleven. He's taken us to Venice for a day. Venice was my dad's version of Disneyland. It's getting late, it's hot, we're lost but there's one last thing he has to show me. I've had enough, I want an ice cream and a go in a gondola. He's irritated, I'm bolshie. We walk around the corner and there it is, there's Verrocchio's condottiere, and I burst into tears, just bowled over, thumped in the soul by art. It's only happened to me twice, both times with my dad. The other was the bronze blind Zeus in Athens. Anyway, he hands me his handkerchief and makes the condottiere live and Verrocchio live and it's one of the best moments of my life.

That's it. The handkerchief, that's my first memory of my father: he always carried a handkerchief. It smelt if pipe tobacco.

We didn't really do outside. Never did that father–son thing with rods and rackets, oars or balls. He never taught me to take a penalty or bowl a googly. We stayed in. In museums, galleries, palaces, castles, ruins, anywhere that had a story. He was the best storyteller. Only later did I realise how amazingly capacious his knowledge was and what a rare and winning gift his ability to impart it. When I first went to school it was a surprise to discover I already knew all the Greek and Norse mythology and a fair chunk of classical history.

Books were our thing. All my adult life, whenever he visited, first thing he'd go to the bookshelves, searching for pilfered strays. He was never a best friend or a mate. I've had lots of friends and mates. He's the only father I'll ever have. We didn't do pubs or garden sheds; we just talked and talked and talked. Always in the deep end.

He's eighty this year, born an only, sickly child of first-generation middle-class parents. He was in RAF intelligence during the war and the occupation of Germany after, read philosophy at Edinburgh – the first member of his family to go to university – became a journalist on *The Scotsman* and then the *Observer*, joined the BBC. Made more than 1,000 art documentaries, filmed Giacometti and Bacon, worked with David Sylvester, John Berger and Kenneth Clark, co-producing and directing *Civilisation*. He made a funny, short 1960s movie that went to Cannes, wrote a clever, idiosyncratic book on the nude in art. Married twice, had three children, four grandchildren and along the way became the widest- and furthest-travelled man I know.

He is a man of his time, that wartime generation of cerebral socialists, instinctive modernists who wanted to build a new Jerusalem on the bomb site of the old world using culture, information and intelligence as their pick, shovel and brick. The last unapologetic intellectuals.

I wouldn't be telling you any of this if something hadn't happened. Prosaically, it came via Age Concern, the Kensington branch. There, a chap called David Clegg has instigated a programme of getting artists to work with the Alzheimered. It isn't art therapy – nothing is as humiliating and demeaning as getting people who have led extraordinary lives to end up colouring in for their own good. This is a collaboration to create a work out of the fractured memory and circular obsessions of dementia.

For some time now Becky Shaw has been visiting Daddy once a week, and together they're creating something. It's meant an enormous amount to him; he's excited by it, and it's so rare to hear of anything positive about our collective treatment of the old, so I went to sit in on a session. I don't know what I expected: stuff about the war, his school days, family things, the shards of life.

When I get there he's sitting on a sofa. In front of him, as ever, there's a scatter of books. He picks one up – H.G. Wells's *A Short History of the World*. We slip into the familiar chat, 'good on the League of Nations and prehistory, not so good in between'. Every time Daddy comes to a pothole in a sentence he pauses, concentrates and searches vainly for the word: 'I can't remember . . . words.'

Shaw arrives with large, chaotic rolls of papers: 'I thought you'd like to see what we've done.' She starts laying down the sheets; the corners flick up and curl. They are densely written with catches of conversation colour-coded and linked by a road map of lines and circles and arrows to make connections to underline repeated themes. There are collaged images from photographs and post-cards, rough line drawings; things are crossed out and new bits imposed and stuck on. The rolls spill out over the floor. Daddy looks at them with a beneficent smile. They are opaquely complex, like a mad family tree or alchemistic experiment.

What I can see is that he's been talking an awful lot about

prehistoric shamanism and the relevance to early religions of domesticated animals. There's a page of ancient horses. 'It's strange,' says Daddy, 'that the horse never became a god: it's the most important and . . . of all the tamed animals but it was never made a god. I wonder why.'

There's miles of it, this stuff about fertility symbols and the role of the earth goddess – then a Mitchell bomber his squadron flew and the Makonde figure he brought back from Tanzania, a photograph of his father.

'What are you going to do with all this; how do you edit it into something coherent?' I ask Shaw. 'Well, I think I'm going to make a museum of your father, a model for a museum with all these impossible corridors, some that connect and some that don't. An architect's model that could never be built.'

Daddy smiles and nods. It couldn't be more appropriate, more right. He is like a curator of a collection that's been sacked by the philistines. He's trying to rescue the objects and memories of a lifetime while the vandals next door rip up the photograph album and smash the furniture. Not just appropriate but awfully poignant.

What strikes me as memorable about this project is that it could only be done with people who are clinging to the wreckage. It's not one of those pitifully hearty bits of do-goodery that pretend to allow the physically or mentally compromised some *manqué* padded version of the able word. Shaw says she reckons the input is 50–50: half hers, half Daddy's. So you're not just being an amanuesis? 'I'm sorry,' she says, 'I don't know what that word means.'

Conversations with Daddy are like talking to someone who can travel through walls. In the middle of a sentence, he can be somewhere else. I have to open empirical, rational doors to follow him. He elides through time and subjects in a way that logic and language prevent me from doing. It's a sort of itinerant freedom. He's still lucid and connected enough for an afternoon spent with him to be funny and emotional and stimulating and real. All this stuff about the prehistory and origins of belief, the theories and suppositions based on ancient ruins and rescued fragments, is inescapably a metaphor, as have been all the conversations we've ever had about history, aesthetics and culture. This was our playing field, the language we used to be together. They were the words between words.

After Shaw leaves I suggest we go for a walk. His face clouds, 'Well, maybe not, I'd rather not, I'm frightened,' he says in a quite matter-of-fact way, as if the fear were just another vandal in another room. But reassured that someone will be here when he gets back, my stepmother gives him a clean handkerchief and we stroll round Holland Park. He used to bring me here as a child. 'I can't have keys now, you know; I lose them . . . Are you going to get another dog?' I haven't had a dog for a decade. 'She's nice, Becky, isn't she? I think the work might be, might be . . . '

We go and sit in the flower garden and I mention how morbid benches are; always dedicated to the dead. It's like sitting on graves. I ask if he'd like a bench here. He laughs: 'No, no. They might put me next to someone I hate. I might get Deirdre Lawrence.' I've no idea who she was, a name snatched from another room.

There is a late autumnal feeling to our time together now. It's the long walk back to the pavilion. We haven't always made each other's lives easy. I was a tedious and irritatingly difficult son; he could be dismissive and short-tempered. But that's all gone now there are no more positions to defend, points to be scored, no more competition. Along with everything else, Alzheimer's has washed away the friction of expectation, leaving us with just this moment. Fathers and sons are an endlessly retraced journey for all men – it is one of the great themes of our lives. For a time every man is a hero to his son and I can catch again something Homeric in Daddy's last lost battle. This slow parting is sad and precious. We have this moment and we've managed to say everything that needs to be said.

Look, I don't want this to sound like a happy ending, some bittersweet violin sob of new-age closure. There is nothing good to say about Alzheimer's. It robs families. It robs the sufferers of themselves. It makes thankless, unremitting demands on those who have to stay and care. The process of loss and grieving is unnaturally mixed with the humbling mechanics of maintenance. Not only will we lose him, but he will lose us. Soon I won't be in any of the rooms at all.

SON

My boy, Alasdair, got himself confirmed a couple of weeks ago. Afterwards, we had dinner – godparents, grandparents, aunts, uncles, the Holy Ghost. It was very nice. For me, the nicest bit was sitting with Ali and my dad. We rarely do. Daddy's Alzheimer's is drawing down the blinds. But it was one of those moments when I didn't feel that my life was heaving and wallowing under my feet, like a tug in a gale. For a moment, it was calm and secure and safe. There was me, my boy and my dad. I'm not a great believer in all that hereditary stuff – the nastiness of blood and bone. It's stifling and prescriptive and morally and socially imbecilic, though I look at my father and see how similar we are. But then, that's down to nurture and enthusiasms.

Then I look at Ali, just eleven years old, and he seems so completely his own chap: a product of his own endeavours, fears, excitements and stubbornness. I can't even get him to sit up straight, so there's not much hope of imparting the collective id and wisdom of a hundred generations of Gillness.

He's a thoughtful, sideways-looking boy, and I'm aware that I don't know the half of him. Fathers and sons are a generically sentimentalised relationship. Mothers and sons, fathers and daughters, come with baggage and connotations. But dads and their lads are as simple as beer and skittles, a lump in the throat, viciously exploited by the advertisers of watches and life insurance.

When you become a parent, the one thing you realise all children have over their fathers is that only fathers remember a time before children. Their arrival is so joyously cataclysmic, comes with such a helium-filled weight of responsibility, that you never quite get over the awe and the shock. But for Ali, I'm just part of the landscape. There was never a time before dad.

It's difficult to know what to give an eleven-year-old for his confirmation. I got him lead soldiers. It's something the three of us share: my father gave me his, and they've been passed on to Ali. It's our one small acquiescence to primogeniture and ancestral property. I gave him a little model of a wartime RAF officer. It could have been his grandfather. The three of us looked at the little blue man, and I realised it was the family equivalent of the Schleswig-Holstein question. Ali didn't know who it was, Daddy had forgotten who it was; it meant something only to me.

But what does he think about having me as his dad? He was at his grandparents. I rang to ask him.

Hello, Ali.

Hi, Dad.

If you had a choice between half a dad and three dads, which would it be?

Three dads. I don't want half a dad.

What's the most embarrassing thing I've ever done?

Once you took me out for a walk. You were wearing some kilt thing. Pretty embarrassing.

What do you think of the car [a bright yellow Bentley with blacked-out pimp's windows that I bought specifically to embarrass the children]? Don't you mind being dropped off at school in it?

It's a weird colour, but it's funky. I like being taken to school in it.

If you could have any car, what would it be?

A Lotus or Ferrari.

What's your earliest memory of me?

You lifting me up and throwing me towards the ceiling. It was really, really frightening.

Oh, I'm sorry.

No, it's a nice memory; that nice scariness.

What's the capital of Argentina?

A.

A what?

A. Just A.

No, Ali. A what?

A is the capital of Argentina.

(Pause for laughter.)

Which bit of sex education didn't you understand and have been too embarrassed to ask about?

I'm not embarrassed by any of it. I understand it all. Well, perhaps it's a little bit embarrassing.

Why do you think they make flavoured condoms?

What?! You're having a laugh. They don't do that, do they?

They do.

We haven't got to that bit yet. Teacher hasn't said, 'Here's a Coca-Cola-flavoured one.' Why do they make them?

To be quite frank, Ali, I've no idea. Do you have names for them? Do you call them rubber johnnies?

(Hoots with laughter) Rubber Johnny – what's that?

Who's the prime minister?

Tony Blair.

. . . of India?

(Quick as a heartbeat) Chief.

Oh, like an Indian chief. How's the dyslexia going? [We're both dyslexic.]

Fine.

No, really, how are you coping?

Fine. Fine, Dad. It's okay.

No, come on, Ali, tell me.

It's fine. I get to miss French.

You haven't really read all the Harry Potter books, have you?

Really, I have, but not the fifth one. I'm reading *The Curious Incident of the Dog in the Night-Time* now.

What are the twenty best things about your father?

He's funny, he has rubbish comebacks and, um, eighteen weeks' pocket money.

And the one bad thing?

Your style, Dad. It's crap. You may be the eighth-best dressed man in Britain, but Robbie Williams beat you.

Isn't there one thing in my wardrobe that you want me to leave you?

Er, the velvet smoking-jacket.

You big poof.

Da-ad!

Do you think you'd like to be a father?

Yeah, I suppose so.

If you could only have one child, would it be a boy, a girl or a Jack Russell?

Jack Russell.

What's the worst row we've ever had?

About cutting off my mullet [cost me £20 in bribes].

What would you change about your life?

My sister.

What are you most looking forward to about growing up?

A driving licence.

What, more than testicles?

Da-ad!

Okay, which is better: popular or famous?

Famous. I'd buy some friends.

Handsome or clever?

Handsome.

Good dancer, good footballer?

Good footballer.

Smelly breath, smelly feet?

Feet.

You manage to do both.

Da-ad!

Snails or frog's legs?

Frog's legs.

What's more frightening; geography exam or sleeping with the lights off?

Geography exam. I'm totally over having to have the lights on any more.

If you could change one thing about you and me, what would it be?

Nothing.

Really?

Nothing, Dad.

And if you could keep one thing the same for ever?

My family.

That's disgustingly sentimental, Ali.

Okay – the dog.

So how's it going so far?

Good, I like my life. It's a standard life.

All right, Ali, thanks.

Love you, Dad.

Love you, Ali. Love to your sister.

Yeah, right.

GOLF

I

Golf: a game invented by the Scots to prove to the world what the English are really like. It seems almost unnecessary, *de trop*, to have to list all that is repellent about golf. It's like having to explain why eating people is wrong. But let's do it anyway. Actually, let's compare golf with cannibalism.

In the left-hand column, what's wrong with golf? It ruins tracts of perfectly nice land and small country hotels. It is, by its very nature, the bottom line benchmark of tastelessness and naff. In fact, naff is a synonym for golf. It is also overtly racist and class-ridden, groundlessly snobbish and humiliatingly sexist. Golf is the standard-bearer and pimp for the worst types of gratuitously wasteful capitalism and conspicuous consumption. Golf is wrist-gnawingly tedious to watch and disembowelling to listen to. It makes widows of decent women and *de facto* orphans of blameless children. And it fucks up baggage carousels. Golf is a fundamentally stupid game.

Now the right-hand column: what's wrong with cannibalism? Tough hamburgers; it makes you a bad neighbour; and Gordon Ramsay would be properly frightening. On paper, then, golf is worse than eating strangers.

The really evil thing about golf is that golfers aren't born, they're made. It's the game that takes perfectly decent people and turns them into fascist, racist, misogynistic, viciously cringing arse-lickers, in 40 per cent nylon. Golf courses don't attract wankers, they turn straight-up blokes into wankers, or Englishmen as they're internationally known. Nothing is so utterly and completely plainly the exposed soul of England than golf. And like most English things, it was invented by someone else. Us Scots. Some heretics try to make a pathetic case for it being Dutch, because the word bears a passing resemblance to *kolf* – middle-Dutch for a bat. Actually, the origin of the world is lost in the mists of the lowlands, but in the beginning, we know it was called *gouff*. I'm not making this up. And to me it will always be *gouff*.

The utterly up-yourself English pretension of pronouncing it 'goff' was – and I'm not making this up, either – an attempt to say 'golf' with a Scottish accent. How pathetic is that? And how many sorry Sassenach tossers still go out on the first tee and do Sean Connery impressions? 'My game, I think, Mr Blofeld.' My nine-iron shoved up your colon, I think, Mr Impotent Wife-Left Loathed-By-Kids No-Mates Sad-Fuck.

Golf courses were built round the globe by Scots engineers, soldiers, doctors and missionaries. They laid them out as ambushes for the English, and just to prove how stupid and unobservant they were, the Scots stuck flags in them, but the gits fell for it anyway, then built clubhouses that wouldn't let women in except on alternate Wednesdays and for dinner dances, and then only if they were accompanied by a male member. Whole new nations learned why they should loathe the English. The Scots crept away sniggering to teach the locals how to play rugby so that they could really cripple the bastards.

All my life, if you had asked me to make three declarations of faith, a trinity of Gillishness, one of them would always have been: I am not a golfer. I prided myself on being, in a metaphysical sense, an anti-golfer. That was until now. You know where all this is leading. As I have grown up, or at least older, I've seen my friends, fellow travellers, slide off the path of good taste to knock balls across fields. With apologetic shrugs, they've stopped being us and gone over to them.

Golf isn't simply an embarrassing part-time reaction, like colonic irrigation or going lap-dancing, it's a life-changer, a barren religion bereft of theology. I suspect it may change people at a molecular level. 'Keen' and 'enthusiastic' are not words that you can apply to golfers. 'Deranged' and 'psychotic' are. Let me relay a conversation between two ex-friends I heard just last week.

First golfer (wistfully): 'You've stopped playing, haven't you?'

Second golfer: 'Yes, you know I only get the kids at weekends, so it was either them or having a round. [Pause, sharp intake of breath.] I had to stop.'

First golfer (with terrible despair): 'Oh God, I envy you. I wish I could. Oh heavens, I wish I could.'

I need to know what it is that happens to people when they catch gouff. It's part journalistic curiosity and part because it's there. I want to try everything. I don't want to get to my deathbed and say, 'Well, in retrospect, folk dancing wasn't a patch on incest, but I wish I'd done golf.'

And it's also because I think it's important once in a while to have Passover in your head, to clean out all the leaven, all the givens, all the absolutes in your life, to shine a light on them, put them through the third degree: why do I think this thing? Do I still believe that? What would it feel like to listen to country music, order the vegetarian option, wear a string vest, play golf?

So I'm going to learn. I'm going to be a gouffer for a year, and I'm going to write a gouff column, twelve of them, and then I'm going to stop and walk away from it. I'll go back to being a decent human being.

I started the quest at the Knightsbridge Golf School underneath Lowndes Square, where Dave and Steve teach everyone to hit balls. But before I started, a man approached me at a party, a stranger. He grabbed me by the arm. He had a haunted, hunted look – the mien of the ancient mariner.

'You're thinking of taking up golf,' he hissed. Well, yes, just for a column. 'For Christ's sake, man, stick to food, telly, frocks, anything. I mean it. You have no idea what you're getting into.' He grabbed my lapels. 'You're an addict, aren't you? An alky, a junky.' Well, up to a point. 'Are you mad, man? You have no conception of where this ends, the depths, how much you have to lose. This is the warning.' And with a glance over his shoulder, he was gone, like a charade of *Invasion of the Body Snatchers*.

You know, I'd been here before. 'I can handle it!' I shouted after him. 'I know what I'm doing! It's only recreational. Look, I can take it or leave it, really.'

My first time with a club in my hand – well, nearly my first – a ball at my feet, Dave and Steve fussing, they couldn't be nicer, friendlier, more encouraging . . . what's the word? Clubbable. Just have a swing, they say. Just try and hit it. You'll probably miss, don't worry.

It's surprisingly unfamiliar, awkward, not like swinging a tennis racquet or a cricket bat, more like getting behind the wheel of a car for the first time. I try to remember what they do on the telly, swing and clip the ball. It skids sideways. Again. This time, there's a click, like someone turning on a light and the ball whacks into the padded wall in front of me. Click, and an impulse sparks up the shaft, through the palm of my hand, along my arm, lodging in the ancient bit of brain that we share with lizards. It's faintly familiar, a remote memory. Dave and Steve, the Fox and the Cat, chuckle and coo and show me how to hold the shaft.

'Look at that, look at that. A natural! See? He can't put it down! Look at him! It fits in the groove just there, doesn't it?'

But I'm not really listening. I'm watching them. Their banter, the way they catch each other's eye, the web of smiles and encouragement. Everything's going to be all right. I'm all right. And I realise what it is, this old memory. I've been here before: this isn't teaching, it's dealing.

II

The moment you pick up a golf bat you're faced with the realisation that this is an unnatural act. Of all the unnatural acts that might end in your ridicule, ostracism, penury and humiliation, this is by far the most unnatural. Games that involve sticks and spheres, hands and eyes as one, generally feel natural; pick up a baseball bat or a tennis racquet and the movement to hit the ball is innate. That doesn't necessarily mean you can do it well, but the principle is already in your arm.

Anything you do with a golf wand that feels right, is wrong. Not just a little clumsy, like the first time you hit a snooker ball, but utterly and completely un-right. The first time you try to hit a golf ball, lifting the stick higher than your elbow, you'll miss. Not only will you miss the ball, I confidently predict you will miss the entire Earth. The world is a pretty big potato. It's a planet, and to miss a planet with a stick while actually standing on it might give you some indication of the difficulty in getting on feel-good terms with the rudiments of golf.

This feels all wrong, I said to the Fox as he taught me to lift the stick back. 'Good,' he replied, 'very good. I knew you'd get the hang. If it feels wrong, it's right.'

'And if it feels right, it's wrong,' I added.

'You're a natural,' said the Fox.

The Fox and the Cat are my ayatollahs of Swing. They have separated the mechanics and mysteries of the hit into four sections. I am only allowed to attempt the backward bit. But before I do that I have to learn how to hold the stick-bat-wand.

To the uninitiated, a golf bat is almost indistinguishable from a broom handle; indeed, I bet if you left a nine iron in a dark cupboard with a couple of brooms and a mop, you'd have a brood of furry putters when next you looked. Now, you could hold a broom three or four ways to make it work. Well, forget that, because holding a golf bat makes you feel as if you've only just evolved opposable thumbs. It makes you feel as if your hands have been attached to the wrong arms. No, it's like someone else's hands have been attached to the wrong arms. I have difficulty with my left and right anyway, but when the Fox says, 'Left hand down,' I look blankly at the stick-bat and squeak, 'What's a hand?'

There are a number of ways your new borrowed hands can arrange themselves around a shaft (no sniggering, get over it) and frankly they're all a bit Freemason. So I plumped for the straightforward one-hand-and-then-the-other-hand. After that, you have to learn to stand. And those of you who imagine that they have been standing still with their feet slightly apart for as long as they can remember, and have never needed a specialist to tell them how, well, all I can offer you is a hollow, dry laugh.

After mastering standing and holding, you must address a golf ball. You feel like your body has been remade by a band of hungry Koreans who only had Meccano and pipe cleaners to work with. Nothing is in its familiar place or behaves conventionally. Addressing a golf ball is what golfers call staring at it meaningfully. In my golf seminar there is a peachy-keen American. When we do addressing a ball he says, 'Hell-o' in a bright and enthusiastic manner using two syllables and a hyphen. Whether this will make the ball go further or straighter I cannot tell. I do know that it's so annoying it will be as good as two strokes at the tee.

I have arrived at some sort of golfing rhythm. Rhythm is everything, I'm told. Along with all the other things that are everything. I turn up at the golf school once a week. And I feel a little less like Douglas Bader doing a Madonna impression each time. I have been made to promise on a photo of Arnold Palmer that I will cease and desist any golfish behaviour between visits. On no account am I to hit, strike, swing or address anything of a spherical nature.

Apparently, it's easier to inculcate golf into someone with no talent than one with talent but bad habits. It's like religion: everyone wants to convert an atheist. On my fifth lesson, the Fox says, 'OK, just for fun, because I know you want to, play the ball. Remember everything you've learned.'

Slowly, I jerk my unnatural body through its foreign paces and swipe at the distant ball. Just at the point of impact the little anaemic bastard dodges out of the way. My bat-stick hits a lump of ground and the ball rolls over and over itself, giggling. The disappointment is as intense as anything from my teenage disco years. The Fox and the Cat and the Yank Who Says Hell-o glare at me with withering ire. 'You tried to hit the ball!'

Sorry, and that's bad?

'The whole point of golf,' says the Cat, with exaggerated Montessori emphasis, 'is not to try and hit the ball.'

Not to hit the ball?

'No, not to *try* and hit the ball. You ignore the ball, play as if it weren't there.'

Right, OK.

The other most important thing about golf: don't hit the ball. Well, at least I hit the world. I'm quietly confident.

III

'The thing is,' I'm told, while looking at the video of the thing laughingly known as my swing, in slow-mo, from behind, 'the thing is, the important thing is, the most important thing is, you need to learn to play golf without becoming a golfer.'

Play golf, but never become a golfer?

'Exactly, that's the trick.'

It's a bit like Kipling: if you can play golf but not make golf your master. And a bit like the Karate Kid: whack on, whack off.

Golf is full of these apparently gnomic aphorisms that don't pass scrutiny, but I know what the Fox meant about not becoming a golfer. It's the golfer thing that we find repellent, the social equivalent of having sex with your socks on. But I'm only half listening. I'm watching my backswing, not looking at the perfect geometry the five-iron is making with the elbow point of shoulder, hip, ankle, ball, Ben Nevis, third star past the moon, and carry on till morning. I'm transfixed by my growing bald patch. It's definitely eroding, a pale bunker in the rough of my head. My hair knows I'm becoming a golfer. For all these years it's held out against hair loss because we were both going to pretend that we were still finger-clicking coolios. But golf has torn it. Too much for the barnet, which is emigrating to live on my back in shame.

This is the beginning of my third month ploughing the furrow that is golf, learning to hit an egg-sized ball with a walking stick. I have a comfortable routine. Two mornings a week I go to the Swing Factory and have a lesson with the Fox and the Cat. Usually the American joins me, and we have breakfast in Harvey Nichols afterwards, like a couple of It girls out on a naughty. So far, in purely golfing terms, I've got half a swing. Having half a swing is like having half a breaststroke. In functional terms, you're still drowning. You're just drowning with intent. My putting's better, though. I do that on my own at home, on the carpet. Here's an interesting thing: I can sink a ten-footer eight times out of ten. But putting isn't golf. Golf is driving. Another of those crapulous cushion mottoes that tells you to 'drive for flash, putt for cash'. It's the short game that wins, but it's the big swinging club that gives you that knotted feeling in the gut and the ejaculatory 'yes!' of release.

You know when girls' magazines always say that sex is really about kissing and stroking and whispering and eye contact? Well, that's chipping and putting. Driving is just whacking it up the fairway – and sometimes whacking it into the rough. But it's definitely whacking and whatever they say, the girlie research proves chaps want to whack. Anyway, I should know, I haven't seen a fairway yet. My whacking's all onanistic and premature.

What I have learned is that this game has the ability to puncture you well below the emotional waterline. Up until a week ago it was all just good fun. I would hit one that would click that pleasing dry note and sail away pretty much straight. And it was enough. It was fun. I got a bit better each time. There was the sense of small achievement, but overall I was bad enough to have little expectation.

But slowly, slowly crept in the resentment. The mass of crap shots, the slices and heels and messy strikes, the twisted face (me and the club). Now I get angry and swear. I get impatient with the Fox and I'm beginning to mind. A bell is ringing faintly somewhere. It's warning that if you start caring, this golf thing will give you more pain than pleasure. And the real bummer is that improving won't diminish the misery of getting it wrong.

'You judge a player by the quality of his bad shots, not his good ones,' said the Fox, after I'd had a tantrum. 'Everyone hits a plum ball sometimes. It's how you play through the bad ones and how bad they are that's the measure of your golf.'

This is a game of ceaseless torment, with brief flashes of possible contentment that are cruel illusions. It builds up mountains of expectation before kicking you down wells of despair, while making you dress up like a twat in the company of 28-carat cunts.

'Listen to that,' the Fox shouted to the Cat. 'I think he's really making progress. We've had a breakthrough. Play golf, don't become a golfer.'

Nonchalantly trying not to look like golfers, the American and I went to Harrods and bought putters in the sale. Mine was splendidly expensive and looked like a piece of veterinary equipment or a ranch brand for homosexual cattle. It's a Futura made by someone called Scotty Cameron. Golf has more designer labels than Sloane Street and I got this golf-ball garage affair that saves you having to dig a hole in the carpet. It spits the balls back at you. The dog adores it. Nicola thinks it's grounds for something punitive.

Now I'm being sent boxes of golf kit. I'm not making any of this up. I've got magic glasses to find lost balls, a pro-aim virtual alignment trainer, glasses with lines drawn on them for accurate putting, a laser putting alignment system that works like the red-dot rifle sights in a Bruce Willis movie, Playboy golf balls, soap golf balls, exploding golf balls, wobbly golf balls, balls that light up and flash, a handy gyroscope (don't ask), a cool grip that is neither cool nor gripping, golf sweets and cuff-links. And this is only the steam off the polar bear piss at the tip of the golf iceberg.

No sport has spawned more juju and voodoo, more lucky-junk-tack, more strap-on miracles and humourless plastic chuckles than golf. What's astonishing is that, considering who plays and the amount of money involved in clubs and kit, it hasn't produced anything of intellectual interest or beauty. Golf has such a chronic cultural deficit. It has become the definition of kitsch tastelessness. Why is there no readable golf writing, for instance, unlike boxing or cricket or football? There's only P.G. Wodehouse, but he only wrote about golf because he was exiled in Long Island, away from his consuming love of bat and pad.

Search the web for great golfing books and you'll find *Life with a Swinger* and another one, *Life of O'Reilly: Amusing Adventures of a Professional Irish Caddie*. I bet he does after-dinner speaking. Then there's *Bullets, Bombs and Birdies: Golf in a Time of War*, my personal nomination for most tasteless title ever. There are no great golf films, unless you count *Caddyshack*. There's no golf art, no painting, sculpture or poetry worth repeating. And my short, glimpsed-between-the-fingers acquaintance with golf clubs and hotels confirms that they plumb unknown depths of plush, grisly nastiness.

Golf is bleach to culture. It's anti-style. And we haven't even got to the clothes. It's not that it doesn't care, like rugby. Golfers spend gazillions on themselves and do everything in front of mirrors. But they still haven't managed to evolve a pair of wearable socks. If anyone out there thinks they have a tasteful or stylish golf thing, send it to me here. We'll show the world. You've got a bag made of killer-whale foreskin? Bring it on. A pair of trousers that don't look like they belonged to Simon Cowell with a double hernia and a kilo of haemorrhoids? Chuck them over here.

There is something endearingly spaz about golf's complete whitewash in terms of its contribution to aesthetics, the *nul points* right across the cool board. It is the G-spot of naff. Only two sorts of people wear one white glove: golfers and Michael Jackson impersonators. Their respective places in the canon of Western culture are pretty much a dead heat, prone at the bottom of the barrel.

The trick is to play Michael Jackson, not to be Michael Jackson.

IV

I'm beginning to think something's not quite right with my teachers, the Fox and the Cat. I'm being taught the ancient mastery of the swing, Scotland's gift to the world of martial arts, in a basement next door to Harvey Nichols in London. It used to be a squash court but it's been taken over by golf, like inner-city Methodist chapels get taken over by al-Qaeda mosques. I've been down here in the permanent daylight twice a week for four months, banging balls into the wall. And I'm yet to be allowed out.

'Please, sir, can I go out now?'

'Ooh, what do you think?' the Cat asks the Fox. 'Shall we take him out?'

The Fox shakes his head.

'He's still too delicate, his swing's too fragile, it could fall apart. Better not risk it.'

I feel like a flasher whose parole's been turned down. 'I'm ready, honest. I won't get it out inappropriately. I won't waggle it in front of impressionable caddies.'

Truth is, I reckon they're agoraphobic. I think they live down here. In fact, I wouldn't be surprised if they've never played golf. I expect they came in here to play squash as young men and slowly evolved into teeing off at walls like those blind fish they find in underground lakes.

Here the walls are covered with photos of famous clients holding up cups. They have hyperbolic encomiums Biro'd on them, effuse gratitude for granite swings. But there's not a single picture of the Fox or the Cat and there is something perfect about just driving into a wall for ever, launching balls at an impenetrable obstacle. It's a fable of optimism and hope, every backswing a glorious evocation of indomitable humanity.

One day I'll strike a perfect ball and the wall will crack and then crumble, and behind it will be a warm first tee of the eighteen holes of nirvana. Either that, or it'll be West Berlin. Whoever considered the bitter disappointment of Berliners when the wall finally came down and there on the other side was just more Germany? This is the sort of thing you think about as you slice balls into a wall.

I know I'm being tested. I've seen the *Karate Kid*, I understand it's my patience and ability to subsume earthly vanity and the desire for instant gratification that's being tested. I should admit that I've fallen short. I haven't blasted into the blue yonder. But I have visited another mosque.

It was the-American-who-said-hello-to-the-ball's fault. He lured me to 'this place where we can play virtual golf'. It's a club in London's Soho that looks like a singles' bar, mainly as it's full of singles. There's a very dateable receptionist and the waitresses wear T-shirts saying 'Who's your caddy?' You stand in a booth and hit balls at a wall, but this one has a golf course projected on it. It calculates speed, velocity, direction and gives you a score.

'Where shall we play?' he asked. Checking in to the virtual snobbery of virtual golf, I said the Old Course at St Andrews. I'm going to cut this short. After nine holes I was playing like Captain Hook, a thrashing hysterical parody of pantomime fury. It was bad. I was staring into an abyss of misery and self-loathing. And it wouldn't go away. It was like being dumped for the first time. I played strokes over and over in my head and then imagined other men playing them. Better, harder, longer men. My crapulous spastic inability to hit a fucking plastic dimple goitre into a fucking wall in a stupid fucking ad executive's sad fantasy of a Nintendo pick-up joint almost made me Google for a drug dealer.

But I took my swing back to the Fox and the Cat. They looked at it, stroked it and manipulated its bandy limbs in the manner of Rolf Harris in *Animal Hospital*. The Cat shook his head, more in sorrow than anger. The Fox shouted, more in anger than sorrow. So I'm still here, teeing off carpet, an underground solitary swinger.

I have discovered the Golf Channel, though. It's awful, with long ads for huge woods. You don't even have to reach for penile puns in golf. I like watching the lesbian tournaments called things like 'The Timotei Virginia Open', and I've sat as time stood still for a doofus in a blazer to show me around the celebrity lockers in the Florida World Golf Hall of Fame.

But I do like to watch the experts give top tips. They're all snake-oil preachers selling a proprietary band of salvation. It's so simply complex; a divine sleight of hand. And you'd think hitting a ball was hardly rocket science until you come across Dave Peltz, the

Jimmy Swaggart of the short game. He was a rocket scientist for NASA until he gave it all up to build a robot that could do the perfect putt. His book is the longest scream for help ever to go into double-digit editions.

I've made a virtual-golf friend, an actor with a handicap so small it's a shrug. 'You must come out with me,' he said.

'I can't. I'm not ready. Swing's a bit . . . delicate. But you could come round and watch the back nine of the Dubai Classic.'

'Oh,' he rolls his eyes, 'they're not very attractive, are they, golfers? Not sensual men. Have you ever thought which one you'd have anal sex with if you had to?'

So I sit here watching the golf channel, this illusion of the outdoors, a beautifully impossible Babylon. Men stride on a viridian sward under an azure sky and waft balls into the distance, their arms arcing with a grace that belies the crapness of their kit and their coarse faces.

Maybe golf is a rudimentary, animist faith, a creation myth of hope and the soaring spirit of goals and journeys. I sit here nursing the grub of my swing, hoping it'll fly and wondering whether, if push came to shove, Ernie Els would give me two strokes on a tight lie.

HUNTING

A house with no road. That's odd for a start when you think about it. Not just a practical business, but the metaphysical questions it implies. Letterewe, it's quite a big house. Seven or eight bedrooms, billiards room, dining-room, study, sitting-rooms, wash-rooms, drying-rooms, walled garden and a gunroom. It has that turrety, crenellated, white-and-grey, hunched look of a place that's turned up its granite collar and is keeping a weather eye. It's typically Scots, a home for boots and tweed and tappety barometers; with deep, gimlet windows and blind corridors. A place that rubs its knuckles over smoky fires. From the eaves, glassy, dust-lidded eyes catch the firelight and follow you with a mournful, flickering disinterest.

You get to Letterewe by boat, from a little jetty on Loch Maree. A long, Stygian, black lake that's separated from the green, Hebridian sea by a strip of battered land, Maree was once famous for its salmon but the fish have grown shy. There are islands where the Vikings briefly forced an uneasy steading. They say a Norse princess is buried here under a strand of storm-gnarled pines, the victim of some improbably operatic love-tryst.

The house is not on an island. It squats on the farther shore. It has no road because there's nothing to tether the other end of a road to. Here is an A but there is no B. Behind it rise thousands of acres of wilderness, traversable only by foot or hoof. Long, crumpled miles of crag and gully, hump-backed mountains, springy, sodden moor, burns and cataracts, high lochans and mossy corries inhabited only by ptarmigan, raven, hawk, the wind and the deer.

I'm not sure quite what this story is about. On the face of it, it's about stalking. Here we are in Letterewe, a stalking lodge. Shortly, we'll go out, walk a lot, crawl a bit, spy a stag, kill it, hump it down the hill and sell it to Germany. That's stalking. But that's not the half of it.

I know what this story isn't. And you should know before you pull on the waterproofs and yomp through miles of heathery prose. It's not funny and I don't think it's terribly exciting. It's not postmodern Hemingway. Or nature notes. I think it's about smoking. And typing. And my grandfather.

My mother's father died before I was born. He was a dentist. He wanted to be an engineer but took to teeth – which must have been a worry for his patients. I have his First World War dog-tags and a photograph of him in a swaggery officer's uniform. His tag shows that he was a non-commissioned motorbike messenger. He has a slightly buck-toothed smile (that must have been another worry for his patients). All I know of him is that he loved to shoot. To stalk.

He would spend all his spare time up here on the hill and he wanted his only child to be a boy. When she failed to grow into one, he lost interest. When he dropped dead in an Edinburgh street, his hunting friends took his ashes away to the Highlands, failing to tell his widow or child precisely where.

My grandfather was French and very proud. After he died, they discovered he was actually half-Indian and plainly not so proud. That's my grandfather: a Frenchman who was an Indian; an engineer who was a dentist; an officer who was a private; a sporting gent who lived in a lower-middle-class suburban bungalow. I never think about him. I didn't know him. Apparently, no one did.

I shot my first stag nearly twenty years ago. A bloke I was staying with came down to breakfast, forked a wheel of black pudding and said, 'Do you fancy shooting a stag today?' And I said, 'Why not?' And I did without thinking. It was August, hot and sunny. The stags were still in velvet, and as the stalker gutted him, for the first time I caught that smell, that heavy, delicious, repellent scent of cud and blood and through it, wrapped in it, came this image, a feeling of my grandfather. It was so intense, so insistently present that it made me start.

I'm not really that sort. The sort who gets vibes and feels things. I don't do 'otherworldly'. I've never been in touch with all that stuff that people always tell you you should get in touch with. But there he was, as plain as the scent on the wind in my face. I didn't talk to him. Nothing weird and wickery. But I took to stalking. I'd go every autumn and shoot a stag and sometimes grandfather would be there and sometimes he wouldn't. And then, one year, I couldn't get up a hill. Well I could, but it took me so long, boys had grown beards. By the time I reached the top, making a noise like a boarding-house Ascot, feeling worse than Florence Nightingale's in-tray, I couldn't breathe. I was drowning 2,000 feet above sea level. It was the fags or the stags. I couldn't do both.

So I retired from stalking. Occasionally, I'd look out of the window at the questing metropolitan traffic wardens and hum, 'My heart's in the Highlands, my heart is not here. My heart's in the Highlands, a-chasing the deer.' But I'd take a drag and think that I'd made the right choice, that urban, cultivated choice, and go back to typing.

And then the damnedest thing happened. I gave up smoking. Just like that. I've loved cigarettes with an unquestioning adoration since I was fifteen, bum-sucked fifty of the little darlings down to their tight brown bottoms every day for thirty years. And I fell out of love just like that. I was shocked. It was borderline psychopathic. Here's the thing with giving up smoking. Everyone tells you how good you are, how strong-willed, how sensible and decent. But it's nonsense. It's not like that. Giving up on fags is giving up on immortality. It's not strong will. It's the spirit submitting to the body. It's the triumph of fear. It's middle age. Stopping smoking is a milestone on the road away from golden, fire-breathing youth towards Crown Green bowls. And I knew it. I felt bad. I could breathe but that's small recompense. So I gave myself a consolation prize. I'd go back to the hill and the stags, which is how I came to Letterewe.

The first rule of stalking is the first rule of life. It's all in the kit. And of all the kit, in all the world, Scots outdoor kit is the bonniest. Stalking actually begins weeks and miles before the Highlands with an intense track round the gun shops and Outward Bound fantasy-mongers of the metropolis, where you can frot waterproof, breathable fabric with labels that are short novels; leer over inflatable stoves and mosquito-repelling wristwatches, while all around you is the siren call of the wild, the slow rending of Velcro. There are boots and gaiters and belts and knives and jackets and fleeces and plus twos, plus fours and the delightful anticipation of new hats. All essential.

The most imperative bit of kit, though, is a cook. A good Scots cook; no snorting, gummy chalet girls with hips like sandbags and 37 Saucy Things To Do With Pasta. We want porridge made with pinhead oats and salt. We need oatcake farls and underage grouse and plump partridge and fat-backed bacon and barley for broth and scones for tea and mutton and rowan jelly and venison and claret and whisky. And Mars Bars. We demand The Full McMonty.

And then all of a sudden it's the airport and Inverness and Jackie from – would you believe – 'Hy Jack Cabs' (the plural is an exaggeration). And the drive across country to Wester Ross and Loch Maree. Which is where we came in. Suddenly, after all the fluster and humping and tickets and lists is just the dying light, the silence and the cool, clean air.

I've shot at lots of things in lots of places. But nothing is like stalking. I can't remember a single pheasant drive with any clarity. I can, though, remember every stag I ever stalked. I can place each one with minute detail. Each is a story, a coherent narrative complete and different. But they all start with the box.

'Do you mind having a go at the box straight away?' asks the stalker. The box is a cardboard, placed a hundred yards off with the target Sellotaped to its side. There's a bit of grotty carpet on the grass 'for your nice clothes'.

'Okay. In your own time, just to get a feel of the gun. Take it easy, no pressure.' I lie on the damp lawn outside the gunroom, still in my London clothes. The stalkers stand back with their fingers in their ears; a brace of pony boys feign indifference. One rests a telescope in the doorjamb and squints. *No pressure.* The telescopic sight isn't the crosshair type of spy films and book jackets. It's the more difficult post site. A blunt, black arrow points up from the bottom of the circle. Where it touches space is where the shot will fall. The stick quests across the tree line, the box bobs as if it were at sea; the target's an indistinguishable dot, a full stop in search of a sentence. The barrel gets heavier, breathe in, then half out. I can feel my heart jarring, everything is made of rubber. Squeeze the trigger like an orange, like a nipple, like a pimple, like it's glass. The tip of the finger, stroking the bottom of the curling tine. There's a tiny, coy resistance, then black noise. The gun jerks up, the report is a startling flat, hard slap like a huge fist punching the air. I look round at the man with the telescope. He searches. 'Och, yeah, bottom left.'

'Have another go,' says the stalker. 'Take your time, no pressure.'

Three shots scattered at random. 'That's fine,' he says, 'Just fine. As long as you're within the outer circle, that'll kill your beast.'

It isn't really fine. I'm not a great rifle shot. I can't produce those neat little clusters of holes but it'll do. And the stalkers know what to expect.

At this point, we ought to do the man-to-man hardware talk: the gun stuff, barrels and triggers, noses, charges and trajectories. But I'm not really interested. I can fake the chat. I just can't remember any of the numbers. Some people care; Germans and Belgians care. They bring beautiful, huge guns that nestle in foam rubber, with calibres that can punch holes in history. But stalking isn't really about rifles. Or, actually, shooting. Not for me anyway. It's about something else. Something that's just out of the corner of my eye, that's shy of explanation.

But, I should tell you what to expect in the death department. You should try to shoot a stag at about a hundred yards. Closer if you can get there, a bit further back if you have to. But a hundred yards is quite far enough. You'll shoot it broadside, standing still. You'll be lying down. You trace a line up the inside edge of the foreleg and continue halfway up the body. That's where you aim. It's not a heart shot. The heart is too low down in the chest. You'll miss or shatter a leg. You aim for inside the diaphragm, anything mucking about there at speed will be mortal. The stag will take a step or two, maybe run a few yards, but it's not going anywhere – except Germany.

And, I ought to tell you what we're stalking. The red deer is the largest indigenous animal in Britain. Even so, it's half the size of the same species across the channel. Its natural habitat is forest. Indeed out of respect, they call these barren, treeless hills a forest – and once it was but now it's peat. The Scottish red deer uses most of its energy keeping warm. All its natural predators are extinct so, as it gets smaller, it grows more numerous and ranges ever further.

The deer are a serious problem in the Highlands. Hinds have a calf each year; the mortality rate in the long winter is high. Stags and hinds live separately until the rut, when the stags come down to gather harems and fight. The rut is set by the weather and perhaps the moon that is now huge and bright and full. And the stags are starting to bellow. That's the Attenborough bit.

The red stag is also stupidly handsome. He moves with the sure-footed lightness of a boxer and the stateliness of a king. He carries cupped in his bony head the weight of his artistic, mythological, poetic and heraldic heredity with an elegant, imperious assumption. Deer are magical beasts. You never shoot one lightly. We don't stalk for trophies. This is important. We aim at the weak and the old, particularly switches – stags whose antlers form a single, lethal dirk.

Letterewe is one of the biggest and, by universal consent, one of the best-managed and environmentally sensitive estates in Scotland. But it'll wait until tomorrow. Now it's dinner and a sleepless bed. The moon shines over the loch, the pines sway black across the pewter sky. And the cry of the loon eddies from the island Valhalla.

7.30 am. Breakfast.

Porridgeeggsbaconsausagesblackpuddingtoastcoffee.

But no kippers – they follow you around all day, like the Ancient Mariner. Stalking is also about conviviality; an individual sport, at best, boasted about to a team. But it's not high-testosterone. A lot of women shoot. They shoot better than men – more accurate, unsurprisingly deadly.

For this trip, I've invited along two chaps who've never stalked before. Carlo, an urbane Italian dealer in very modern art with a severe dose of the English wannabes. He's kitted out like Lord Peter Wimsey. And the actor Ross Kemp, whose top half looks like it's going to garrotte towel-heads and his bottom half is going to a gymkhana.

Outside the gunroom, the stalkers – David and Norman – and the pony boys and eager-beaver terriers and the frightful midges wait patiently. Stalkers are singular men, like the captains of ships. You employ them as servants, but, out on the vastness of the hill, their word is iron law. A stalker says what you shoot and when. If he says lie down and crawl, you crawl, even if you are wading a burn. They have an almost uncanny knowledge of country, a sensitivity to wind and the best of them think like stags. They all have soft voices and hard hands and in rural communities they are held in high regard, though their pay is Victorian, their work medieval and their prospects gloomy – rheumatism, arthritis, bent backs and a long, shuffling retirement in a cold bothie, collecting firewood. I've met stalkers that I didn't like, but never one that I didn't admire.

On the first day, Carlo went for his stag and came down the hill caked in gore. It's tradition: after your first stag, you are turned into Driller Killer. Usually it's just a strip on the cheek but Carlo copped a couple of pints because of his impeccable neatness. Norman informed him with a fearsomely straight face that he had to wear it until midnight or have bad luck for ten generations. And being Italian – and therefore more superstitious than a convention of clairvoyants in a ladder factory – and not wanting to flout protocol, he kept it on for dinner, cracking and peeling like an Old Master.

The next day, I shot my stag, an old chap we found sitting on his own on a high plateau. He looked a long way off, but through the sight I could see the individual hairs on his neck, the sweep of his wide head. The tension before you shoot is as extreme as anything I've ever known and there's a moment when you really see what you are about to do. You stare and will the bullet home. There's the double thud, the echo that arrives in the splitting of an atom as the shot strikes. The beast jerks and tenses, absorbing the massive shock, walks a few steps, stands and sways, head dropping under the weight of his crown, flanks heaving, straining at the bubbling wreckage of lung, bone and muscle. And gently he settles onto his haunches so that from the firing position all we can see are his black antlers; slowly they slide sideways, like the masts of the sinking ship.

David, crouching, crabs forward, takes his thick-bladed knife and jabs it into the base of the beast's head. Searching for the axis at the top of the spine, he works the steel back and forth, edging it between the bones. The deer doesn't move; its tongue lolls, still with the fresh grass on it. The soft muzzle shivers with faint breath. David taps the dark eye with the flat of the blade.

I'm always astonished that even in so violent and sudden a death, how gentle and fragile is the departing of life. You can sense it stealing away, evaporating with the slightest whisper. He slits the cheek to age the teeth and he's about ten – younger than he looked. Must have had a hard winter. I gralloch him, slitting the stomach from sternum to pizzle. I reach into the hot cavity, feeling through the slimy entrails for the spleen to grip the top of the stomach and reach the whole ninety-nine yards out onto the heather for corbies (crows) that are already circling and cawing. David sits and smiles and says, after a bit, 'My but that's a fine and expensive watch you've left in there.'

On the last day, Ross and I go for his stag. This is what I like best. The joy of the stalk. Someone else to shoot. We are going to search the distant march of the beat. Stalking is all about wind. Stags have uncanny hearing, excellent sight in black and white; but their black noses are their most reliable long-distance warning. You travel all day with the wind in your face. The wind constantly eddies and backs, bouncing off cliffs and down blind glens. Worst of all are the days when there is no wind, but they're rare in Scotland.

We start out at 8.30 am, working our way up. First thing is always up. You have to be high to spy the deer. And high up is where the stags like to be, for the same reason. Up there, the wind is true. Up, up in slow lung-tugging zigzags: a thousand, two thousand feet in the first two hours. Now, there's a point on every stalk I've ever done where I think with absolute conviction that this is the very last time I'm ever going to do this.

Trudging up a one-in-two incline, with a drop beneath you and a summit that keeps retreating above, I think, 'What a ridiculous piece of asinine, male bravado.' And then you reach the top and breathing is less like sword-swallowing and you look up from your feet for the first time in an hour and it just takes your breath away all over again.

To say that Scotland is beautiful is to turn out a predictable truism, but it's the quality of that beauty. There is a keening melancholy in the emptiness. This is a sad place. A sad country. I've often wondered if I'd enjoy stalking over some other landscape. But I've never had the inclination to shoot fat stags in German oak forests, or scramble up Switzerland for hairy goats. It's the emptiness of the place. It's not an untouched, pristine emptiness. The Highlands are bereft.

We walk up and up and in the neck of a glen, by a sandy loch, a spellbinding place, there's the footprint of a croft. They are dotted all over the hills. I try to imagine the life up here, the savage winters, the unforgiving soil, the shin-splintering rock, the impossibility of comfort, the weeping loneliness. The families who once lived here are now probably bankers in America, shopkeepers in Canada or lawyers in Australia. Scotland's long history of disappointment, heroic failure and exodus has made this stoic, granite landscape a memorial to a million small, personal wars lost to despair, politics and time. Scotland is not that much smaller than England. It has a population of five million, four-and-a-half of whom live in the conurbation between Glasgow and Edinburgh. The rest of it is stone memories.

We walk on, up and up; a covey of ptarmigan fly beneath us, calling like someone winding a large clock. The day grows into a sublime wonder, the light dapples and sidles over the hills. The deer are always ahead of us. In their eerie corries, we can hear the stags roaring to each other; they're rolling in peat, painting themselves black, hanging garlands of grass and myrtle from their antlers. They're maddened and bold with pummelling hormones; too excited even to eat; their necks swollen to make their challenging bellows. Across a glen, we sight a river of them, five, six hundred stags raving across the hillside. Some are huge, holding their great heads up and back to support their crowns of bone. On and on we walk, drinking from tumbling burns. The ravens fly past, their wings creaking like starched linen. And then we're on a crag, a serrated spine of rock above the clouds. Far below are two bible-black lochs with cascading waterfalls. To the east, beyond a rainbow, this rolling, blasted moor flows into the green fields of Inverness-shire. And to the west there's Loch Maree and the sea. And over the sea, the great Cuillin mountains of Skye and, beyond that, shadows in a glittering ocean, the Outer Hebrides, Lewis and Harris. I can see from coast to coast, from North Sea to Atlantic.

Ross finds his stag at about 5.30 pm. He has a tricky, awkward stalk. At 6.30 pm, there's a shot. Gingerly we make our way down and there he is, as red and bald as a pillar box, grinning fit to split.

We drag the stag down to a plateau where the ponies can reach it, heft it onto the complicated Victorian saddle with its dozens of belts and buckles, the head twisted up over its shoulder, leather pulled tight under its breast bone. The ponies are fat, stubborn garrons, the indigenous Scots horse. Sure-footed, unflappable, they pick their way through the bog and shale, carrying the great dead weight, dripping sweat and foam and blood.

Walking back is easier, the wind behind us, the setting sun ahead. I can't disengage my feelings for Scotland from this landscape. They're all one. I suffer the heightened sentimentality of all expatriates. I live in London. I sound English but I was born here. I have a feeling for it that's beyond words. This place is the only inanimate thing in the world that I miss. It's all wrapped up with history and my grandfather, the little, dark Frenchman who escaped here from Verdun. How astonishingly peaceful and grave and grand it must have seemed to him.

We get back to the lodge at 9 pm, eleven hours' hard walking, eighteen tricky and treacherous miles. That's Scots miles, mind, which are longer than your soft Sassenach ones. Then whisky as the moon rises, teasing and banter. A bath, a grouse, a bed. And tomorrow, London, where I can go back to being a Scotsman who sounds like an Englishman, a hunter who stalks with a keyboard.

SHOOTING

I once took a friend from New York shooting. A small, traditional, driven family shoot in Gloucestershire set around a country house, not unlike another house of lore – P.G. Wodehouse's Blandings. Driven shooting is when the hunters (or guns) stand still and the beaters or servants do all the walking about, and the Chinese birds do the really energetic aerobic running, shouting, flapping, and then falling from a great height. This is different from hunting, which is . . . the uneatable in pursuit of the unspeakable or the other way round, as Oscar – yes, that one – said constantly. Hunting involves a fox being chased by hounds being chased by horses being chased by merchant bankers, gay interior decorators, farmers, resting criminals, nymphomaniac girls with faces like farriers' anvils and asses like airbags, and Camilla Parker Bowles chased by psychopathic vegan animal liberationists chased by fat policemen chased by paparazzi chased by insurance-claim lawyers.

My friend turned up at breakfast ready to hike the Rockies. He was swagged and bonded like a Japanese sex toy. When he walked, his high-visibility neoprene sounded like a lizard orgy in a cornflakes box. His boots had three sorts of lace holes. The rest of us wore dung-coloured tweed and bedroom slippers.

That evening he tipped up in the drawing-room for pre-dinner drinks resplendent in a dinner jacket with wing collar and bow tie, patent shoes, and glittering studs; he looked like he was about to make an acceptance speech or burst into song. The rest of us were in old, stained, balding, saggy smoking-jackets with open shirts, jeans, and those carpet slippers again. He took me aside and said, with just a hint of peeve, 'This is a joke, right? You all put on collars and ties and wear cuff-links to kill birds in muddy fields, but for the formal dinner with the butlers and the ladies in frocks you wear jeans and open shirts.'

I shrugged apologetically. What could I say? It's shooting. It's the country. It's the English. I tried to explain that the thing with shooting is that it's almost all to do with kit. It's not about dressing up, it's about dressing down, and, frankly, it's absurd. That's the thing about an awful lot of traditional life. If we stopped to think about it for a quiet rational moment we'd blush scarlet, change our names, and never dream of doing anything that ludicrous again.

Englishmen who shoot spend the close season from February through August pining like widowed swans. They yearn for the smell of cordite and the crippled flutter of wounded birds trying to escape the jaws of hysterical spaniels. Then, when shooting starts again, they'll turn up for a weekend with a suitcase big enough to require a zoning permit and they won't sleep a wink the night before. And then they'll come down in the morning with odd socks, a shirt that hasn't fitted since they were at school, an egg-yellow pullover (inside out), the wife's hat, and some mud left over from last year.

Shooting clobber is that peculiarly English thing: studied, posed, rubbish. This is not to be confused with the French existentially studied nonchalance or the Italian casually studied exhibitionism. Every single bit of shooting kit should look like it has been put on in the dark by a depressed Method actor. To look this ridiculously ghastly takes great application, and just in case you're ever caught out by an invitation to shoot stupid birds in England, here's a tip: the central mystery of shooting is not skill – nobody gives a fig whether you can shoot or not as long as you don't kill someone who was at school with your father. And it's certainly nothing to do with food or hunter-gathering, or love of fresh air, or nature, exercise or, heaven forbid, male bonding. Male bonding is one of the things Englishmen carry guns to deter.

The central mystery, the core belief of shooting, is tweed. Tweed of the father, tweed of the son, and Holey Tweed. The indigenous national costume of the British Isles in winter is tweed. Compared with the lightweight, temperature-controlled, breathable, waterproof, utilitarian, stylish and comfortable materials readily available for all sorts of outdoor fun and games these days, tweed is antediluvian lunacy; it's like wearing thatch.

Englishmen will tell you with tears in their eyes that because it works for sheep and their grandfathers, tweed is unimprovable. This is a hairy, ignorant lie. One of the many lies that make English weekends what they so richly are, and, anyway, what other aspect of your safety or comfort would you entrust to the example and experience of a sheep?

First and last, tweed is hellishly uncomfortable. English country tweed isn't that soft, languorously draping material you associate with Cary Grant and the Duchess of Windsor. This stuff is so solid you park it in the closet rather than hang it. The trousers feel as if you've got George Michael's chin between your thighs. It's invariably far too hot, except for those mornings when it's bloody freezing. An Englishman claims tweed is magically water-repellent. It's not. It's water-absorbent – not the same thing. And as shooting takes place in the Arctic monsoon season, it gets an awful lot to absorb. A decent tweed jacket can suck up three times its own weight in liquid and then retain it like a miserly camel. It will also smell like a miserly camel. Most shooting tweeds still have areas of last century's dampness.

Ideally a tweed should be inherited. You should wear your father's or the remnants of your grandfather's. There is no such thing as tweed that fits – it just sags. There is, though, one big plus with tweed: the cleaning. It's very simple. You can't do it. You can't dry-clean tweed because it turns into chipboard; you can't put it into a washing machine because it morphs into a dinosaur's fur ball. The recommended method for cleaning tweed – and I'm not making this up – is to 'lie it in a cold bath and then dry it flat.' Well, I'm sorry, but what in all creation was ever cleaned by being laid in a cold bath? And it would take eighteen months to dry out laid flat.

And who in the history of dressing up ever thought that plus fours or plus twos were a practical and attractive addition to the male wardrobe combined with long woolly socks, which are usually characterful, coming with amusing stripes, patterns, and occasionally knitted swear words?

The English also make their keepers, beaters, pickers-up, flag-men, and stops (all servants) dress up in tweed, like extras and suspects from an Agatha Christie mystery. Old or grand estates have their own tweed, like a clan tartan. Some of them have an ancient and modern tweed, some have separate ladies' tweeds – stop me if this is getting just too outré. Having been designed by the English county class, most of these bespoke tweeds challenge the eye. Shoot servants all have to wear the same pattern so they trundle around the heather and the bracken looking like a game of hide-and-seek played by scatter cushions.

Everything about shooting is retrospective. The shotgun I use – an Edwinson Green side-by-side, from a good extinct maker, not a best extinct maker – was made in the year that Zola died and Conrad wrote *Heart of Darkness* and the first Rhodes scholarship was awarded. A modern gun would be far cheaper, more efficient, reliable, and easier – so would Gore-Tex boots, but we all trudge about in gumboots and ancient leather hobnail shoes. Given the choice of something that is efficient, light, and easy to use, and something that's complicated, heavy, ugly and unreliable, we'll go for the latter every time. We'd rather hitch a lift in the wheezing Land Rover than slip into the warmth and comfort of the Japanese 4x4.

The English aren't alone in having a special dressing-up box for shooting. The French and the Spanish have wonderfully subtle, elegant shooting clothes, and the Austrians make the most beautiful hunting kit in the world – deer-leather trousers with decorative embroidery, loden jackets with horn buttons. It's elegant, dashing, practical and warm, while the English insist on looking like poachers and tramps. The worst faux pas – far worse than looking like a Canadian rambler – would be to turn up at breakfast dressed as an Austrian archduke, unless of course you are an Austrian archduke, in which case it would be excusable. But you'll be relentlessly teased for your arch-ness.

The smelly ugliness of shooting kit plays up to a particularly English trait of wanting to rise and shine in despiteness. The English want to be loved, despite their teeth, despite their voices and stupid names, despite their chronic studied shyness and irritating faux self-deprecation, and most of all despite their erotic-as-Tupperware country-weekend clothes.

It's not masochism or intransigence or fear of innovation, it's a sort of role-playing nostalgia. A feeble belief that if you repeat a thing over and over it remains valid, even if its original purpose is dead and gone. And that, like the hymnbook, the ancient and the modern can happen together, at the same time. If you dress up in the clothes of the past, if you suffer the damp and cold draughts of your grandfather, then in some way you're taking part in a practical sense in something that communes with the past and fits in with the rolling round of the seasons.

Autumn arrives the same every year, and although everything about it is new and different, it's still an immutable and comforting repetition. We'll get up while it's still dark, and dress with an exaggerated quietness so as not to wake the other half of the bed. We'll pull on the damp kit with its familiar buttons and smells, we'll hiss for dogs and lift heavy bags and steel out into the pewter dawn, cursing the cold and swearing that next week we're definitely, definitely going to get a new sensible coat.

And when it's all over, everyone who shoots has had the experience of stopping on the motorway for petrol . . . standing on the neon forecourt, with the sudden, horrified shock of catching sight of himself on the security monitor looking like an utter prat, a ghost from some Dickensian film. And behind him the lumpen men of the twenty-first century queue up and snigger and whisper behind their blinged-up fingers.

My New York friend enjoys shooting. He likes it for all the reasons we try not to. He likes the 'guy thing'. I now lend him my kit. He wears tweed and plus twos and gumboots and a flat cap from before the war. But he still looks like an eastern Democrat, like a Yankee in the court of King Arthur. The clothes seem to reject him like a transplanted organ. His squeaky, blonde, suede-and-flats New York girlfriend came to have tea after a shoot. She took one look at him and laughed like a hyena. Later he told me they'd had really elaborate sex afterwards.

'She wouldn't let me take the tweed off and wanted me to talk dirty like an Englishman,' he said.

'What did you say?' I asked.

'Well, I said I was going to tie her up with an old school tie that I wasn't entitled to wear.'

Ooohh, *rude*.

DOG

I'm looking at a bunch of flowers. It's expensive, hand-plaited and knotted, £70 minimum. They're for me. I've been bunched. Someone wanted to say it with flowers. The note that came with them says, 'Sorry' but the flowers say, 'You're a fucking monster.' They say it in *a cappella*, colour-coordinated, greenly scented harmony. They're from a man. When men send each other flowers it means one of four things. It means one of them is a gardener, one of them is an interior decorator or cheating on an interior decorator, one of them is dead, or one of them is a monster. The man who sent them to me was an editor, so none of the above. I checked my pulse and it must be me: I'm either the interior decorator or the monster. I have become a diva, the Pavarotti of print. I'm toying with the idea of insisting on my own personal sub-editor. I want Mario to do my picture and Nicky my hair. I want my name above the headline. I want my name to *be* the headline. I want my prose in bold. I want editorial control of readers' letters. I want control of readers. I want, I want . . . How did it end up like this? How did I get bunched by an editor? Because I'd behaved like Lady Victoria Hervey at a TV soap opera awards party.

My Great-Aunt Netta used to say, 'If it's a choice between being brilliant and being nice, be nice. And if you don't have the choice (and you don't) be nice, because you don't have to be brilliant to be nice.' I know what kicked all this off, when my inner monster came out of its closet. It was the dog. An editor (not the floral one, another one) called to enquire politely, nicely, about a piece I owed. It was late, exceedingly late, later than a Bulgarian tackle, later than the USA joining a world war, later than Jools Holland and David Letterman, so late, in fact, that the entire magazine was waiting on the printers' slipway, so did I think perhaps I might let them have it?

Instead of saying sorry, which would have been the Aunt Netta, nice option, I said, 'I'll give you the piece by Friday, if you give me a puppy on Monday.' And instead of saying, 'Fuck off, you megalomaniac little madam,' which would have been the normal sane reaction, the editor waited a beat and said, 'What breed?' And then instead of me saying, 'Ho, ho, ho, I was only joking,' I stepped through the door marked Barking Monster and growled, 'A Parson Russell Terrier. A bitch with a pedigree.'

And so it was that I morphed from mild-mannered hack to loony man of letters and became an eye-rolling anecdote: 'What's the worst job you ever had?'

'Getting a small bitch for that A.A. Gill.'

With a disturbing sense of unreality I filed the piece on Friday and on Monday a pair of editorial assistants, who presumably had double-firsts from ivy-clad academe and had beaten off hundreds of other applicants to gain a toehold in publishing, presuming that it would be, well, God knows what people presume magazine publishing would be, but certainly not driving to Norfolk and back pretending to be a puppy-less couple on behalf of some columnist with a stratospheric ego crisis.

'It's very sweet,' said one of the young over-achievers, 'it's been sick on my lap twice. We called it Biscuit.' *Her* Biscuit.

'Did you? Can I get you anything? No, well, bye-bye.'

I was beginning to understand why very famous, very mad people are often seen as bad-mannered and distant, and can end up as recluses. It's the look on other people's faces, the shadow of mild disgust insufficiently covered by polite disbelief that exposes the bad behaviour.

So there I was, alone in the house, with a Parson Russell puppy, long-legged, wire-haired, a question-mark tale, a tan face with a white blaze. She became Putu, the Zulu word for maize porridge. Naming pets is a glimpse into the prosaic flights of ego, like the naming of celebrity children. You're not giving the thing an identity; you're putting a label on the new extension of you.

Now I'm not going to give you a long, winsome description of dog and man: the runs through the long grass, the amusing little adventures in the shoe cupboard, the heartache of the worm pills, the crisis of the turd in the early morning kitchen. Humans' stories about dogs come just after their stories about dyspraxic children for their utter hell. Suffice it to say, in the language of Californian self-help gurus, I had a dog-shaped hole in my life that Putu filled neatly.

What's always fascinated me is how our species ever got a dog-shaped hole in the first place. Why didn't we have a sloth-shaped or a Noah's Ark-shaped hole? I understand this is rather deflecting the subject from my bad behaviour, but actually it's more interesting. Dogs are the oldest of all domesticated animals. Before sheep or cattle, long before horses and arable farming, man shared his hearth and his bones with dogs, and no one knows quite why. The relationship between horses, sheep, chickens and men is obvious. We eat them and sometimes fuck them. With dogs it's not as straightforward. The hominids that walked out of Africa came with dogs at their heels, but why?

The first question that everything in the world asks itself every morning is: 'So, what's in it for me?' It's not clear what was in it for man or dog at the start. Later, of course, dog would herd, guard, catch crooks, find people in earthquakes and be Shep. To see what's in it for the dog, you only have to compare the number of dogs with wolves. Domestication is a vast advantage for a species. The original progenitor of the domestic cow is long extinct. Happily, animals don't have romantic, new-age, green problems with a free life as opposed to a housebound-and-fed life. But in the beginning, the hunter-gatherer and the dog must have been competitors. Packs of dogs would have been after exactly the same food as people and it's safe to imagine that given the opportunity they'd have killed and eaten each other.

Selection and survival are all about opportunity. What the precise set of circumstances was that made dogs and men cohabit we'll never know, but a likely scenario is that a clan of hominids found orphaned puppies. They wouldn't have been an immediate threat, neither would they have been much of a meal. And a human, probably a child, looked at them and went, 'Ah!' And in that instant there was one of those turning points for a species that is the difference between an evolutionary early bath and a seat on the sofa with your own doctor. It was a moment that went into slow motion and had violins as a soundtrack. The dogs recognised the opportunity. This was what dogs had been born for. This was the once-in-a-lifetime opportunity for an entire species.

Hominids and dogs were opportunistic. Most animals made their living by being specialist tradesmen, working to be the most efficient in a particular habitat or circumstance. They play all their evolutionary cards in one hand. But some are generalists, doing a bit of everything, always competing with specialists but able to adapt. It's tougher to begin with, there are a lot of risks and a lot of casualties, but in the end it seems that nature favours the dilettante. Adaptation is the name of the beautiful survival game. And these puppies saw an opportunity. They saw something they couldn't understand, but they saw that they might exploit it. The puppies noticed that humans had a range of expression and behaviour that was outside dog experience, but that 'Ah!' showed they could manipulate it. They were the first animals to see and understand the importance of human emotions. To live with men, dogs had to do a pretty swift makeover. You can't have small kids and an adult wolf in the same tent, trust me. So dogs do something called neoteny. They remain in a juvenile state for their whole lives. Domestic dogs grow up to be childish wolves, never getting to adulthood because that would make them unpredictable and violent and a blanket.

Dogs are naturally pack animals so they found it easy to fit in. The biggest problem in becoming domesticated is not for the species who can't live with humans, it's for the ones who can't live with each other. For thousands of years we tried to domesticate cheetahs. They're readily trainable, but you can't breed them because they're solitary. Cheetahs have never managed to get over themselves and now they're endangered. Dogs, on the other hand, now live on every continent and country on earth. They've gone into space, though they didn't know why and they didn't come back. They managed to do one other incredibly clever thing: they mutated faster than any other animal. A new variety can be made in less time than Ferrari can make a new car.

You might say that inventing breeds is wholly human – and choosing the colour swatches and size is – but it can only be managed with the acquiescence of the dog. We've been breeding horses for 3,000 years and a horse is still a horse; there's nothing like the variation between a Chihuahua and a Great Dane. Dog species may come and go but their genes are pooled infinitely.

The first dogs realised that, alone in the natural world, humans crave variety. Everything else wants continuity and certainty; people want novelty. And dogs provided it. What they came up with is the cleverest thing in all of nature: reverse-Darwinism – not the survival of the fittest but the survival of the least fit, the most needy. The Chinese Crested is a completely naked Chihuahua except for a tuft of old man's pubes on its head and tail. It has large, lachrymose eyes, huge ears and a tiny little nose. It feels like dry chamois leather and it'll go floppy in the crook of your arm and stare up at you. It's imitating a human baby. What's even cleverer is that its temperature is a couple of degrees higher than normal. It's imitating a sick baby, so you'll care for it. As an animal, it's a fucking disaster. As a dog, it's supremely successful.

Dogs have understood that they can use their genes to become smaller, furrier, weaker, worse hunters, reedier-voiced. Wolves went on being better and better wolves and now they're just behind the cheetahs in extinction's waiting-room. Dogs, meanwhile, have their own doctors and holiday homes, their own laws, their own human police force (the RSPCA), their own professional association (the Kennel Club), and they have welfare. They live with all the benefits of the most civilised humans. They even have people who follow them round picking up their shit. (This is an utterly inexplicable waste to a dog, but then everything we do is utterly inexplicable to dogs.) They recognise our emotion. Over a thousand years they've learned to read it and react to it, but they can have no idea what it means or why we do it. All they know is how to exploit it.

The most fascinating thing about them is that they are no closer to understanding what it is to be human than they were 10,000 years ago, but they pander to our feelings with an infinite subtlety. It's like a play where only half the cast understands the language it's written in. The irrefutable rules of evolution say that there must be something in this relationship for us. And plainly there is: dogs sniff, lead, herd and fetch slippers, but those things don't account for 1 per cent of dogs. They do something more complex for us. They're nature's yes men. A dog is the ultimate lifetime sycophant. A junkie tramp sitting on a pavement in his own wee can have a dog whose look says, 'You're a god among men.' Dogs allow us to be stars in our own lives. They're an endlessly appreciative audience, our most assiduous fans and obsessive stalkers. It's not for real, of course. They just read us in the way a wolf reads a caribou, and if the caribou had opposable thumbs and a tin opener then the wolf would probably let it get dinner instead of ripping its throat out.

When you fall over and break your hip and can't reach the phone, your dog will try his damnedest to help. He'll bark and jump and whine and wag. But when no one comes, have no doubts: he'll eat you. He's a dog. In the way of things, when I turned the corner and stepped through that door marked 'Ooh, get you!' and became the monster, God and Darwin (who are an item) had a bit of a laugh and gave me an antidote, brought on the Fool to my Lear.

As I write, Putu's lying on her chair that used to be my chair, and she's watching me. She can watch me for hours and hours. Her expression looks very like devotion. The eyebrows twitch. She rests her chin on her paws in adoration, except she doesn't. Those emotions are exclusively human. What she's doing is learning me. She's reading me like a book. The truth is, I'm the Fool to her Lear.

Dogs are bigger and better monsters than we can ever be. They've found the weakness in our huge brains: we're slaves to our sentiment and emotions. For dogs, we're just a resource. We're prey.

BEETLES

Being the day of the Princess of Wales's funeral, it sticks in my mind. My watch was still on London time as I stepped off the little plane onto the baked red-earth airstrip. Eleven o'clock – time for the two-minute silence. There was nothing but silence. For as far as the ear could hear, just the shimmering, humming halogen silence of the desert.

The Kalahari is a place of few words. It cares little for princesses, though it knows a lot about death. There are rules here, and you had better understand them. It is unforgiving of innocent mistakes. Things that do decide to make a life for themselves here tend to be curmudgeonly, suspicious, tooled-up specialists. There aren't many dilettantes in the Kalahari – lifestyle experiments tend to end up as someone else's opportunity.

I love it here. The Kalahari is one of the last places on Earth without a hint of sycophancy. At its heart, a day's slow, tooth-jarring, thorn-whipped drive from any direction, are the Makarikari salt pans. This is an extraordinary place, so flat and featureless you can turn 360 degrees and see nothing but the curve of the globe. In the wet season it becomes a shallow soda lake, overrun with flamingos. For most of the year, though, it's a baked crust of salt. Nothing lives here, things only die. Flocks of exhausted finches lie preserved in bas-relief. Elephants' footprints, perhaps a decade old, pad nowhere. For thousands of years, the San people, the bushmen, have trekked out here to collect salt, which they bartered for tobacco and beads. Salt – the oldest currency in the world, the origin of our word 'salary'. Its main value is as a preservative, but it's also a poison. It sickens the earth, turns men mad, and burns and sucks the moisture from the living and the dead.

So while picking over the glittering white crust, I was surprised to come across a beetle. A couple of centimetres of questing, streamlined black oval. How had it got here? Had it been blown from the relative fecundity of the desert by the hot wind? And then there was another. And another. This was no unlucky shipwreck – the beetles must live here. But why, and how? It was one of the little mysteries of a desert where all life is something of a mystery. I collected a couple in a film canister, put them in my pocket and forgot about them. Weeks later, back home, with nothing better to do, I went to the Natural History Museum in South Kensington to see Martin Brendell, the lead curator of beetles.

I've always adored Waterhouse's monumental mausoleum to Mother Earth on Brompton Road. It is the closest thing this city possesses to a humanist pantheon. To get to beetles, you go through the terracotta hall, up the grand staircase, left past the bust of the remarkable Frederick Selous, on through monkeys and the 'Darwin Experience', past the stuffed drongo, until you come to large double doors marked 'Entomology Library'. Here you step into the secret part of the museum. Museum is not the right word for this business – less than 1 per cent of its collection is on display. It employs 900 people, 350 of them natural scientists. This isn't merely a temple or a museum, or even a resource, it's an ark. Up another flight of stairs – through a locked door with a sign asking you not to bring in unwanted live specimens – are beetles. Row upon row of cabinets that reach twice as high as a man, each filled with thin, wooden, colour-coded drawers. From a Hobbit-like den in a corner popped Martin Brendell. Now, to say that people who devote their lives to animals take on something of the nature of their work is a lazy journalistic truism. But Brendell really does have a beetlishness about him. A compact, alert man with a grizzled beard, he moves with a mechanical directness, legs bowed, one arm held awkwardly at an angle. I'm afraid there's no other way of putting this – he beetles down the labyrinth of his habitat. He has the personable manner of a man whose inquisitiveness is at odds with a natural reluctance to socialise. I'd guess that he was once a solitary foraging boy with disgusting pockets.

To say he's obsessed with beetles is not enough. He is possessed, and has been since he was seventeen, in the 1960s, when he came to the museum and wanted to work on mammals. 'But there wasn't an opening, so I got beetles,' he says, with a shudder of someone who narrowly escaped a life-deforming accident. He has been here ever since. In a few years he'll have to retire, and it doesn't bear thinking about, so he doesn't, and burrows on. I gave him my little beetle and waited. 'Yes, well, it's carnivorous, a predator.' Called? 'Oh, I don't know. It's probably an unrecorded species.' You mean I've discovered a new beetle? 'Perhaps, I'll have to check.' My mind races – a new species. I see papers in serious magazines, lecture tours, awards, honorary fellowships. A grateful nation. A beard – and a name: my name, appended to the great roll-call of life. 'Gill's salt beetle.' And I can't understand why he isn't slapping me on the back, reaching for the dusty bottle of amontillado kept for just such occasions.

This is exciting – a new beetle. It's more an observation than a question. 'Ah,' he says, with the apologetic reserve of a man who's about to piss on a stranger's fireworks. 'Let me show you something.' And he goes to a filing cabinet and starts pulling open drawers. Dozens of them. Inside each are hundreds of beetles, like a fairy's jewel case. Glossy big ones, bright little ones, ones with horns and flanges. Ones with stripes, spots and runic filigree. There are beetles that look like leaves and twigs, and one or two that just look like beetles. 'All these beetles,' he jerks a foreleg, 'are unnamed. They came from one corner of the Venezuelan rainforest last year.' He looks at my offering.

'About your beetle – we'll give you a call.' And two weeks later, I got a terse call from an assistant: 'It's a *Pogonus* of some sort.' And that was that.

Over the next four years, once in a while, I thought of *Pogonus* and the metropolis of beetles, and promised that one day I'd go back and find out more. And then one wet afternoon with nothing better to do, I did. I sat in Brendell's little higgledy-piggledy den, with its piles of papers and books, curling postcards, paperweight beetles, jokey fridge-magnet beetles; the First World War army knife with its spike for horses' hooves and its blade sharpened down to a nub, the little magnifying glass and the bottles of pins. And I said: 'Tell me about beetles.'

It was, I now realise, not a question to be bandied about lightly, a question that should have come with the unspoken caveat of not how long have you got, but how long do you propose to live? It was like asking someone to bottle Niagara Falls with a spoon. He took a deep breath, rubbed a mandible on his thorax and said: 'Beetles are by far and away the most successful creatures in the world. One in every four animals is a beetle. Every fifth living thing is a beetle. In one genus of weevils, there are 2,000 species. That's equal to half the total number of known mammals. In the beetle department, there are 10 million named specimens, and 2 million unidentified ones. This is the most comprehensive collection in the world. The Smithsonian may be larger, but it's got a lot of repeats. Paris may have more, but no one knows where anything is. This museum has more variety, from more habitats, in more places than anywhere else. Let me show you.'

And he's off again, pulling open drawers. 'Beetles have colonised every conceivable habitat, from the edge of the polar ice cap to the middle of the hottest desert. The only place they don't live is sea water. There are beetles that live in ants' nests, imitating ants; there are thousands of plants that have their own specifically adapted beetles. There are beetles that look like bird shit and ones that are smaller than dust particles. There is one which is the size of a hot dog. There are beetles that eat opium and strychnine. There are beetles that specialise only in beaver hair. The whirligig beetle has an eye that's bisected – the top half sees in air, the bottom half underwater. There are beetles that live in collections of beetles; the museum beetle. And one, *Blaps gigantean*, lived for seven years in a goldfish bowl on my fridge; it was called Barnacle.'

Stop, stop. Look, I've got to get a mandible on all this – how many species of beetle are there altogether in the world?' 'Ah,' he said, 'you need to speak to Peter Hammond.' Hammond pops out of another den. He too has metamorphosed into his calling – perhaps a little more weevilish than Brendell. He smells strongly of Old Shag.

'It's an interesting question. Up until now, there are about 450,000 described species. There will definitely be 1 million beetles, probably 2 million, possibly 5 million, conceivably 10.' So let's get this straight – at the most conservative estimate, we know of less than half the beetle population of the world? 'Very conservatively, yes. There are only 2,000 people in the world working on *Coleoptera* [beetles].' Christ, then beetles must be Darwinishly mutating at a rate of knots? They look at each other, then at me, with a fathomless pity. 'Beetles,' says Brendell, 'were perfect . . . '. ' . . . 10 million years ago,' finishes Hammond.

So, with that much diversity, what makes a beetle a beetle? There is no one thing that all beetles have that no other insect has. But the general definition includes an exoskeleton, biting mandibles, six legs, and elytra – that is, the hard wing coverings. Incidentally, beetles, though not generally great flyers, have wings that can be five times the size of their cases. They fold them up like origami umbrellas. And they have four distinct lives – as eggs, grubs, pupae and adults. Though not all beetles necessarily have all of them. Brendell's off again: 'Some beetles that live in the desert have fused elytra, and form an air-conditioning system. Some are soft-bodied, some are hairy. There's one that never really develops from the larval stage . . . '

Stop, stop. We pass a man working at a desk, surrounded by specimens. What's he doing? 'Well, all the beetles in the collection – which, by the way, started with Joseph Banks's specimens from Captain Cook's *Endeavour* – are stuck on pins, set at a specific height through their right elytron. But the old pins are brass, and have copper in them, and the copper reacts with the fatty tissue of the beetles and causes verdigris – which makes gas, which in turn can make the beetles explode. It's a problem, so that all have to be repinned and labelled. It's a delicate job.' But there are 12 million. 'Hmm.' Good grief. Imagine a lifetime spent defusing exploding beetles. I realise the more I know, the less I understand. So Brendell gives me a duffer's guide to *Coleoptera*, the standard work, a reference book of scientific terms, a couple of papers and a chair. It's all beginner's stuff, and after an hour I'm drowning in the vastness of the subject. So I go and look at more beetles.

What none of us has mentioned is how awesomely, arrestingly beautiful they are. Each tray is an aesthetic wonder. With their neatly written labels and amazing patterns, they bridge the chasm between science and art. Here, I'm afraid, I have to stray into the heresy of anthropomorphism. I wondered what I found so fascinating about them. Though their vast divergence is hard to encapsulate, there is something singular and ethereal about beetles. They all share an essential beetlishness, a stolid sense of purpose. Beetles are, by and large, defensive rather than aggressive. They don't sting, though they can be poisonous, like the Spanish fly or the arrow-poison beetle. They can be fearsome, like the amazing bombardier beetle, which mixes in its backside two inert chemicals that squirt boiling hydrogen peroxide at anything foolish enough to cross its path. But as a rule, beetles advertise their deterrents on their backs. They are cunning and brave but not devious. They do just what they say on the box. In short, beetles embody all the talents of the middle classes. They are not aristocratic, vain esoterics, like butterflies and moths, or communists like ants and bees. They're not filthy, opportunistic carpetbaggers like flies. They are professional, with a skill. They're built for a job, and get down to it without boastfulness or hysteria. And there is nowhere that doesn't, sooner or later, call in a beetle to set up shop and get things done.

And as I pull out drawers, I slowly become aware of the importance of a corner of science I haven't ever paid attention to: taxonomy. The science of naming. From the Greek *taxos*, 'arrangement', and *nomos*, 'law'. With something as vast and varied as the *Coleoptera*, precision in naming is vital. The Aborigines believe that a thing without a name doesn't really exist. And what we call biodiversity is a meaningless and formless emotion if we can't put a name to its parts. If you order red snapper in a restaurant, you could get one of thirty different fish, all called red snapper. Aristotle tried to organise the haphazard colloquialism of the world. He called beetles *Coleoptera* – 'sheath wing'. But it wasn't until 1758 that a Swede, Carolus Linnaeus, later ennobled Baron Karl von Linné, devised the binominal nomenclature system – a generic name coupled with a specific name – and set out to name everything all over again. So, for instance, my beetle is organised as, first, a family name: *Carabidae* – of which there are 30,000 to 40,000 members (beetles have over 200 families); then a generic name: *pogonus* – which is quite small, only about thirty known species, all *halophilous* (salt-loving); then, a species name: *gillae*. Except it's not called that yet, because a drawing of its willy has to be made and reputably published first. Beetle willies are like Yale keys – no two species are the same. And it's not the done thing to name a species after yourself, although Brendell has more than fifteen named after him, including a hawk moth. Your peers do it for you – coleopterists look after each other in the immortality stakes.

For 200 years after the Linnaean system, beetles were discovered and named in an amateur way. Since the war, it has all been more purposeful and scientific. Still, there have been enough species discovered since the beginning of the eighteenth century to account for one every six hours. In the trays, some specimens wear the discreet award of a small red dot. This means they are holotypes, original examples, against which all other contenders have to be measured. In some species, only one has ever been found. The Natural History Museum holds more holotypes from across the natural world than anywhere else. They are of huge value, and are sent to other scientists to study. This collection is, in fact, a priceless resource. Brendell once asked an obscure German museum for a holotype specimen, and got the curt reply: 'Your RAF bombed it.'

Hammond has a theory – he thinks that the success of beetles can be put down to two things: sex and crunchiness. I don't entirely understand the sex bit, but I think it's something to do with the fact that beetles are apparently easy lays. They don't go in for complicated displays and courtship; they're not picky. And the crunchiness is the ergonomic robustness of most beetles. They're utilitarian and can live in places that would put off other orders. They have a tough confidence.

I could have, should have, finished this story in a day. But I drag it out. The truth is, I'm hooked. There is a trendy new scientific word – biophilia, the innate emotional affiliation of human beings for other living things. Until now, I've been pretty immune to biophilic tendencies. I'm a city boy – the only natural world I'm drawn to are things that come on plates. But there's something about beetles, a connection. A pheromone of empathy. Perhaps it's a recognition of fellow bourgeoisie. Then, one morning, Brendell pops out, beaming: 'I've discovered something about your *Pogonus*. I've found a paper published about a similar one in Tanzania. *Pogonus rodolphi*. It's a predator that has regressed to eating algae. Were your salt pans wet underneath? That'll be it, then. I expect it'll still be a new species.' Even after all these years, he's shiny with pleasure. During Brendell's time here, the collection has doubled. He and Hammond have collected everywhere, from the dank rainforest to the high Himalayas. Always with difficulty, often with danger, and with a passionate patience. They collect using light traps, nets and sieves, smoking the canopy and using cadavers. 'I find a goat's entrails are particularly effective. And shit. Human shit's marvellous.' They use a specialist piece of equipment called a pooter – a glass jar with two tubes. You suck on one, and the beetle is pulled up the other. You mean you suck at rotten entrails and shit? 'Yes, it's disgusting,' Brendell laughs. How many beetles do you think you've killed? 'Oh, thousands and thousands.' They use a fumigating poison that smells like nail-varnish remover, or a syringe for the larger specimens. 'But I mind it more and more. I find myself picking individuals, and being pleased when they get away. I'm getting old. When I was young I collected like a madman, but now, well, they're so wonderful.'

Being a coleopterist is as close as anyone can get to living the dream of being on the Starship Enterprise. You boldly go and find new habitats and weird life forms, then kill them. Beetles are as strange, marvellous and varied as the most vivid sci-fi imagination. We tend to think that the brightest edge of science is quantum physics, but there's so much left undiscovered and unanswered right here. The last frontier is at your feet, under a rock.

Brendell and Hammond look at the beetle collection and see a resource, a record of diversity and a monument to the awesome achievement of beetles. I see something perhaps they don't: it's also a monument to human achievement. Mostly unremarked and unregarded – lives devoted to the fundamentals of life on Earth, minute and inconsequential, but also transcendent. Brendell and Hammond find God in small things. Every one of the 12 million specimens here in South Kensington carries with it a story of huge diligence, enquiry and the open-mindedness that is the defining characteristic of our species, *Homo sapiens*. *Sapiens*, the ability to think, to question. If the world were to end tomorrow and we could choose to save only one thing as the explanation and memorial to who we were, then we couldn't do better than the Natural History Museum, although it wouldn't contain a single human. There is, oddly, no Linnaean holotype for man. But there doesn't need to be. The systematic order, the vast inquisitiveness and range of collaged knowledge and its consequential beauty would tell all that is the best of us, and pinned into a corner of this encyclopaedic wonder would be my little beetle, *Carabidae pogonus* (sod the orthodox procedure and proper channels) *gillae*.

EDWARD HOPPER

'Nighthawks', Edward Hopper's picture of an all-night New York diner, is one of the most famous and familiar images of the twentieth century. One of the scant handful of museum pictures that have made it over the gallery wall, escaped the frame and become part of the popular visual vernacular, along with Warhol's 'Marilyn' and Munch's 'The Scream', 'Nighthawks' has been plagiarised, parodied, lampooned, collaged and cartooned. Ask the internet what it knows about 'Nighthawks', and you'll get 110,000 sites.

The picture spawned a Tom Waits record, a Broadway play, a Liverpudlian-American football team, the F-117 fighter, a Sylvester Stallone movie ('Only one man can stop him') and millions and millions of posters beloved of depressed teenagers and their Habitat-friendly parents.

The appeal of 'Nighthawks' is instantly accessible, but – just as instantly – it's fugitive and inexplicable. This is not an immediately winning subject. A rather dull window into a dull café; the bright light inside shines out to cut the darkness of the street. The room is plain to the point of banality. All we can see are two metal urns, a strangely improbable triangular counter, a yellow door, the tops of empty stools and four figures. It's not painted with verve or in great detail. It lacks excitement, occasion and spectacle. The more you look at it, the more its frame seems contrary.

Every commentary on 'Nighthawks' – and there are thousands, because people seem continually moved to write about this image

– mentions the word 'loneliness', usually in the first sentence. It is an evocation of the uncaring, deep loneliness of the city – but why? Look at it again. Here is the waiter washing cups, a man doing his job. Apparently he's talking to a couple, a man in a fedora and a brown-haired woman in a red dress. They aren't apparently lonely. There's a sense of bonhomie, even the intonation of sexual tension, about them. Then there's the fourth man with his back to us, cast in shadow. He's too unspecific to carry the emotional weight of the picture alone.

But undoubtedly there is a sense of loneliness, of dislocation. It isn't in what we're looking at. It comes from somewhere else in the shadow. Just as the scream in Munch's painting doesn't emanate from the figure but is in the surrounding, so the overwhelming atmosphere of loneliness in 'Nighthawks' comes from outside. It's from us, the viewer, standing alone in the cold and the dark, looking in at the light through the window. The emotional tug isn't to be found in the picture: it's in our profound reaction to it.

'Nighthawks' was painted in 1942, just months after Pearl Harbor sent the United States to war, but there's no sign or intimation of it here. Hopper had spent the First World War obliviously painting rocks at the seaside. His art inhabits a time all of its own, unrelated and unbothered by events. His last pictures of interiors, painted in the 1960s, are populated by figures still dressed for the 1940s.

Now, Tate Modern has created the largest retrospective of Hopper's work outside the US since 1981, at a time when his country and its politics, its overconfident, overbearing and over-here culture are subjects of extreme anger and rejection. How does this strange, awkward, parochial painter, so typically American, remain immune to the current cultural shudder?

The US has always produced art that exists simultaneously but separate from its politics; a culture that seems to come from a parallel nation that only lives in words, music and images. Vicente Todoli, the new Spanish director of Tate Modern, says that Hopper finds a particular resonance in Europe because he paints an existentialist isolation and angst that's a central concept of our old-world art. Maybe, but it hardly begins to explain the enigma of what makes Hopper such a consistently popular artist with the public and the critics.

For a start, he's not a very good painter. His brushwork is often clumsy and numb, the paint has the consistency of clotted cream, his drawing is no more than competent, with that predictable, workmanlike, chunky gracelessness that's been taught for a century in American art schools. His subject matter is wilfully dull, as if chosen to repel interest. Neither was he a painter of his time. His contemporaries, Pollock, Motherwell, Rothko and the other abstract expressionists whom he despised, were taking art and making it psychoanalytical, jazzy and modern, while Hopper was left with his nineteenth-century, Frenchish conventions, and images that were Teflon to intellectual observation or extrapolation.

Hopper was the end of a cul-de-sac. Nobody came after him, and yet there is this palpable atmosphere about his work, his compelling gaze. He glazes the mundane with menace and dread. His work is often compared to dozens of things and people, as if to compensate for their emptiness: Raymond Chandler novels, Steinbeck, Nathaniel West, pulp-fiction dust jackets, de Chirico, Corot, Sickert. But it's film that seems to be the most obvious influence on his images. The odd points of view, the angles, the portraits of houses that look like establishing shots. Hopper looks at things from above or below, moving a composition so that it resembles a frame pulled from a panning shot. He takes the convention of *film noir* and marries it with the older convention of landscape painting. The result is a disturbing sense of unease often described as loneliness. The cinematic nature of his pictures implies that often the true object or subject isn't recorded at all. It might be happening outside the frame, or is about to happen. As with Hitchcock movies, the tension builds over purposefully mundane and innocent images, but we know that something shocking is imminent. The longer it takes, the worse the suspense. Well, in Hopper's picture of black-windowed houses and deserted urban landscapes, the suspense keens like a continuous violin note, always unresolved.

One of the most threatening and successful of these bland images is 'Gas'. It's simply a picture of three petrol pumps on a long road. The subject is so anodyne, so utterly familiar, yet it appears as threatening and fearful as a Goya nightmare. Again the focus of the disease is not actually in the picture. Hopper connects with the viewer's shared experience of driving long distances in North America, the low-level worry of running out of gas on a deserted road. And then that surreal feeling of stopping in one of these little oases set in the vastness of the continent. Many films, from *Stagecoach* to *Duel*, use the weirdness and danger of fuel pit-stops. It's become a set-piece cliché of American cinema, as old as the mythical islands in Homer's *Odyssey*. Hopper taps into all of that with this simple painting. He's also been linked to Kerouac and the beat poets, an association you suspect he would have resented. None of this verdigris of outside influence should detract from Hopper's innate brilliance in accessing it. It's a miraculous act of artistry, as clever as any bit of mannerist chiaroscuro.

I've driven past this petrol station on Cape Cod, where Hopper spent most of his life. I went back with a copy of the painting to find the viewpoint and to stare. The pumps have changed, of course, but it was still recognisable and completely, utterly bereft of any atmosphere, any frisson of menace. Nothing. Todoli of Tate Modern says this picture is a great American Calgary, a crucifixion. The three pumps represent three crosses, and petrol is the holy spirit of America, he adds.

Once you've shown an interest in Hopper, the locals of Cape Cod will point out any number of his views, shots, clapboards, dunes and coast. All have a benign, cosy, good-looking blandness. Cape Cod is a fine, windblown, elegant place, but it's hardly like discovering Tuscany or Umbria for the first time and suddenly seeing the early Renaissance fall into the landscape like a missing bit of jigsaw. Hopper country resolutely refuses to look like Hopper. The people here, though, have a look, an atmosphere and a style. The Americans of the north-east coast are a type. They are big and gangling, often handsome in a bony, unflashy way, with clear, pale eyes and competent hands. They dress for longevity and warmth, and are understated people. They are naturally intelligent, having produced more than their demographic share of American culture, but they have an equally natural distrust of showing off. The original Protestant pilgrim virtues and vices are inherent here. And it's these people who Hopper lived among, and you see the lonely, existential anger and fortitude of his pictures behind the pursed lips and hooded gaze.

Hopper is chronically crap at painting people. It's another reason he may have the laurels of that most coveted and argued-over plaudit, 'the very best bad painter ever'. There's not a natural bone or pose in any of his cast. They enter his pictures like the cut-out characters in Pollock's theatres – something else he shares with Hitchcock, who famously said that all he wanted from an actor was someone who could remember lines and not bump into the furniture. Hopper goes one further. He paints people as if they were furniture. They are given the most rudimentary interior life. Mostly they possess a look of stoical blankness, and yet some of his greatest images are of these silent, lonely, gimpy people: 'Nighthawks', the girl drinking coffee in 'Automat', the usherette in 'New York Movie', the couple in 'Room in New York', and the secretary doing filing in 'Office at Night'.

The model for all Hopper's female figures was his wife, Josephine. She insisted on it, including being the stripper in 'Girlie Show' (1941). Theirs was a difficult marriage. They argued continually and viciously. He may well have hit her. Yet they remained together. This miserable marriage was one of the two defining relationships of his life. The other was his relationship with everyone else. He didn't think much of us. He was short-tempered and fractious, frustrated by critics, the media and the art world for misunderstanding his work and for championing abstract expressionists. He hated being pigeonholed, but resented being ignored. He read a great deal. So no different there from a great many artists. But I suggest that his New England, prickly, intelligent contrariness is what gives his characters their stiff awkwardness.

Using his bitter, bickering wife as a model for every woman has removed the slightest hint of sexuality from his female figures. He is possibly the least erotic twentieth-century painter. Even when he puts his characters in bed or in intimate rooms, as in 'Morning in a City' or 'Eleven am', they are utterly without sexual intent. Even when the burlesque stripper strides gawkily onto the stage, the most prominent member of the audience has his head turned away, seemingly uninterested.

There is a peeking element of voyeurism in Hopper's work. He stands outside, looking in at people glimpsed through windows or surreptitiously spied across the carriage, the lobby, the next table. He seems to be stalking buildings and rooms. Here again is a reference to Chandler and the private detective creeping in crêpe-rubber soles through the mean streets, sated with the hopelessness of humanity, recording the banal data of sad, immoral, venal existence. But where a Marlowe will ultimately enforce justice, Hopper spies without intent, judgement or compassion. These are not the images of someone who is empathetic. He simply witnesses the loneliness, the quiet despair and the small attempts at joy with a forensic eye. That's a really difficult thing to accomplish, and it borders on the psychotic. All through his life, Hopper made pictures of couples. It's a motif he liked. They exist together on the canvas, often obviously married or long-term partners, deeply familiar to each other, but invariably they are separated by acres of silence. There's never any warmth or connection between them. Occasionally the image can be seen as one person's unhappiness and the partner's inability or reluctance to help. Most often their separateness defies narrative or plot. It is just an existential understanding that ultimately we are all alone. There is, though, a ray of hope in Hopper's view of existence, and it's in the sunlight. Many of his subjects turn to face the light; a moment with the sun on your face is a beneficence, a small blessing. People stare out of windows in their lonely rooms and are baptised in an almost celestial light. It's light that saves Hopper from nihilism. Light is a solid thing, an emotion. Humanity may be lonely and silent, but the sun blesses all. His pictures are often known for a time of day.

It's as if the light were a theatrical performance or a church service, evensong, matins. Crepuscular light has a particular philosophical, theological resonance, promising hope for a new beginning or an earned rest. Electric light is mendacious. It casts complex shadows, makes untrue colours, turns faces cadaverous. But the sun shines. It scrubs the picture's surface, creating clean, flat planes. Light is the only unequivocal good. Whether this equates to a formal belief in God, I doubt. Hopper is not a religious artist in any theological sense.

Cape Cod is famous for its light. Hopper is, above all, a painter of light – not in the impressionist sense of saturated colour, but as the expressionists used it, as a metaphor, a symbol and a tool. In his works, the light makes no judgement.

Two subjects that Hopper returns to are the lighthouse and the cinema. They are symbolic of loneliness and hope. The escape and solace of the movies, and the lighthouse, safety and guidance. Light shining in the darkness. Hopper, with his wooden characters, his doughty subjects and his snapped composition, uneven paint, hovers on the edge of being tastelessly kitsch. I've just been sent a Sotheby's catalogue in which Jack Vettriano, the mordantly sentimental and emotionally incoherent popular-postcard painter of dancing butlers, is compared favourably to Hopper. And he was just the other side of the page from Norman Rockwell, the illustrator of nostalgia and Americana, freckle-faced apple-scrumpers and prayers at Thanksgiving. Hopper avoids the drop into Vettriano bathos and corn syrup by never taking the easy option of sentiment and parable.

Paul Klee memorably said that the art of drawing was the art of omission, and no artist leaves out more to greater effect than Hopper. He offers us sparse sets and characters without dialogue; we bring the emotion, the associations and the plots. And perhaps the reason he remains so popular, and why this exhibition is so timely, is that he shows an America that is lonely and unsure and altogether more insecure, but a great deal more profound and thoughtful than the one that we have been seeing such a lot of recently.

CARTIER-BRESSON

Genius is a word that has been adulterated to dross. Hairdressers get labelled geniuses, motorcars and mobile phones are supposed to embody genius. It has even become a cliché to point out that genius is a cliché. But if you were to reclaim the word back for society's most exclusive club and ask who is a genius, there's only one unequivocal, unarguable living member: Henri Cartier-Bresson. He is the real deal, a photographer who defined the purpose and power of photography, a recorder of life who seemed to have second sight.

He's ninety-four now and famously won't give interviews or be photographed. He hasn't taken a published snap for three decades. So when you're asked if you'd like to go to Paris to talk to him, 'I'll just check the diary' isn't an option. The reason he will now talk is that a definitive book of his work is being published, and the French government has awarded him a foundation that opens this month in Montparnasse, Paris. Funded by British charitable trusts and French donors, it houses the Cartier-Bresson archive and showcases the work of other photographers.

Cartier-Bresson lives with his wife, the Magnum photographer Martine Franck, above the tourist headscarf shops on the Rue de Rivoli. As I walk there, I run through his CV. Born to a wealthy mercantile family, he studied painting, was associated with the surrealists and bought the newly invented Leica camera, which he was to turn into the most fetishised, venerated artist's tool of the twentieth century. He jumped a cargo boat, became a game poacher in the Ivory Coast, was captured by the Germans during the war, escaped to join the resistance, photographed the liberation of Paris, the partition of India, the fall of the Kuomintang in China, and worked for magazines all over the world.

He started the photographic agency Magnum with David Seymour ('Chim'), Robert Capa, George Rodger and William Vandivert. It created the standard for modern photojournalism. What he's famous for is the phrase 'the decisive moment'. The composition of his images is so aesthetically exact that, an instant before or after, the picture wouldn't exist. The decisive moment is the ability to capture the precise fusion where light, shade, expression and gesture come together to make a perfect composition that is greater than the sum of its parts. Cartier-Bresson doesn't just do this once or twice, but over and over again. It's remorseless, uncanny; it's genius. Martine Franck opens the door, a handsome, elegant woman. Behind her, silhouetted against the window, is Cartier-Bresson leaning on a stick. Behind him is the panorama of the Tuileries gardens and the Louvre. He doesn't look a day over seventy, a tall man with pale eyes and strong hands. We sit opposite each other across a little table in the unassuming living-room. There are no photographs on the wall, but some small paintings and a lot of ethnographic objects. I apologise for not speaking French. Cartier-Bresson speaks beautiful, slow English with a hint of an upper-class accent learnt in Cambridge.

'What are we having to drink? I suppose it's too early for a glass of wine?' (It's 11 am.) A cup of coffee for me. He goes for the wine anyway. I start by telling him I have no prepared questions. 'Good,' he replies. 'I have no prepared answers. Perhaps we could sit in silence. Silence is the most wonderful thing.' He smiles: 'I have no more interest in photography.' Equally famously, he has become a self-denying genius, reluctant to say anything about his former career or photographs. So our conversation is long on silence and that particular Gallic pout that could mean so many things, or nothing.

'I draw; that is far more important.' For the past thirty years he has devoted himself to art. 'I can't draw from imagination – it has to be in front of me.' His work is competent but unexceptional; what strikes you most is the composition. It's terrible. The tops of heads are cut off, landscapes are crammed into the page, objects bend to find space. The genius emerges only through the view-finder. The most he'll say about his photographs is that he was lucky. It's all dismissed as mere luck.

Are you pleased about the foundation? He makes a face and sighs. 'It's a mausoleum.' Franck laughs and says: 'He's pleased it will help other photographers.' Young photographers, I add. 'What is young?' He taps his arm. 'Young is in the blood.' I have brought an advance copy of his book. They hadn't seen it yet. Franck is excited. She grabs her Leica to photograph him looking at his photographs. He regards the definitive collection with wariness. If he's interested, he's disguising it well. Gingerly he opens it and turns to the family photos at the back. 'Here's my nanny, my grandfather.' His fingers trace the faces of long-gone school friends and army buddies. He flicks back through the images of a peripatetic life. That was in Mexico, wasn't it? I ask of one of his most famous pictures. 'I don't remember,' he shrugs. 'Maybe Spain.'

'I don't remember' and 'I don't know' come up again and again. He may mean 'I don't want to talk about it' or 'It's unimportant' or simply that he really can't remember.

He stops at a picture. 'This was a whore in Pigalle. She had a beautiful friend. Here is a photograph of a Taoist burial. You know what this says?' He points at some pictograms. 'It says "funeral". It could have said anything – "Coca-Cola". It was lucky it said "funeral".'

In the portrait section, he pauses over Matisse holding a dove. Matisse was his mentor and friend, and here's Bonnard. He stabs the page. 'He was the best.' What was he like as a person? A long silence. 'Secretive.'

There's a picture of a man swimming with a naked girl, her bosoms framing his head. 'She was a buxom wench.' 'You haven't forgotten all your English, then?' laughs Franck. There's Truman Capote, looking sullen. 'A little devil. We travelled together. Oh, you don't want to look at all this.' He shuts the book. No, no, I do. I really do. 'Would you like a glass of wine?'

Is the title yours, I ask. 'It was originally called *The Image and the World*,' says Franck. 'We added "The Man" because it's so personal.' He says something in French. She translates: 'It's nonsense.' 'A polite way of saying bullshit,' he adds, and laughs.

Tell me about starting Magnum. 'No, no, I didn't. Not really. That was Chim and Capa. I was travelling in the Far East.' But you were a photojournalist, 'No, I was never a photojournalist.' Look, I'm sorry, but you just were. You almost invented the job description. You worked for magazines. 'They paid me, but I worked for myself. It was Capa who told me I should call myself one or I wouldn't get paid. We were very different, him and I. We were friends but we didn't work the same way.'

Were you ever frightened? 'No. You just feel.' But when you were a prisoner and you escaped, that must have been frightening? A shrug. 'What could they have done. Shoot me?' A long pause. 'I'm interested in prisoners. I sympathise. I've given a library to a prison.' He calls to his wife to read out a testament he has written. She translates. It finishes: 'In the end, what's important is love and friendship.' You must have had many friends? 'No.' A long pause. 'Not many, but many acquaintances.' Do you make friends easily? 'When I'm in trouble, yes,' he laughs. 'Would you like some wine?'

I open the book again and slowly turn the pages. His pale eyes flick over the decisive moments. We sit in punctuated silence. 'Here I was with Pasolini . . . Here I lived in Harlem. Sometimes they mistook me for white.' What are you, then? Pause. 'I'm wherever I am. Americans are so violent.' Pause. 'They're sour.'

He won't be drawn on photography, meeting every question with a shrug. 'Oh, everyone is a photographer,' he says dismissively. 'Everyone has a camera. I don't know what it means now.' None of these pictures appear to have been cropped, I mention. 'No, no. I never crop them.' You can't fake the synthesis of a decisive moment. And it turns out that even this aphorism wasn't Cartier-Bresson's. Dick Simon, his American publisher, took the title of the ground-breaking book *The Decisive Moment* from another source for the English edition of *Images à la Sauvette*. (The literal translation would be 'Hurried Images'.) So much has been made of the decisive moment, it has become mythic. Sometimes the subjects seem to be just figures in a formula. But what is remarkable is their deep humanity, the affection for the subjects: the drunk, the frightened, the jolly, the ridiculous, the amorous and the pompous. They're all treated with an extraordinary tenderness and respect. Each moment is decisive. Without sentimentality, there is something of the divine in these fragile records of humanity.

There is a short film of Cartier-Bresson working. The camera is in his big hand, his gangly body dances in the street, always on the balls of his feet. He trips and pirouettes around the crowd. The camera appears for a moment and disappears again. This peerless collection of captured time could be seen as a silent love letter to the world. 'I'm an anarchist,' says Cartier-Bresson. 'A peaceful anarchist.' And an optimist? 'Yes.'

He inscribes his book with an elegantly childlike hand and gets up to say goodbye. He points his stick at the floor. I think he wants me to move a chair. He points again. There on the carpet is the little Leica.

NUDE

I distinctly remember my first time. I guess he was in his late forties; a short, muscular man who had run to fat, his shoulders drooped into short arms, with chubby hands and stubby fingers. His back was covered in dark, wiry hair; like a lot of fat men, he had a surprisingly small and shrivelled bottom, which drifted into thick, furry legs and little spatulate feet with overlapping clawed toes and a bunion. His haggis stomach rested on his thighs. Underneath drooped a penis of supreme ugliness, a Quasimodo todger, bent double, shouldering the weight of a voluminous, rucksack scrotum. He sat on a chair, one hand on his fat knee, the other hanging at his side. He stared at a spot on the wall and settled into a professional torpor. This was my initiation into the central mystery of high art. My introductory week at art school. He was a naked civil servant. This was my first life-drawing class.

Having settled my drawing board at 45 degrees to his belly button, I tentatively drew a line and discovered the great truth of art and love and existence. The difference between nude and naked, as the art historian Kenneth Clark said, is that to be naked is to be without clothes, but a nude is the body re-formed – a creature that exists only in culture, that pertains only to civilisation. The man sitting in front of the class was unquestionably, grimly naked. We, in our clumsy ways, were trying to elevate his corporeal presence and render him nude. The fact that we have two words for the same state is telling of the contradictions implicit in how we see our bodies as nature intended, sky-clad. As so often with English, the older, rougher version, 'naked', is from the old Frisian, while 'nude' is effetely Frenchified via Latin. It was inserted into the lexicon in the eighteenth century when aesthetes needed a word to differentiate the higher moral and philosophical calling of art from base, human nakedness. The art historian, critic and Svengali John Ruskin is said to have fainted with horror on seeing his wife naked on their wedding night. It was the pubic hair that particularly disgusted – absent, of course, from classical female nudes.

The two most energetic, exuberant moments in the western art canon, classic Greece and the high Renaissance, raised the nude to being a central totemic subject. In the public mind still, the ability to render a recognisable body is the measure of an artist. Nudes in painting or marble embody the highest attributes and the loftiest quandaries. They reflect the humanity in God and the godlike in man. There isn't a human emotion, desire or thought that can't be symbolised with a nude. Nudes exist in a world untroubled by bodily functions. Put biblically, man was born nude and was expelled for discovering that he was naked. The nude in high art is a body re-formed in Eden.

And then came photography.

Photographers borrowed the visual language of high art, but they discovered almost immediately that people in photographs are naked, never nude. And the subject that drove the nascent craft of photography was the same one that propelled video, DVD and the internet – pornography. A histrionic pose, a Greek urn and a leopard skin don't fool anyone into seeing a pocket-sized snap of a chubby Parisian call girl as an allegory for courage. The fact that a photograph captures the literal truth, that these are figures who have taken their clothes off for the sole purpose of showing you their bits, means the naked body can never become nude. It will always inhabit an everyday world. The figures in photographs sweat and sneeze and wipe their bottoms and get dirty.

The power and the joy of photographs is that they can be openly and urgently sexual. Art before cameras might have been erotic, it could intimate every lascivious desire, but it could never be openly sexual in the way a photograph can. It's nothing to do with realism, everything to do with art history, aesthetics, heritage and expectation. We look at a photograph and know that it's a moment captured. We look at a painting and know it's a moment imagined. Photography gave the two-dimensional body back to grunting, smelly, sticky sex and it also invented obscenity.

In a painting, any amount of fleshy invitation, rape or murder, mutilation, bondage and orgy is perfectly acceptable, even pleasing. But quite bland nakedness in photography can be much more offensive. We see the difference in the male nude. The rule of thumb is that paintings and sculpture minimise penises, whereas photographs maximise them. The mechanical image always draws the eyes to genitals and breasts where a painting doesn't. But the thing that makes photography instantly erotic is the gaze of the subject. It's the eye contact that is the invitation – and it's why so many photographers crop or obscure their subjects' faces, thereby objectifying bodies and distancing them from pornography or personal involvement. A face is just too much information. A headless body is a sculptural form, an object. Photography can never claim to view the naked body with innocence. Only art can represent purity and virginity with a semi-naked girl with pert nipples and no pubic hair.

The invention of photography changed for ever the way traditional artists and their audiences could look at and use the nude. Painters began to put nudes into unequivocally everyday situations, as they bathed or worked as prostitutes. They used photographs instead of models. And the nude lost its metaphysical calling, its wings and halo, and became like the rest of us, human and sexual. Manet's Olympia, a courtesan lying provocatively on her bed, was accused of obscenity because of her direct, knowing, photographic look. In the strange painting 'Le Déjeuner sur l'Herbe', the picnic with a nude girl, the surreal sense is that the nude belongs in the familiar painted landscape; it's the clothed men who are out of place.

Today it's not possible for an artist to compose a nude without reference to the hundreds of millions of images of nakedness that every adult in the western world has seen. We are all naked now. Never nude. We've lost that touch of divinity. In a toweringly kitsch picture, the great French studio painter Gérôme painted the myth of Pygmalion, the sculptor who falls in love with his own creation and whom the gods allow to become real. The point is that once the marble has become flesh it can never again be put back onto the pedestal. We will never get back Eden.

Photographic images of naked women pixelate our visual environment. Our bodies have become clichés for brain-dead advertising. Nakedness has been bankrupted by its own inflation. The ubiquity of body parts to sell papers, spaghetti and scent, drive the internet, DVDs and satellite TV, has cast out the nude. Photography's devaluing of nakedness has made the nude, with its delicate and complex baggage of symbolism, mythology, metaphysics and poetry, extinct. Nude and naked existed side by side, in juxtaposition, each confirming the existence of the other, but now the overwhelming body count has made the nude unintelligible. We can't 'unsee' the pornography, marketing and the cheap attention-grabbing, the fast food of naked images. They have destroyed the nude's habitat. For an artist today it's virtually impossible to make a picture of a nude that is not an ironic comment on nakedness.

As well as naked capitalism, there's been naked politics. Bodies have wrestled in the cause of feminism, freedom of expression, freedom from sexual hypocrisy, and just the freedom to be young. Nakedness is a political statement – from Delacroix's Marianne with her bared breasts storming the barricades, to suffragettes slashing the Rokeby Venus, to the student poster of the knickerless tennis player. All this has made the *haut* rendition of artistic nudes impossible. The nude is dead. The naked triumphed.

Last week, I walked into a room and on the wall was an Yves Klein, the artist who painted girls blue, then pressed or flung them against canvas, as a mixture of titillating happening and soft Playboy pop art. The Moroccan-blue imprint of breasts and legs was unquestionably a nude that echoed cave paintings, childish finger smudges and the absurd stars' imprints in cement, but it was also strangely moving. Time has lent Klein a retrospective gravitas. Here is the last dance of the nude, the final act. And like the Turin shroud, it was a winding sheet bearing a ghostly imprint. Even though we're deathly, cynically numbed by the cliché of photographic bodies, still we fall for their cheap trick. We always look twice. We can't help it. We're addicted to the clicked image of ourselves. And when we look again, when we linger, perhaps it's because, despite our experience, we're searching for something more in the blindingly familiar flesh; some hint of the divine spark, some lyrical couplet, a metaphor for the human condition. Perhaps the nude isn't extinct. Maybe it's hidden, clothed in nakedness.

THEATRE

Prologue: a single spot

The audience discovers a character on a stage. 'Tis I. Audiences are always supposed to be discovering stuff on the stage but it's theatre, they've bought tickets, finding an actor is hardly a discovery. It's hardly buried treasure. Perhaps I could walk on and discover the audience. No, no, that's so cheesy. And hammy. It's a toasted theatrical cliché: actor does double-take at audience. 'Ooh, there you are.' Shading eyes, perhaps. No, no, it's ghastly. Maybe I should just sit and talk to myself, like an internal monologue, so the audience overhears. No, too Beckett. Too weird. Right, kill the spot. Lights go up. I walk on. And just start.

This is supposed to be a monologue to get you to like theatre. We assume that you probably don't. Liking theatre doesn't fit the *GQ* reader profile. I don't know if I can do that. I don't know that you can make someone like something just by telling them you like it. It's like trying to set up your mate with a dodgy older woman. 'What's she like then?' Well, funny, smart, really good company. 'She's ugly, isn't she?' She's clever and attractive. 'She's a dog. You always say "clever and attractive" when you mean coyote. And you've had her, haven't you?' Well, she's not a film star . . .

So I don't expect I can sell you a theatre ticket. But you know, theatre's not like Marmite. It's not a love-it-or-hate-it deal. Oh, by the way, you might want to skip the prologue altogether. A lot of directors do. It's often just the author clearing his throat. But then again it's background, character and atmosphere. Suit yourself.

My first time. Well, not actually my first time. I'd done it before, fiddled about with pantomime, kid's stuff, shouted that I believed in fairies. But the time I think of as being the first time, it was amazing. I was thirteen. My mum took me. And it was with Laurence Olivier. The thing was, I didn't want to go. I really, really didn't want to go. Thirteen's a bloody age. You probably remember better than me. It's desperate, half in, half out. Not one thing or the other. My voice was all over the place, there was body hair, I was precocious sometimes and remedially childish at others. I still made model bombers but named them after existentialist writers. My mum said I had to go, she'd been given the tickets. They were rarer than pleasant, grateful and polite thirteen-year-old boys. I had to go.

It was *Othello* at the Royal Court. However you arrange your ears, Shakespeare's fucking difficult. It's 500-year-old language and, on top of that, Shakespeare's inventing words all the time. Changing their meaning, punning, making jokes. And even though he precedes the first dictionary by a couple of centuries, his vocabulary is still three times the size of most of ours. Shakespeare's just not easy. And anyone who tells you he is doesn't know the half of it. Literally. The plot of *Othello* is stuff that a boy whose balls are still up the shallow end is really not going to get. So I slouched in the stalls, sighing and eye-rolling, and the curtain went up and I discovered an actor on the stage and it was better than buried treasure. It changed my life.

Afterwards I was taken back and stood on the stage. The house lights were up, the stagehands were clearing the set, I was surprised by the rake, the slant of the stage, it was like walking sideways round a hill. Stepping into any proscenium is to grow an inch or two. I walked to the point where Othello had stood to kill himself and I could feel it, a frisson of electricity came up through the boards. I wasn't then, and I'm not now, a spectrally sensitive bloke. It's never happened to me since, but I could feel Olivier's performance. It was still here.

Theatre is made up of three things: writing, performing and

witnessing. What got me that night was a performance. I hadn't really seen *Othello* or understood Shakespeare. I'd witnessed Olivier. I know who the rest of the cast were but I couldn't tell you a single thing about Maggie Smith's Desdemona or Frank Finlay's Iago. I couldn't take my eyes off Othello.

It was a huge performance, Olivier's last great classical part. It's the sort of acting that doesn't exist any more. A style that grew and was polished before film or television, before analysis, the Method or workshops. A performance of gesture, projection and presence. Big acting. Acting up. Acting out.

If there are three theatrical things, that gives us three acts.

Act I: performance

Scene: my garden in the middle of the night. Sitting round a table lit by candles, Ralph Fiennes, Michael Gambon and me. Look, I'm not going to apologise for name-dropping. Theatre actors are the only stars that make me blush with shyness, the only fame I'd consider getting an autograph book for. Actually they're just extras in this act. Gambon and I have just been to see Fiennes in an Ibsen play, *Brandt*. It's fantastically bleak, titanically Scandinavian, the story of a Calvinist vicar's struggle with total faith. In three hours there isn't so much as a giggle. It's unrelenting, everyone dies. Unsurprisingly, it's rarely performed. But now at the Theatre Royal, on a boiling hot night with no tourists, it's packed. It's a single, monolithic performance, and performances are what most people go to the theatre to see. If you only go to the theatre once or twice a year it'll be to see a star. If you're lucky, you'll also get to see an actor. Gambon, by the way, was a spear-carrier in Olivier's *Othello*.

Theatre acting is compared and confused with film and TV. Actors do all three. Fiennes and Gambon are electric stars but there's a gulf of difference between celluloid and stage, and it's not just the difference between talking softly and raising an eyebrow on film and waving your arms about and spitting on stage. There's a physical difference. Stage actors turn up, film actors don't. You can watch the dead on film and it makes no difference. That's an obvious truism but it's also a metaphysical one. Film performance is a vanity, it's done for a mirror, it's passed through a hundred hands. The audience is an abstract. There's no middleman between you and a stage. Every time you see Olivier perform *Othello* on film it's the same. You make no difference. What I saw on stage was unique. Incidentally, Olivier's film of *Othello* is truly awful.

Fiennes says, 'I can remember every play I've ever seen, good, bad and indifferent. That's not true about films. Even the brilliant ones fade.' And that, in a sense, is the fundamental truth of theatre. Its presence makes it memorable and real in a way that film never can be. Film may be far more realistic but it's never as real. I saw Simon Russell Beale play in *Othello*. He was Iago. Now I can't remember who played Othello. When I first saw the play it was about the power of jealousy, with Simon it was a study of evil, the most evil man ever conceived by fiction. That's what actors do on stage. You can see the same play again and again and it utterly changes. Every performance leaves a footprint, but it also leaves the text pristine and untouched.

As I grow older, plays grow old with me. Their meanings change, the emphasis is different. What made me laugh as an adolescent makes me maudlin now. Suddenly a familiar speech becomes about you and your life. I bring the memory of other performances to the theatre. Plays and characters embroider the hem of life.

If I had to choose one Desert Island Play, after much gnashing and renting, it would be *Cyrano de Bergerac*. I think it's the finest observation of the power of words and the calling of journalism. Of course, you may think it's about having a big nose and getting your end away. I watched Derek Jacobi play Cyrano and had one of those complete breakdowns which happens more in theatres than anywhere else. I sobbed, Jacobi sobbed. Cyrano ends with one of the most heart-rending *coups de thèâtre* ever imagined by a Frenchman. It was heaven. And then later I watched Anthony Sher murder it. He took the part and the play and he mummed and stamped and gesticulated the life out of it. It became merely about a bloke with a big nose wanting to get his end away and I hate him for it. It was years ago but I hate him like it was yesterday. I know he was just play-acting and isn't really a bad man but that was my play. It affects the quality of my life. So I hate him.

Now I could never say that about any other medium. Only actors can do that. And when you see how dim and insecure most of them are that's a terrifying responsibility.

Act II: the writing

Scene: a schoolroom full of teenage kids, restless, mucking about. The teacher, a humpy man who's constantly pushing his spectacles up his nose. Without looking up, he shouts, 'Judge Danforth.' At the back of the room a boy, me, starts reading from a text, stumbling at first, then with more confidence. The room slowly grows quiet, becomes a court. In turn, other children speak their lines. Reading *The Crucible* was one of the high points of school for me. Unfolding this stark parable about fear and orthodoxy took over my O-Level class for a term. We lived it, understood how art, literature, history, politics and ethics all came together.

We are all basking under a rather fruitful time in theatre at the moment, it is a lot more exciting and energetic than novels. Our best writers are writing for the stage. But it's not like a book. You can't get it at Waterstone's or borrow your girlfriend's. Plays are a moment and now is your moment. Theatre is the senior service of storytelling. Novels are a mere couple of hundred years old. There are plays performed today that were written 2,500 years ago. Our whole sense of plot, our understanding of narrative, action, nemesis and hubris are derived from the theatre. The stage cast the role models of our relationships, between parents and children, loves, mistresses, siblings, the individual and the mass, us and God, they all came from the theatre. It's the ring which describes the business of being human.

There's an old play, *Antigone*, by Sophocles, about a girl who defies her uncle, who's a dictator and her prospective father-in-law. He forbids her from burying her renegade brother. With a stubborn clarity, she refuses to bend and forces him to exercise his power and suffer the consequence. Everyone dies except Creon, the dictator, who is doomed to live. It's a play that's older than the arch, written in 441 BC. A Frenchman, Jean Honneuil, made a translation and put it on in Paris in 1942. Parisians flocked to it, realising that it was a parable, an act of resistance. The girl, Antigone, was France, she was their Marianne, refusing to surrender. The Germans also went to the theatre. They didn't ban it, or shoot Honneuil, because what *they* saw was the story of a strong-willed protector sacrificing his personal happiness to duty, and shouldering the heavy responsibilities of power.

Act III: witnessing

Scene: the theatre at Delphi. You can stand on the stage here and talk in a conversational voice and they'll hear you clear as an oracle at the top of the stone bleachers. It's a magical place. Of course, just because something's old doesn't make it good or interesting or relevant. I don't expect the practice of origami and macramé have changed much down the centuries. But in all essentials, theatre is precisely as it was 2,000 years ago. Shakespeare would be able to walk on to any London stage and feel at home, as would Sophocles. Theatre was conceived word-perfect. It must have been created to fulfil some collective need. From it all other narratives flow.

This third act I've called witnessing. It's a sort of embarrassing, poncey way of saying the audience. But audience implies passivity, that you're merely a viewer. Films and books carry on whether you're there or not. Theatre only exists if you see it. If you're a witness. Like a murder. Like a marriage. Like a voyeur. Like a jury. It only happens if you're there. A man playing Hamlet in his bedroom is not theatre. It might be a movie, though. I once sat in the Ivy with Sam Mendes talking about theatre. I was an Olivier Award judge. Sam asked how I could stand to sit through so many bad evenings in the theatre. And I admitted that I quite often left in the interval. But that cumulatively I loved it. We worked out a universal theory of culture, the one in fifteen rule. One in fifteen creations is good, one in fifteen books, one in fifteen films, TV shows, paintings, poems, pop songs, everything. One in fifteen is what culture needs to chug along. The trouble is that even if you counted a regular theatregoer that means buying a ticket a month. So you could go for a year and a half seeing nothing but dross. And that's why so many people are put off theatre: 'I went once, it was crap.'

The fact is, when you catch a good one it changes the way you see, the way you think, who you are. Maybe only for an evening, perhaps for a week, sometimes for life. And that's better than winning the lottery, and the odds are healthier, but you've got to be a witness. I sat through a really ropey play called *Shopping and Fucking*. It had been awarded a double arse-licking by *Time Out* and the *Guardian* and was packed with an audience who plainly dreamt of being Tom Paulin's friends. It doesn't matter what the play's about, not much. It was rough, and halfway through there was a gay bloke spread-eagled over the kitchen table with his keks round his ankles begging another geezer to bugger him with a serrated knife, because that's what his dad used to do.

The audience watched respectfully, with a studied, impassive cool. All except for the American in front of me who had been sold tickets for himself his wife and daughter under false pretences. He was outraged. He stood up and started shouting back at the actors, 'This is disgusting! How dare you?' The culture-vulture audience turned like housemaids startled by a mouse and gasped. It was a Bateman cartoon, 'The Man who Spoke Back in the Theatre'. They were livid, foaming with righteous anger. It was a glorious moment. A bloke getting shagged with a steak knife? That was theatre. A man shouting from the stalls? That was an outrage. You really ought to have been there.

THE RGS

A granite obelisk stands in a remote and dank region of Kensington Gardens. Few people pass this way; it doesn't compete with Peter Pan, the Diana adventure playground, or the maudlin gothic gaudiness of the Albert Memorial for attention. Those who do stroll by rarely stop to read the inscription. It simply says 'Speke' – not a name that conjures much these days.

John Hanning Speke was an explorer from the brief, grandly mythologised age of imperial discovery. It was he who unravelled the greatest of all historical-cultural-geographical mysteries, answering the question that had been posed for almost 3,000 years since Herodotus: where and what was the source of the Nile – the umbilical cord to one of the first great civilisations of antiquity, and from there to classicism, and thereafter to the triumph of the West? Speke was the first westerner to discover Lake Victoria Nyanza, bordering Kenya, Tanzania and Uganda, while travelling across Tanzania with fellow explorer Sir Richard Burton in 1858.

It was an expedition largely considered a failure: marred by expense, desertion and illness. Burton became too sick to travel, so Speke set off alone – to Victoria. He came to the mistaken conclusion that this must be the Nile's vast reservoir, but failed to travel the length of the river to confirm his theory. He returned to a torrent of disbelief, sneering and character assassination, not least from his one-time friend and travelling companion Burton.

Burton was a handsome, dark, bullying polymath who spoke half a dozen languages, travelled in disguise to be the first

Christian to visit Mecca, habitually dressed as an oriental pasha, translated *The Perfumed Garden* into English, and swaggered, seduced and shocked society with his graphic essays on polygamy and eastern sexual kinks. He and Speke were at opposite poles of the Victorian obsession with discovery and knowledge. Burton was a self-publicising adventurer, Speke a painfully solitary explorer. The day he was due to face his critics in a public debate with Burton, and deliver his paper on the source of the Nile, Speke shot himself – officially a hunting accident but possibly suicide. Poor Speke. He could face the danger, the disease, the natives and the terrain of an expedition to the heart of Africa, but his nerve gave out at the prospect of a room full of bearded geographers.

The Royal Geographical Society (RGS) was a truly frightening organisation. Speke had won its highest honour – the gold medal. It was the final arbitrator of the physical world. It granted or withheld funding for expeditions. It could unlock fame and fortune or draw down impenetrable shutters. It was the umpire of Empire, and not since Genesis had one organisation had so much power over the way the world looked. Today it still stands opposite the park on the corner of Exhibition Road in the small square mile of London called Albertopolis, the prince consort's new town built for the Great Exhibition for the permanent temples of enquiry and order: the museums of natural history, science, geology and design, Imperial College and the Albert Hall.

For an organisation that looked outwards to the ends of the Earth, the RGS has never encouraged people to look in. It is based in a large converted house set back from the road, with the addition of the best lecture theatre in the city, from whose windowless walls stare the bronze effigies of David Livingstone, that strange, driven Scottish missionary, explorer and Victorian hero, and the Arctic explorer Ernest Shackleton – the only statue in London of a man in a balaclava and mittens.

Inside, the RGS has the quiet feeling of a midweek golf club or a lesser prep school on half-term. There are the portraits of bearded old boys and busts of the worthy and reckless. Speke and Burton are both here, at a discreet distance from each other. The large rooms with high ceilings and sash windows stand to attention, trying to ignore the cheap-as-chips utilitarian furniture. There is the ghostly feeling of the shades of many, many bachelors who paid little attention to décor or comfort but liked things to stay where they were put. There is a genteel shabbiness, as if polished by millions of tweed elbows and scuffed by thousands of sensible shoes. In the tearoom a large dog sniffs at the biscuits; the piebald blotches on his back look suitably like a map. This is the sort of place where a chap can go to work with his hound.

Only the ranks of gilded names in the entrance hall, who might be rugby captains or dead scholars, tell you that this isn't some nostalgic crammer or secretariat for a ball game. This is the list of the RGS's gold-medal winners, one of the most admirable awards in the world. It includes Burton and Speke, Livingstone, Stanley and Shackleton, Scott and Hillary.

Most of the names mean little to us today, but they are an unmatched collection of ingenuity, scholarship, imagination, rude fortitude and staggeringly hard work, and above all of astonishing bravery. Whatever else you can say about the history and purpose of the RGS, have no doubts about the sustained courage of the men who went and mapped, measured and confronted the globe. Whatever the grander motives of the nation, these adventurers were driven simply by the desire to see what was on the other side of the mountain.

The quiet in the halls of the RGS is the one before the storm. For the first time in its history it is about to welcome the public. Until recently you weren't even allowed in for its Monday-night lectures, except as the guest of a member. It's never been what you would call welcoming, though it did begin to admit women in 1892. But that's all about to change. A £7 million project is just coming to fruition. A glass-walled gallery and a new reading room and library open officially on 8 June.

The society has amassed a remarkable archive: a million maps and half a million photographs, many on glass plates, ranging from the first photograph of Mecca to a picture of Scott in the Antarctic. The maps run from fifteenth-century Ptolemaic guesses to recently declassified Soviet military maps of Mongolia. When the army needed to get to the Falklands sharpish, the RGS had the maps for them, as it did for Afghanistan, originally mapped in secret by spies. It holds a priceless collection of journals, diaries and papers, bound specialist periodicals and speeches – 250,000 books at the last count. It has Livingstone's hat and Stanley's helmet, an Eskimo's wooden sunglasses, and ethnographic drawings from all over the world, including the first map of Easter Island and South Sea tattoos. There is a section of the tree trunk under which Livingstone's heart was buried. The two servants who brought him back to England were given a pension by the society.

This collection is without parallel in the world. Laid out, it would measure one kilometre. The new RGS wants to emphasise its educational potential for schools and, thank God, schoolteachers. Anyone with children in uniform will know the infuriation of the current geography curriculum, which seems to be about everything except where places are. The RGS, which is even putting the collection online, also aims to be a resource for those who want more from their holidays than sunburn and bikini envy.

Immediately I finish writing this, I'm off to Chad. Within half an hour of mentioning it, I was given four pages of reference works, books, maps and memoirs of the central Sahara. The archive is already a vital working tool. Ecologists use it to study erosion, climate, deforestation and environmental damage. But there are also many papers, books and photographs that have hardly been examined since the society got them. It is a huge treasure trove.

People from the old Empire come to trace their families. There's a comfortable irony in West Indians coming here to find old St Lucia or the Gambia, but there is also a more uncomfortable heritage for our multicultural, politically correct society: the RGS has baggage. It was an instrument of empire and exploitation: it painted maps pink, and the maps themselves were tools of manipulation, with lakes, mountains, seas and deserts named after bits of royalty and aristocracy, and occasionally after the geographers themselves.

Do you know the Nepalese name for Everest? It's Sagarmatha, meaning Mother of the Universe. But we call it Everest, because in 1865 Sir Andrew Waugh pretended there wasn't a local name and called it after his predecessor as Surveyor-General of India, Sir George Everest. The RGS is big on Everest. It holds the archive of all the British climbs, starting in the 1920s. One of the pictures it is most often asked for is the famous coronation one of Hillary on the summit of Everest holding the flag. Wearily, the society always has to decline. The picture is not of Hillary; it's Tensing. Hillary had the camera and Tensing didn't know how it worked. Occasionally people ask why there isn't a picture of them both together on the summit.

Maps shape the world. The Mercator projection shrinks the equatorial poor world and enlarges the wealthy north. The RGS is keen not to be painted pink by its past. We are, it stresses, geographers, and geography is neither good nor bad, simply an observation of the natural world that overlaps with history, sociology, economics, anthropology, biology, geology – in fact, just about every 'ology' you can think of. If people have used geography for evil purposes, that's not their fault.

Perhaps the greatest problem that has faced the RGS is its legacy from the golden age of discovery, when Victorian explorers raced to be first to get their flag on the map. The feats of cartography and surveying are now done by satellite and it's a generally held belief that there is nowhere left to explore. Geography is seen as a defunct subject.

Unfortunately, travel writers are also responsible, peddling a rueful nostalgia, constantly pointing out how fabulous places must once have been. The RGS will not get involved in the ever-more-ridiculous spectacle of sponsored endurance voyages or gap-year adventures or millionaires' midlife crises. It is only interested in supporting science. Given its history, it could have sat back in its sagging chesterfields and rotted. It could have sold the lot and stayed a rich, cosy talking shop of ageing travellers' tales. But by opening up to the public it hopes to show that geography is not about being the first to name something or stick a flag in it;

everywhere is discovered anew by everyone who sees it. Geography is a journey, not a destination.

The view of the world changes with each generation. Speke and Livingstone might still just recognise parts of Africa, but they'd be utterly lost in today's Britain. The world is not coming closer together; it's being pulled and pushed further apart. It's more different and strange now than it was 200 years ago. The poles of possible experience – economic, social, cultural, political, spiritual – are more disparate than ever before. This is the new, gilded platinum age of discovery. And so the RGS sits by the park and waits to be discovered. Having sent so many abroad, it now nervously arranges the furniture and polishes the knick-knacks. I don't think it has any idea what's in store for it.

But then that's the joy of exploration. The RGS: now less intimidating than the Congo.

There

HAITI

The only world leader of any note to turn up for Haiti's bicentenary party, prophetically, was Thabo Mbeki of South Africa. He'd seen the obvious parallels in a black country that had successfully thrown off colonial rule. He took a lot of flak for it in the South African press. He took some in Haiti too. They shot at his helicopter. He can't have foreseen that he might be asked to return the hospitality quite so soon. Jean-Bertrand Aristide begins his exile back in the continent where Haiti's sad story began. He was its best hope in 200 years and its worst disappointment.

The events in this article took place at the beginning of the coup. I flew into Haiti on the day of the largest mass demonstration against Aristide's rule. The Artibonite Resistance Front, aka the Cannibal Army, had taken control of Gonaïves, a city in the north. There was a lot of intimidation by government-sponsored thugs. The chancellor of the university had had his legs smashed in his office; students barricaded themselves on campus; and the Oloffson, the spookily gothic hotel in Port-au-Prince made famous by Graham Greene's *The Comedians*, was empty except for passing tight-lipped evangelical missionaries sipping fruit juice on the veranda, and voodoo covens spitting rum in the tangled garden beneath them. Hanging over the city was an expectation of change. The barometer of anger and retribution was rising; it was insufferably hot, close and dirty. There was drumming and screams in the night, Port-au-Prince was as mad as hell and it was its birthday. Blow out the candles, the petrol bombs and the burning roadblock and make a wish. Haiti.

Two centuries ago the divinely named Toussaint Louverture, a latter-day Spartacus, raised up a black army of slaves and beat Napoleon's grand army, therefore joining that tiny elite club – along with Hannibal, the Zulus and the Ethiopians – of African armies that have beaten western ones in battle. But the Haitians alone went on to win the war and form a third of the island of Hispaniola into the first and oldest black republic in the world. So why isn't this the biggest global feel-good, politically correct whoopee anniversary of the year? Why isn't there a mini-series and holiday programmes and delegations of western left-wing politicians parading their collective white-arsed guilt, junketing in solidarity? Well, mostly because it's bloody frightening; really, properly, deeply scary. Haiti is a political and economic dead man walking, and it has been for most of its 200 years. The colonial powers in the Caribbean make sure that no damn slave republic was going to prosper – bad for business. So Haiti has staggered from one corrupt, bankrupt, vainglorious, mad government to another. Poor, friendless Haiti has been cleaved by self-imposed racism between black and mulatto, private armies of thugs and the pervasive influence of voodoo. Ten years ago, Aristide swept to power for a second time – his first crack at the job in 1990, when he was elected in Haiti's first free elections, had been spoilt a bit by a military takeover. A one-time liberation theologist priest, he was going to be the Caribbean's Mandela – part Gandhi, part Eva Peron. He became an embattled, paranoid recluse who suspended parliamentary elections, ruled by increasingly irrational diktat, had his own death squad, and was widely believed to be fundamentally corrupt, steeped in drug money. The anger, the heat of betrayal in the streets, had reached boiling point.

Thirty-three coups and two elections sounds like a political joke. It's Haiti's CV. Politics have always been a seesaw of violent regime change followed by ruthless consolidation that inspires violent change punctuated by occasional foreign intervention. The Americans have tipped up three times, once staying for more than a decade. The French, with a solipsistic vanity, imagine that partially Francophone Haiti is in their sphere of influence. Each new regime scrapes ever more frantically at the empty barrel. Haiti has nothing to offer the outside world except the threat of refugees, and precious little to offer Haitians. There is 70 per cent unemployment and the worst Aids infection in the new world, a problem of sub-Saharan despair. With nobody to stop them or help them, Haitians take to internecine violence of a Hammer Horror ingenuity.

Haiti is the poorest country in the western hemisphere, and the skintest bit of the poorest country in the western hemisphere is Cité Soleil, a sprawling slum of 250,000 God-and-mammon-forsaken souls on the seashore at the edge of the capital, Port-au-Prince. The one thing everyone who knows about Haiti agrees on, the top piece of advice they all give you, is: don't go near the City of the Sun, it's just too dangerous. Nobody has tried to solve its problems, only exploit them. Even Haitians, who are born living dangerously, say that the city is desperate, its main industry kidnapping, its only law gangs of nihilistic youths. It was advice I was happy to take after a week in this country. And then Louis, my driver and guide, a weary, prematurely aged man with more worries than joys, quietly mentioned, apropos of nothing, that he could take me to Cité Soleil if I wanted to go. 'But wouldn't that be suicidally foolish?' I whimpered. He shrugged: if I wanted to, he'd take me. I so wish he hadn't said that. Leadenly I took the offer to the photographer. We don't want to go, do we? I mean, poverty worldwide has an ugly sameness, a characteristic it shares with uncountable wealth. And, frankly, us going wouldn't make the slightest difference to the inhabitants or anyone else for that matter; no story is worth risking your life for. Being a photographer, Gigi said simply: 'It's what we do; it's not our job to make a difference. We witness and we report.' Damn, damn, damn. I wriggled on the hook for a week, but I knew we were going.

From atop the surrounding hills, Port-au-Prince looks like God aimed the ethereal kitty litter at the sea and missed. It's a pale splatter of mud brick, breeze block and corrugated iron set in a plate of congealed, dried sludge. In passing I should mention that Haiti is a first-rate, Hydra-headed ecological disaster. The richest soil in the Caribbean is being blown into the ocean. The crumpled land is a dusty, dun-coloured, cracked lino. It's easy to pick out the border with the Dominican Republic, because that's where the green starts. That's where the money starts. Picking my way through the streets of Port-au-Prince, I'm prodded by the twin conundrums of late capitalism. Why is it that the poorest travellers have the most luggage, and that the people with the least make the most rubbish? Rubbish is Port-au-Prince's leitmotif; a passing Martian would say that the manufacture and marketing of filth was the city's principal industry. Nowhere has the accumulation and hoarding of garbage reached such obsessive, constipated zeal as in Haiti. Filth flows through the streets and alleys and down the canals and through the squares like slow, slimy magma; rubbish creeps in through doors and windows, absorbing homes and parked cars. People live in and on it, like grubby, glistening surfers. The abiding essence of Port-au-Prince is its smell. Fumes from thousands of exhausted carburettors and the sweet stink of gutter decay and warm piss. Despite all this, they are an astonishingly handsome people. We honk and stutter our way through town past the dock, where market stalls are cut-open sea containers full of contraband. Past the charcoal market, where the barges bring in the charred remains of Haiti's hardwood forest. Past the rolling, smoky rubbish dump that's the size of Rutland, and on to the end of a narrow alley that peters out to nothing. Here, Louis stops the car and we walk across no man's land to the City of the Sun.

In the roofless wreck of a breeze-block hut is a gang of boys, the oldest probably in their twenties, the youngest, five or six. Louis talks quickly and softly in Creole. They stare at us with blank faces; I take off my sunglasses and smile winningly. Two lads in their early teens slide off a wall and walk ahead: our guides and bodyguards. We slither over a field of effluent towards a stand of beaten corrugated huts on the banks of a river of sickly effluvia. We slide and shuffle to the dark side of the sun. I'm something of a passing slum expert – a tourist of poverty, a misery day-tripper –

but let me tell you, nothing, nowhere, not the squatter camps of Cape Town, the *favelas* of Rio, the famine centres of Sudan or the hideous Stalinist gulag of Kaliningrad come close to the squalor and deprivation of this place.

This is a city built on shit. That's not a euphemism: it's a stinking, sick dung mire that stretches as far as the eye can see, riven with streams of diarrhoeic runny shite that splatter the beaches and leak out to sea. It's like the battlefield of some gastric Somme, with sunshine. Nothing grows here but shredded plastic and disease. It's so disgusting and inhospitable that there are barely any flies. Naked children sit and play in slimy holes, their houses rusted corrugated lean-tos that teeter and clank; occasional brick sheds squat with black, paneless windows.

The next thing you notice about the City of the Sun is how quiet it is. Slums are generally raucous, energetic places, but there are no roads here, no traffic, no electricity, no generators, nobody to venture out for fun or companionship; no shops, no business. In the shade of a hut, a man with a cleft palate and harelip sits on a brick and bangs a nail into a square of tin, over and over. He's making coconut graters. The boys laugh at him. This place is where Aristide's most ardent support came from. They grasped at him for a saviour. It's from here that he recruited his muscle, but now there's anger and resentment. One of my guides points at the picture of the president on his faded free T-shirt, and searches for an English word, jabbing his chest. 'Fucker,' he says, 'big fucker man, okay.'

There's a saying in Haiti: 'What you see, it's not what you think.' People say it all the time. It explains the inexplicable and makes a mystery of the mundane. I pay a handful of notes to the gang elders. Our guides grin and shake hands. One asks, with a faltering intensity: 'You come back?' We drive into Port-au-Prince on the busy main road behind the little 'tap-tap', the brightly painted pick-up truck that serves as public transport. They all have religious exclamations painted on them; this one promises that Jesus is the saviour. A couple of youths are mucking around on the back step, and then they jump off to fight in the road; that rutting grappling that young men casually commit in streets everywhere. We stop, and as if by sleight of hand, now they are fighting over a pistol, holding it high in the air, grabbing each other's wrists. They struggle for the gun, and then one boy seems just to lose interest; he lets go and turns to amble away. There is a pop, pop, pop; guns make such a tinny, silly little noise. The one lad who was firing wildly, I think he's missed, but the other boy, now the victim, stumbles and turns with his hands out, in an imploring but unsurprised, almost bored gesture, and I can see the huge exit wound spreading over his yellow T-shirt. He slumps onto the verge, down on his back. Another lad jogs up; together, with an aggressive, cocky, adrenal strut, they walk into the middle of the road and just stand there, holding their guns, staring into our car.

Louis is shouting: 'See, see, see what it's like here! See, see, how we have to live!' He's livid with fear. The shot boy raises his head from the gutter. His murderer notices the sign of life and trots back: pop pop, pop pop – point-blank, he fires into the yellow shirt. He skips back to his mate, and they amble down the centre of the road. 'For God's sake, let's go!' I shout from the footwell. But Louis is immobile, knuckles white on the wheel. 'We must go,' he repeats, but doesn't move. I shake his shoulder. The car stutters and almost stalls. Back in the hotel, clutching a beer bottle, he re-creates the scene, dancing back and forth down the bar, playing the roles. The guns grow: there are two, three, maybe four, more guns in belts, more shots, more boys, more blood, more murder. That night, I can't sleep. I'm childlike scared in the dark. The killing's the secret I can't talk about for fear of tears. It plays over and over in the corners of the room, flickering under the door. Why didn't the dead boy fight harder for his life? How could it all be so banal and awkward, and clumsy? Who'd choose to die in a yellow nylon hockey shirt? Why do I feel this fragile? It was such an amateurly improvised drama. Such brutal bad luck? 'What you see, it's not what you think.'

On our first day in Port-au-Prince, with Aristide still clinging to his rule, we went to the riot. It was the medical students' turn.

Somebody demonstrated most days. The government had just announced that it wouldn't put up with any more demonstrations. The police had orders to clear the streets with force. At the medical university, they were patting down visitors for guns. In the courtyard was a display of classroom chairs with bones on them, and placards demanding stuff. On a dais was a coffin with a skeleton in it. It represented the president. There were speeches and pop music. When everyone was shaken up and fizzy enough, they took the coffin round the corner to burn in front of the American embassy, the traditional venue for burnings if you want your picture in the foreign press. Then the police turned up and so did the Chimères. I should perhaps stop here to explain the *dramatis personae*. There are the police, your regular standard banana-republic corrupt cops; then there are Cimo, the riot police – semi-house-trained by the Americans, they come with Action Man body armour, M-16 rifles, pump-action shotguns, pistols, clubs and tear gas. Then there are some paramilitary palace guards. Haiti has no army as such. The army was responsible for so many coups, they got rid of it. It left a hole; there was no ultimate safety net, no forcible full stop.

And then there are the Chimères – they do come up with great names – from 'chimera', the mythical creature: part goat, part snake, part lion, park cockerel. They're the latest version of the ousted dictator 'Papa Doc' Duvalier's secret police, the Tontons Macoute. These are gangs of thugs who drive around in unlicensed SUVs and hang out on street corners and in front of public buildings, intimidating and extorting, drug-dealing, beating, breaking, raping and killing. It's said that most of the money the administration accrued, legal and illegal, went to pay the Chimères. On the other side, the opposition was most people, but by no means all people. Aristide had support: Louis, my driver, for instance, thinks the French were paying the students to riot, which is no dafter than everything else you hear on the street. There hadn't been much of a popular organised alternative to Aristide, just a lot of folk who don't know what they want, but know what they don't want. There's not much press in Haiti, and the TV is state-run. Real politics happens on the radio, everybody listens, and opposition is organised and advertised on pirate stations. Roving journalists report from mobile phones direct into cars and shops and homes. It's impressive. DJ is a high-risk occupation in Haiti, and some of them have enormous influence.

And finally, there's the Artibonite Resistance Front: these are more young gangsters with guns and pick-ups and bits of nicked, cool army kit and American ghetto sports clothes. They're opportunist drug peddlers, extortionists and pimps, and originally they were Aristide's men. But their former leader, Amiot Metayer, was ritualistically murdered, on the president's orders, and the word on the street is his heart was ripped out and put in a jar to go with twenty others for harvest festival. I know that sounds unlikely, but it's what many believe. And if they don't believe it specifically, they believe it's possible. Voodoo is a recognised official religion, practised by 90 per cent of Haitians, most of whom are also Catholic. Aristide was a Catholic priest. Now it's said he was a voodoo priest who had babies pounded in mortars with pestles, like African mealie meal, till they were pulp. Most people believe this is possible, probable.

This mixture of West African animism with a cloak of Catholicism and mystical witchcraft and goblin vendetta, underlies everything in Haiti. It's the spiritual prism that distorts and unifies. Voodoo means that nothing is what it seems. That everything, however obscene or absurd, is believable. I was driven one night out of Port-au-Prince through the pitch-black, potholed roads across the empty fields where the zombies lurk, to the middle of a hissing stand of sugar cane, to see a voodoo ceremony. It was like an evangelical church social, in a barn. There was barbecued jerk chicken and beer. Kids ran around and teenagers flirted. Old women cackled and swayed their hips. The vicar was direct from some hip-hop Ambridge. Nothing was sacrificed: no animals were hurt in the making of this worship. But often they are. Usually it's chickens. Voodoo runs between these hearty rhythmic hoedowns to sacrifices, vendettas, revenge, fear and murder. In the dark corners of markets, you can buy spooky faceless rag dolls with real pubic hair for the pricking of pain and vengeance. Voodoo is one of the few uniting factors in this fragmenting society. It's also the cause and focus of much of its fear.

At the demo, the medical students decided to take the show on the road and march in the general direction of the royal palace. There were about 300 of them; perhaps another 1,000 passively supportive people watching. The riot police in their home-made armoured trucks read their version of the riot act, and the march started off with a lot of heat. The riot cops got out and held their M-16s at high port. There weren't enough of them, a dozen or so, they're nervy and aggressive. And there weren't enough press, only a couple of photographers. In fact, there isn't enough of anyone to offer safety of confidence in numbers. Louis looks round and says: 'This doesn't look good.' He's noticed two truckloads of Chimères who have arrived behind us, blocking an exit. We turn a corner and, no warning, there's a volley of shots. Very loud, very close, all aimed at me. Around me, bodies blur, we're all running, falling, hitting the ground screaming. I haven't been in a riot for thirty years.

Inside I'm Wile E. Coyote: my legs are a whizzing oval blur; I'm motoring on turbo adrenalin. Outside I'm an arthritic tortoise, wheezing and plodding up the desperately exposed street. I'm way, way too old for this. Ahead is a line of very frightened and excited riot cops in balaclavas and American helmets waving their guns at chest height. One of them steps forwards and grabs Gigi's camera; she shouts at him and grips the strap. They tug, both yelling. He's seven-foot-plus in his parachute boots, a highly trained authority figure with guns and a lot of mates; she's a slight girl. I spring into action: 'For Christ's sake, give him the fucking camera!' I can tell by the look she flashes at me that she appreciates my wisdom and tacit support. The cop yanks it out of her hand and chucks it into a truck. Then, in a very Haitian moment, Louis bravely sidles to the cop and gets the camera back, minus the film: 'I recognised him – he's the boyfriend of one of the waitresses in your hotel. I said she'd be angry with him.'

The riot fragments into a series of running fights through the streets. We dodge and chase the police and students for a couple of hours. Within yards of shot and stone and petrol bomb, people get on with their day: shining shoes, selling little bags of drinkable water. We drive to a crossroads and into a cloud of tear gas. It smells like minicab air freshener, and feels like someone scouring your sinuses and eyeballs with a wire brush and Harpic. Over the radio we hear that a protestor has been shot and rushed to hospital. The riot's been reconvened there. On the street, they say a little girl's choked to death on the gas. Outside the hospital are the remains of burning tyres. Inside, the medical students wait. The wounded demonstrator turns out to have been shot with a tear-gas canister. It must have been fired at point-blank range to go into his back. On the operating-theatre table it explodes, killing him and filling the hospital with gas. The police storm the building, shooting one, possibly two students, whose bodies disappear, and they throw one or two others out of second-floor windows. We go back to the hotel. The city quivers with expectant anger, gunfire crackles, radios spill a breathless deluge of exaltation: they have a martyr. Tomorrow there'll be a funeral. Over dinner on the veranda, the photographers commiserate with Gigi over her lost film. They compare tear-gas vintages: not as peppery as Israel 2000, but with a stronger choking aftertaste than Serbia '98.

The next morning, the funeral. It's a long march through Port-au-Prince. The students are here, singing and chanting. There's a bit of a band, there's the riot police, there's a mourning family, and the Chimères hide in ambush up side streets, and there's an atmosphere. But the procession goes off without incident until it reaches the city's rambling walled cemetery. When the coffin goes inside, the rest of us mill about in the street. A rubbish cart turns up; it's state-of-the-art, with hydraulic tippers and pushers, and a postilion team of men in rubber gloves and overalls. It huffs and puffs, trumpets and leaves; it is, I notice, pristinely empty. The Chimères at the entrance stop anyone entering the cemetery. Louis whispers that he knows another way.

It's often a truth that graveyards mimic life in death. This is a chaotic slum, a morbid city of decomposing disorder. The tombs seem to clamber over each other. Thigh bones and spines poke out of cracked catafalques; dead rats rot. Among the Catholic imagery is the smell of rum and the blackened, waxy altars of voodoo. With help, we find the boy's grave, the plaster still wet; there's no name, no flowers. On the way out, Louis points at a mound of broken bricks, shards of plaster, smashed bottles, choked and overgrown with weeds. 'That is the tomb of Papa Doc Duvalier. The people, they came and destroyed it, the body's not here – stolen for magic.'

Aristide came to power promising so much: international recognition, reparations from the French (who took the equivalent of $4 billion in an 1825 divorce settlement). He promised what they all promise: jobs, peace and prosperity, a chicken on every altar. They were never his to give. Haiti's biggest money-earner is expatriate Haitians living in North America, sending home crumpled dollars from their jobs as busboys, maids and drug-dealers. Haiti's depleted soil grows a little sugar, a bit of coffee, some fruit. They used to make baseballs, and those labels that say 'made in' somewhere else, but it's cheaper in China. Aristide's failure was catastrophic: his corruption and cruelty, the heart-breaking trashing of trust and hope – but whatever comes next is unlikely to be much better. It's a nation of guns and protection and fear, which deals in superstition, second-hand drugs and bad horror-movie scripts.

On the road out to the airport, there's a body, bullets in its head, police standing around the long slick of blood, looking pissed off. 'Chimères,' they say. Later we're told he was one of Aristide's bodyguards, killed by the police for some internal infraction. And it turns out that the boy who died in the operating theatre wasn't a martyr after all. He wasn't even a student: he was a docker and Chimère. He was dead, though to beat it all the funeral, it turns out, wasn't even his: it was another kid, killed in a drive-by shooting the week before. In Haiti, 'What you see, it isn't what you think.'

GUATEMALA

Walking around Mexico City's archaeological museum, a reasonable man has to come to the conclusion that the Aztecs and the Spanish thoroughly deserved each other. They were the two most vicious sets of sixteenth-century xenophobes, a righteous blind date.

I suspect from looking at Aztec culture that their lives were a cross between a Nuremberg rally and the Folies Bergères, but then you walk into another room and here are the Maya. For most of us, American artefacts are a cultural margarine test – can you tell Aztec from Maya? Nine out of ten can't, until you see them side by side and then instantly you know the Maya were the good guys, altogether more ethereal, amused and enquiring. Where the Aztecs are all threats and instructions, the Maya are all observations and questions. They were a collection of agrarian city states, connected by a common language, a culture, some religion and a hierarchy that flowered in what is now the Yucatan peninsula, Belize, Honduras and Guatemala. They flourished for 700 years each side of the birth of Christ. At the very apex of that remarkable civilisation, the Maya suffered a catastrophic, vertiginous decline and vanished.

'Whatever happened to the Maya?' may not be a question that furrows your brow, but for beardy, Birkenstocked chaps with trowels and Indiana Jones complexes it's one of the great mysteries of humanity, and to find an answer you have to go to Guatemala, heartland of the Maya.

'Guatemala,' I was told by an enthusiast, 'is like Mexico was fifty years ago.' And that's a good thing, is it? To start with, you bypass Guatemala City, the capital. It's a sprawling, snarling, bad-tempered mess of a place, and potentially dangerous. These things are all relative, of course: it's an adventure playground compared with ten years ago. Guatemala suffered an intractable civil war that started in 1960, instigated by the CIA on behalf of American fruit companies. Thirty years later, nobody could remember what it was they were fighting about, so they decided to give elections a go, and we're in the middle of one right now. The country is papered in posters sporting smiley, 'trust me', open-necked candidates. Every tree, rock, wall and telegraph pole is daubed in slogans, and you realise at least in the electronic West, television is somewhere to put political graffiti.

Forty minutes down the road from Guatemala City is Antigua, which used to be the capital. Guatemala's had bad luck with capitals. The first colonial one was overrun by Indians, the second was buried under a mud slide, and the third, Antigua, was wrecked by an eighteenth-century earthquake so severe that the shaken population upped sticks en masse, leaving the dead to rot in the streets. Today it's a miraculously beautiful, crumbly Spanish colonial town. Sometimes neglect is the best thing that can happen to a place. It's set in the lee of three towering volcanoes, one of which smokes and dribbles malevolently. It's a low grid of pastel- and earth-coloured shop fronts, courtyard houses, picturesquely ruined churches and runaway tropical gardens. It has an outré expat population who all seem to be escaping from something. Antigua is a Butch and Sundance hideout for the comfortably off and the harmlessly dotty.

The weather, they boast, is permanent springtime. On the streets, riotously embroidered Indians carry bundles of blankets on their heads. I took Matthew, my photographer, to the local market, which was so bright and exuberant it made your eyes strobe and teeth ache. We ate corn porridge with black beans and chilli. 'Bloody hell,' he said, 'we've landed in a Tintin book.' It does have a simple, primary, timeless feel to it. Guatemala is innocent of what the holiday trade call a top end: there are virtually no luxury hotels, or at least none that fit their billing, and the tourist infrastructure is pretty much everyone else's infrastructure – that is, like Mexico fifty years ago. What there is instead are lots of bed-and-breakfasts set in wonderfully evocative period houses. We stayed in Quinta Maconda in the middle of Antigua. It's owned by John Heaton, a stalled adventurer and escapee from the First World who managed to be a beguiling cross between Keith Richards and Cecil Beaton. He has been collecting curios and votive objects from Central America to make a house and garden of eccentric beauty and tasteful comfort. He appointed himself our guide and travelling companion, which turned out to be something of a godsend, though whose god I'm not entirely sure. Most tourists in Guatemala carry their beds on their backs and are walking through Central America as an act of stamina before doing something grown-up or media studies. Very few locals speak any English, there are no road signs in any language, and indeed often not much road either.

Guatemala has proportionally the largest population of indigenous Indians in Central America. These are the descendants of the Maya. You see faces that could have come off limestone reliefs a thousand years old. Nobody could pretend that history since the conquistadors has been kind to them. This is still a racist, exploitative and hierarchical society. Unemployment stands at around 40 per cent, wages are tiny, corruption a matter of fact, but everyone we met was quietly polite and as helpful as mutual incomprehension allows. But there is overall a miasma, a maudlin sense of loss and of resignation. There is little exuberance about the Maya: their body language is folded and hunched. Mourning becomes the Maya. I was having breakfast in a village, and I noticed something odd about a washing line. It was made from barbed wire. It seemed very Guatemala, that – emblematic, appropriately awkward.

We travel out of Antigua and visit great crimson football fields of poinsettias, named for the poor Mexican girl who could only offer weeds to the baby Jesus at Christmas, but whose piety so touched the Almighty that he turned them red at the altar. And then a coffee *finca*, where the parcel-farmers and day workers wait in line with bags of beans to be weighed and paid for. The global price of coffee has fallen to the basement, and it shows on the resigned acceptance of their faces. Coffee is Guatemala's principal export, so of course it's impossible to find a decent cup. Occasionally it manages to be too repellent to swallow at all. Their other thing is cocoa, but there's no chocolate either, just weird little packets of 1950s biscuits that taste of dust and rationing. We go on, up to San Andreas Iztapa and a shrine to Maximon.

Guatemala is a Catholic country converted with torture and blackmail. But the Indians developed another underground religion that is half hidden behind the plaster saintly images of the church. Maximon is an idol originally involved to protect women from being raped by the Spanish while their men worked in the field. Bizarrely, he is part Pedro de Alvarado, the conquistador who conquered Guatemala, and part Judas Iscariot. The manifestation in this chapel is called San Simon: he's another, rather absurd mannequin dressed as a classic early-twentieth-century landowner or lawyer. He sits awkwardly on a podium in a black suit and hat, with a stick-on moustache. His shrine is covered in votive plaques thanking him for miracles. A few squat peasants queue to ask him favours. They offer booze and fags as gifts; a man kisses the corner of his scarf with a barely restrained fervour and hoarsely implores some desperate desire. It's almost funny, like watching someone talk to a ventriloquist's dummy – but then it isn't, because the belief and the need are so nakedly intense. Outside in the courtyard, a drunk with rheumy eyes and an idiot's grin tries to sell us good luck: he doesn't look as if he has much stock. Invoking the spirit of people who have massacred and subjugated you looks like spiritual masochism, but it's explained that the idols represent unimpeachable power. That's what the impotent peasant needs. Power, like electricity, is in itself neither good nor bad – you just have to plug into it – and who could be more powerful than Judas, the man who killed the conquistadors' God?

We travel on to the river Dulce, and the countryside is

ravishingly beautiful. There are mountains and lakes, woods and fields of corn and beans. Farmers in white cowboy hats trot small horses up bumpy roads, and skinny dogs lie in the dust. The river runs through some of what's left of Guatemala's rainforest. This is rainforest lite, in that it doesn't rain the entire time, it isn't full of bugs that have been designed for horror films, and it doesn't smell like a mass grave. The river is so flat and clear that it reflects the sky like a mirror. Occasionally we drift by buoyant fields of water lilies, and islands covered with Christmas decorations of white egrets and black cormorants. Pelicans dive with the insouciance of small boys jumping off piers, and the humid air is punctuated by iridescent butterflies and green parrots. John has a banana-roofed guesthouse on the river. When the oil lamp is blown out, I lie moon-eyed under the mosquito net, listening to the jungle scream and chirp. It's real, as real as the spider like a child's lost glove on the bedroom floor.

Next day, we putter down-river to a gorge that's forty storeys high, a limestone cliff and hanging tropical forest. At the end of it there's Livingstone, a surprisingly-named town that is only accessible down this river or from the sea. Ostensibly it's a fishing village that started life as a hideout for British Caribbean pirates, but it's now home to one of the strangest races I've ever come across. Locked into this run-down little port on the Caribbean are the Garifuna, whose story is a singularly romantic saga. They were the male survivors of two shipwrecked Spanish slavers from Nigeria who were washed up on the shores of the island of St Vincent, where they defeated the indigenous Arawaks (now extinct). Taking Arawak women, they ruled St Vincent until the British, thinking they were a bad precedent, fought a vicious war against them, finally rounding the survivors up and marooning them to starve on a rocky outcrop. The Spanish governor of Honduras rescued them to become skilled craftsmen and mercenaries, and they ended up here, where they still have their own language, their own food and music and religion. They really couldn't be more different from the Maya, who suspiciously say that they are a matriarchal society and that the women have a language passed down from mother to daughter that the men can't understand.

By chance we arrive on their national day. The streets are full of ladies swaying staccato bottoms exuberantly; they all wear hand-made frocks in ginghams and checks, and Sunday-best hats. The men flaunt a studied eccentricity of floral shirts, three-piece suits, co-respondent shoes and pork-pie straw hats. Barbecues grill jerk chicken and sweet potato, and the whole town vibrates to African drumming, singing and laughter. There are a surprising number of pick-up trucks on the couple of hundred yards of drivable road that goes nowhere. Livingstone is fortuitously positioned between Belize and Honduras; they say its business is not entirely subsistence fishing, but still the old family trade of smuggling – drugs, mostly.

Tikal is the grandest and largest of all Mayan cities. The thing to do, I'm told, is to get there at dawn, so at 6 am we race to the ruins and hike up a rickety staircase to the top of the temple – which makes you gasp and think that 2,000 years ago, the Maya built this stone edifice ten storeys high in the middle of a jungle, and today they can't build a wooden ladder that would pass Russian health-and-safety. At the top, confronted by the stares of half-a-dozen bony-kneed, spiky-haired gap-years, I sit next to one who's scribbling in his travel diary. Why is he here? 'Because I want to see where the rebel base was filmed in the first Star Wars.'

Tikal's impressive: a bit like a Mayan Windsor. What I liked better was Uaxactun, twenty kilometres away. Here the ruins are still hidden in the jungle, the great sabre trees towering over crumbling walls and fallen gods. Here you can sense a connection to the past. A small, serious boy appoints himself as our guide and leads us into a musty, dark chamber. He holds his hand up against the wall, examines its shadow and says: 'It's about twenty past twelve.' I look at my watch: this room has only lost two minutes in 1,700 years. The Maya had a complex knowledge of astronomy and mathematics; they discovered the concept of nought, which I'm assured is a great achievement. They had a written language in the form of glyphs. They grew interminable corn and beans, but without ploughs. They had no cows, sheep, chickens, horses, oxen or pigs. They did, though, have the first rubber ball, and played the first ball game, pelota Maya – a sort of football where you don't use your feet or hands, but your hips, elbows and occasionally your rolled-up enemies. It is being reintroduced by a gently dotty Swiss gent, who wants to get it into the Olympics. Seeing as the Maya regularly sacrificed the winning captain to the gods, I wouldn't hold your breath. They also used to puncture their foreskins with skate barbs: I just add that for local colour.

To find out what did happen to the Maya, we go to Chiminos Island Lodge, a remote collection of spartanly comfortable guest huts in the rainforest. There's a semi-tame ocelot, which stalks me back to my hut at night and frightens me more than I'd like to admit, as did the howler monkeys, which in the wee small hours make a noise that is an eerie cross between the M6 and the torment of lost souls. If you're coming to Guatemala, you shouldn't miss this ecologically soft-footed camp. First thing in the morning, we hike through the damp jungle and clouds of mosquitoes to Aguateca, a fortress on top of a cliff cut off by a deep natural chasm. It's around here that the Maya civilisation finally disintegrated in the eighth century. According to recently decoded glyphs and archaeological digs, they fought each other to mutual unsustainable destruction. They became too fearful to farm outside the protection of their cities; the delicate, thin soil became eroded and barren, and lakes silted up, bringing more desperate raiding and violence. The peasant population couldn't sustain the huge and expensive priestly noble class; the great temples and palaces fell to become paranoid defensive fortresses for the starving and sick in the terrifying jungle.

During the 1960s, the Maya became popular because their apparently peaceful, ecological nature was an echo of the flower-power times. Now their internecine violence and suicidal environmental destruction also has a timely resonance. But what is still inexplicable is why they just left their civilisation – all that investment, all that effort, all that pride, achievement and heritage. They just ran away. People still lived in Rome, Athens,

Cairo and Constantinople after their empires expired, but seemingly not the Maya. Whatever it was that happened to them, it was too awful to live with. All this speculation, though, comes from the universities of the West. Nobody seems to have thought to ask the Maya. They're still saying nothing.

BRAZIL

I'm told that if you're in the second-hand passport business the top of the range, most sought-after nationality to blag isn't American or Brit or Canadian or Swiss. It's not any of the top-dog nations with international clout. If you're looking for an off-the-peg, easy-fit, attractive, fashionable new identity then slip into Brazilian. And you can see why. Everyone could be a Brazilian. There is no shade on the human colour chart that isn't indigenous. Here you can find cities of blue-eyed, blond Germans and Prada-black West Africans. Brazil boasts the largest expat population of Japanese outside Japan. And there are millions of Italians to add a dash of humour to the Portuguese. You could be called Cohen or Smith or Schmitt or De Souza or Datsun or just Sting's mate and wear your passport in your lip.

Brazil's catchy favourite cliché is, 'Hi, melting pot is us.' A rich stew of hot homogeneity. It's not true. Brazil's actually more like God's home improvement swatch: plenty of colours, they just don't all go together. The only people who'd have trouble fitting in to a Brazilian passport are fat people. Brazilians really don't do fat, so you can't be Brazilian unless you can touch your toes.

Brazil is everyone's reserve country. It's a truism all over the world that when your lot are out of the cup you support Brazil. We like to feel that spiritually, rhythmically there's a little samba in all of us. The connotations and associations of the place are almost all good. There's football and bottoms and all that rainforesty new-age stuff. There's *Carnaval* and samba and the beach and bottoms, coffee and nuts and wax and sun and bottoms. And they've never fought a war – well, not a serious one – against anyone except Paraguay. And they deserved it. Do you know anyone who wouldn't rather be in Brazil?

Looking at the little map on the video screen in the plane, you realise the one defining truth of Brazil. It's vast. Now, of course you always knew it was vast. We all know it's a big place, but big is comparative and Brazil dominates Latin America. It's almost the same size as the continental United States. To travel from east to west is like going from London to Moscow; north to south from London to New York. It borders ten countries and has a third of Latin America's coastline. It contains states that are bigger than France but have only three policemen. It's so big it uses Wales as a ruler. But two thirds of the population live in a thin strip on the coast and half live in cities.

The rest of it contains every mineral you've ever heard of and a dozen you haven't. It's got gold, diamonds, sapphire, emeralds and oil. It's got heavy industry from steel to the original Beetle and the cars run on sugar. I'm not kidding. You can go to a pump and fill up with sugar alcohol or you can drink it in a caipirinha. Brazil grows the complete supermarket from cattle on the pampases of the south to wheat, manioc, potatoes, coffee, nuts, sugar and every fruit and vegetable known to Stella McCartney. And then a bewildering amount of stuff from the interior unknown outside its borders. Plant a walking stick in Brazil and it'll sprout chilli peppers at one end and mangoes at the other and then grow another walking stick from an immense quantity of exotic hardwoods. Brazil is one of the few countries that is truly, completely self-sufficient. Not just physically, but spiritually and aesthetically. It has an indigenous culture based around music and dance but that includes film, books, painting, photography and a television industry that isn't just badly dubbed episodes of *The Waltons* and *Benny Hill* but actually exports dramas around the world.

Oh, and one other thing: Brazil contains 20 per cent of the world's surface water. Now that may not sound exciting, but 50 per cent of the world's water is so polluted, degraded or salinated that it's now barely fit for consumption. Water is becoming the globe's most precious resource. Forget oil, you can run your car on sugar. You have to drink water. Brazil's got it, California needs it. That's the geography lesson. It poses one insistent question: what the fuck went wrong? Why doesn't Brazil work? Why is one of the top ten world economies still living in the basement of a Third World country, taking handouts from the Americans and stay-in-after inflation lessons from the IMF? Why can't you name three famous Brazilians who aren't footballers? OK, Gisele. Who are the other two?

Brazil is either one of the great might-have-beens or yet-to-bes. They're still deciding. It's a complicated question.

Rio de Janeiro is not a particularly beautiful city but, more by luck than judgement, it found itself a fabulously beautiful setting on a bay surrounded by mountains and lagoons and rainforest. Its peaks look like children's drawings and above it all hangs the greatest Art Deco sculpture ever built: Christ blessing his new world. And the first thing you notice are the Brazilians. They're all beautiful, even the ones with Zimmer frames. You walk down the streets and into lampposts. And then when you look again you notice that actually she's not that amazing. She's short, her eyes are too small and she's got the thighs of a power lifter. But, whack! She's still the sexiest thing you've seen in years. The weird truth is that Brazilians exude a fabulous self-confidence. Not a flaunting Hollywood exhibitionism, but a slow-burn physical contentment that translates as an engrossed, syncopated sexuality. They don't dress well or much, but I've never seen a collection of people who are so alive and comfortable in their bodies. They wear themselves as if they were bespoke tailored.

The next thing you notice is that this isn't some cheap imitation Miami. So much of Latin America is burdened with a weary economic envy and the tatty trappings of avarice. Here there are no advertisements for Marlboro or Coca-Cola or Levi's. No one speaks English. Brazilians are not in that long, sad, invisible queue to be wetback migrants cleaning Californian toilets and serving hot dogs. Brazil hasn't finished discovering itself yet. And then you notice little things like the money. There isn't enough of it. So they Sellotape coins together to make sensible dominations and then you just go back to noticing their bottoms. And you think, 'That's quite enough noticing for today.'

My first day in Rio, we land at breakfast time, check in to the Copacabana Palace and my guide says, 'How would you like to go to a football game this afternoon in the Maracana Stadium, a local derby? Of course you could just relax on the beach and watch girls.' Now I'm not a great football wonk but I'm a huge wonk for girls, particularly on beaches. But even I know that turning down the Maracana Stadium is one of those decisions I'd be made to regret for life. This is the Vatican of the beautiful game. It's up in the poor, rough north of the city, still a handsome, concrete oval, that seats . . . well, it seats loads, as many as they can cram in. It was built for the 1950 World Cup. It was the biggest stadium in the world. Brazil is the only country to have reached the final stages of every World Cup and this was the first to be held outside Europe. And the first after the interregnum of the war. It was, the aficionados say (everyone is an aficionado), the greatest Brazilian team ever. They got to the final. The capacity crowd squeezed in another crowd to sit on its knee. They were playing Uruguay, not some distant gringos but their tiny neighbours. It was one-one and then ten minutes before the whistle, 'Goooooaaaal!' Uruguay scored. They say that in that moment the Maracana Stadium broke a world record. It held the biggest collective silence ever. Ten minutes later, people started jumping off the roof. The loss still affects Brazil. It's like a bereavement. You get on, you love again, but the pain never goes away.

Our match, Fluminese *v.* Flamengo, two Rio teams, was a bit like Chelsea *v.* Arsenal, but only a bit. In truth, it wasn't a great game – a lot of niggly fouls and playground dives, but it was still unarguably Brazilian. They'd rather lose the ball than pass it. Defence is remedial, attack continuous. Wingers with the ball actually slow down to let opposing backs catch up so they can beat them with a patent dummy and flick. The crowd, though, was fabulous. They barely take up half the stadium but make enough noise for it to be deafening. The drumming is incessant, the rhythm syncopates to the echo. It's a lot more sophisticated than oafs humming the theme from *The Great Escape* to a dodgy trombone. Men all around me shout 'Son of a whore' continuously, while pointing incredulous outstretched palms. It's nice to see that the greatest depths of livid obscenity are reserved for members of your own team so dumb and talentless that they occasionally have to obey the laws of gravity. It's a one-all draw, which pleases no one.

This is like a British game only in the sense that there's a ball and grass. There are girls here, real hip-swaying girls, not those manky baritone geezer-lite trouts we get back home, with builder's crack for cleavage. Football was originally brought to Brazil by Scots engineers. Fortuitously, the Brazilians grabbed the rules and ignored the Alan Hansen team talk. Their particular fluid dribbling game they say came from the black players. Blacks were only allowed to play with white chaps in the twenties on the understanding that they didn't touch anyone, hence the reliance on ball control.

Racism is endemic in Brazil, on a sliding scale from Baltic-white to Gambian-black. Ask someone up the pale end and they say it's nothing, it's not racism, rich blacks are accepted everywhere. What they mean is that money's white. All black footballers have blonde Nordic wives. Apparently it's a rule. White is status. It's a truth that most poor people are more black than they're white and rich people are more white than they're black. When the government tried to take affirmative action on university places there was patronising laughter from the taupe folk who puffed that they all had a touch of black. How black is black? To which the answer ought to have been, ask a black man.

Another little thing. Lots of girls dress so that they show off the marks left by their bikini tops. It looks odd but there's a reason. It's a way of letting you know that they're actually lighter than their tans. I may look mulatto, but really I'm white.

Poverty is Brazil's great sickness – the scale and the relentless grip of it. It's often said of all Latin America that the insoluble problem is that there's no middle class, as if car dealers and insurance salesmen were the Oxfam of economics. Brazil does have a huge middle class, it's just that the poor are still so far below them. Another little thing: drink a can of Coca-Cola in Rio, don't bother putting it in the bin. Just leave it. Within seconds it'll disappear. They're very proud of their recycling of tins. What they don't mention is that this means there are thousands of people for whom a desperate competition for rubbish is their only livelihood.

One of the many causes of poverty is endemic corruption. By its very nature it keeps wealth and power in a small, closed circle. But there is also a strange, contrary counterpoint democracy about poverty in Rio. It's not hidden in distant suburbs or squatter camps, though it's there too. It's right here in the middle of the city. The *favelas* – the slums – crawl up the hills and have the best views. The poor folk and the rich folk stare into each other's windows. On one side of the street there are electric gates and bougainvillea, on the other rough sewerless shanties. They say that if you want to stay rich in Rio, look poor. Everyone dresses the same, shorts and T-shirts, bits of sports clothes. You don't see any jewellery, women don't have big hair and glossy make-up. There's surprisingly little fashion, indeed no style worth the mention, just an enormous sashaying flirtatious self-absorption. *Cariocas* (the colloquial name for people from Rio) innately have the stuff that clothes are meant to give the rest of us. But theirs is real and not off the peg and they all have it, rich or poor.

Cariocas like to talk up the danger of their city in the way New Yorkers used to. The *favelas* are *terra incognita* for them, as forbidding as the great rainforest. But tourists go and have tours. You can get in an open, jungle-green Land Rover with guides dressed in safari costumes and big Ernest Hemingway hats. I'm not joking. The indignity and the irony of treating humans like a game drive doesn't seem to strike the gawping tours of Italians who trip out to snap pictures of beggars and buy Amazonian fruit juice.

The first *favela* was made by nineteenth-century soldiers returning from a regional revolt. They were promised land and money but were given a useless hill and no cash. They named it after a hill they fought over – '*Morro da Favela*', referring to a plant from the Bahia region. What's interesting is how the *favelas* were built. They crawl higgledy-piggledy up precarious inclines built with bricks stolen by construction workers. Houses rise five or six storeys. All have flat roofs, in case you need to build again. Most have satellite dishes. There are shops and internet cafés and supermarkets. It turns out that what people build when no one's watching are seventeenth-century southern European towns with stolen electricity. The *favelas* are poor but they're not the poorest. Even a handmade slum has value. The houses are bought and sold. There's a communal postal service. A few bohemians and some foreigners are starting to move in, a sort of hardcore exotic Brixton.

One of the things they tell you about the *favelas* is that local people leave their doors open. There's no crime, they say, because there are no police and there are no police because they're run by drug gangs who like to keep things quiet and unexciting. In the sixties, Brazil had a gang problem. It also had a variety of left-wing revolutionaries. The military junta locked up the gangsters and the intellectual Marxists together, and they found they had much in common and formed a new, improved criminal class. The drug cartels are ruthless, corrupting, murderous and romantic. They have better guns, lawyers and judges than the police and they tell you that the only major crime committed here was a bank raid. The drug-dealers caught the culprits, who turned out to be – you're ahead of me – policemen.

But the *favelas* are also the engine of culture, which means music and dance. The best parties, the best clubs are up here. There was a dance called the 'Little Train'; popular with nubile youth, it was a sort of lap-dancing conga. There were reports that teenage girls were getting pregnant not after the dance but during. Now that's a party. The samba schools that organise the *Carnaval* come from the *favelas*. Being poor in Brazil is as grinding and life-shortening as anywhere in the world, but it's not dowdy and it's not joyless.

I'd always imagined the *Carnaval* was a sort of Las Vegas girly show on a truck; a sort of bigger, brighter, sexier version of Notting Hill. Actually, having a verucca removed is sexier than the Notting Hill Carnival. No one had told me how serious this is. Properly serious fun. For a start each samba school's float, or rather collection of flat-bed trucks, takes about eighty minutes to go past. Thousands of dancers, drummers and performers are involved. Each school has its own celebrities and an annually composed song and a theme. You look at the photographs and you think, 'That must be Group Sex and Feathers or Competitive Smiling', but you couldn't be more wrong.

This year there were floats devoted to the illegal trade in body parts for transplant surgery – hundreds of spangly dancers with great big kidneys and eyeballs on their heads and girls doing the samba in specimen jars full of water. There was a school devoted to piracy that started with Captain Hook and ended with intellectual copyright and fake designer labels with dancers dressed as CDs and with Nike trainers as epaulettes. There was a history of Judaism; exhausted little menorahs and Pharisees trudged back in the wee small hours to the *favelas*. The winning school was a *Panorama*-style exposé of homelessness that ended with a big head of Lula da Silva, the new President. The energy and commitment to *Carnaval* is unlike anything I've ever seen anywhere. Hundreds of thousands of people, ecstatic for hours and hours. As an outsider you can only judge this by what you already know: girly shows and cabaret. But we're only getting the sequinned tip. I'm transfixed by the feathers and buttocks, the pantomime and the pumping rhythm, but *Carnaval* has a cultural and political significance that is uniquely the experience of Brazilians.

An enormous amount of hope and goodwill rests on the shoulders of Lula. He's the first head of state to come from poverty. They desperately need him to clean out the stables of Augean corruption. Brazil is a big country to turn round. Its vices are tenacious. But still there's an aura of optimism. Maybe this time.

Just one word about rainforests. There's a great chunk of original growth outside Rio. It's not Amazonian, it's what's called Atlantic rainforest, which is rainforest without the rain. And to be frank, despite what the Body Shop tells you, it's pretty dreary and reminded me of nothing so much as a Homebase pot plant sale. Almost everything you've seen in office atriums. It's really very, very Surrey.

Salvador. When you get past bottoms and football and think about Brazil, you think about Salvador. Up on the northern coast, this was the original capital. This is where the slaves came to. Brazil was the world's biggest importer of slaves. Over three million West Africans – and still Salvador seems closer to Africa than Europe. This place is the cultural beat of the nation. This is where all the artists and musicians come from or to. The city's poignant, crumbling colonial heart shimmers in the heat and reflected light of the Atlantic. There's an atmosphere you can taste. It's dark, intense, sad, beautiful and dangerous – a city of exuberant churches and desperate prayers. Every Catholic sect set up a department store here, and now that protestant evangelists have arrived from the US it's like God's Brent Cross.

The Franciscan monastery is a staggering crusted gold example of what they call tropical baroque. The finest, gaudiest, good God-rich church in all the Americas. When the slaves were finally freed they built their own monumental church in gratitude. They pooled their crumpled, sweat-damp pittances and bought a monument to the religion that had enslaved them. It took fifty years but still underneath the beliefs of Africa flourish. Candomble, a complex and semi-secretive religion based on ancestor worship and animist spirits. For centuries it was woven in among the Catholic saints. Capoeira, the dance fighting from Angola that those two red T-shirted nancy boys are doing on the BBC channel ident. It's a spinning, incredibly muscular shadow fighting.

The food in Salvador is a fusion of Africa and America. Big stews that taste of salt sweat and hot tears. One night I went to a dance in a packed, open-air bar that shimmied and bumped. A group played *forró* music. It was brought here by English engineers, of all people. They'd hold parties on Sundays 'for all', which meant for blacks as well. The instruments are a sailor's accordion, a triangle and a drum, which sounds like the musical equivalent of *Ready, Steady, Cook*.

On the street men push portable cafés, Thermoses of coffee and sweets with a sound system. After work people sit on the beach in the slanting afternoon light. Boys practise their cartwheels, fishermen clean their catch, hawkers sell cheese to be grilled on braziers, bootleg CDs and silver earrings. One of the many great things about the beach in Brazil is that if you smile and say no thanks they smile and say OK. A little lad washes the sand from my feet with a watering can. Salvador feels as if it's built out of secrets, gilded dreams and remorse. You half-sense things. There's always something happening in the corner of your eye but when you turn to stare it's gone. It's surrounded itself with the fetishes and comforts of a distant, long-gone life. Salvador is a place out of place that's both subtle and brutal. It blew me away.

The beach is central to Brazilian life. Back in Rio, Copacabana and Ipanema stretch for mile on pulchritudinous mile. Everyone comes here to play games: rounds of keepie-uppie that last longer than football matches, a type of volleyball called footvolley that's played to the rules of football. Imagine volleyball played without hands. There are schools and gyms on the beach and men making sand sculptures. The *Cariocas* come with just enough money to rent a chair and buy a drink. The little *cabanas* on the beach have boys that'll do everything for you, including taking phone calls from your office and laying down punctured hosepipes to sprinkle cool paths in the sand. People don't lie around much, they stand and chat or run or do sit-ups or bat balls or do Olympic flirting. Brazilians flirt with a purposeful, tireless élan. As far as I can make out they're all pushovers.

And then there are the bottoms. What can I say? The finest, ripest, richest, most joyous arses anywhere. Bottom is a national obsession. It should be on the flag. They like them big and muscly with thighs to match. Oddly, no one goes topless. Breasts are a side-order. The personal ads in the paper don't print pictures of faces. 'Hi, I'm twenty-six, enjoy dancing, long walks and keeping fit. Looking for like-minded man for a good time.' And there's this smudgy snap of an arse. Brazilians stand on the beach looking back over the rolling surf towards the ancient, disparate countries they came from. Behind them is the dark, green, sweaty interior. You still get the sense of a new community trapped between the forest and the ocean, amusing themselves whilst still waiting after 500 years. At night, the incandescent Christ seems to float in the sky.

PAKISTAN

Perhaps the shop could best be described as a sort of Pakistani Evans the Outsize, or Pathan Connection – or Burqas 'R' Us. If you want a burqa, and a surprising number of women do, this hole-in-the-wall swagged salon in Peshawar's Storytellers' Market is where you come. And I want a burqa. Can I have a burqa please? 'Certainly,' replies the manager, an imposing man who's sensibly dressed in a *shalwar kameez* and wool waistcoat with matching white beard. 'Any particular colour?'

Ah, I wasn't prepared for a choice of burqa. The thing seems to imply an absence of choice. But I can see they come in bile green, nappy sienna, sepulchral white and two shades of blue. The blue, I think. 'Ah yes,' nods the manager, 'the most popular choice. And what size?' Oh, about my size. The assistants catch each other's eyes. I feel like an ugly fundamentalist transvestite. It's for my girlfriend, I add lamely. They talk rapidly in Pashtu. A boy at the back titters. I don't need a translation. 'Oh, get her, it's another one of those ridiculous reporters trying to cross the border. You know, we had John Simpson in the shop . . . '

I'm given a blue one. It's beautiful, with needle-sharp pleats and embroidery down the front that stops coquettishly just below the crotch like a teddy. When I finally get it home I'm enchanted to see that it looks very fetching with fishnets and suspenders.

It's made of nylon, the kind that produces enough static to run a short-wave radio. Don't you have anything in cotton? 'Certainly, it's cheaper. The women prefer nylon.' Then he gives me one of those quotes that make you think the world has tripled in size and we're all separated by insurmountable cultural distance. 'Nylon is the modern fashionable choice.' The idea that anything about a burqa could be deemed either fashionable or modern proves that we are singing from very different hymn sheets.

One of the first shocks of getting to Peshawar is seeing so many refugee women wearing burqas. I'd have thought the first thing they'd do at the border was rip the humiliating, hot, sweaty, incapacitating things off and yell for joy. But then I come here with as many preconceptions and prejudices as everyone else. In the West we assume the burqa to be a totemic symbol of everything we're using bombs to stop: totalitarianism, fundamentalism. But long before the Taliban made it a uniform of oppression, it was the cultural, not religious, overall of conservative rural tribeswomen, and represented safety, respect, conformity and belonging.

We drove into the city past little piles of khaki rubbish bags in the gutter. Then I realised that refuse sacks would be a laughable extravagance in Peshawar, and that these were widows – burqaed and begging – who had lost their families to spiteful serial wars. To have no family on the frontier is to be nobody; giving to the needy is one of the tenets of Islam; being a recipient, one of its greatest humiliations. The burqa may cloche aspiration, intelligence, individuality and beauty, but for these women it hides their shame and makes them anonymous, mute Mother Courages. Stony, stoic war memorials.

You can get to Peshawar from the north down the Khyber Pass, or from the south up the Grand Trunk Road, a fork in the ancient silk route. Dodging the careering lorries, brightly painted like fairground rides, you come to a town called Attock. Here the road meets the confluence of the river Indus, on its way from the high Karakoram mountains, and the river Kabul, which draws down from the high country of Afghanistan.

The Indus is clear mountain water, the Kabul a soup of brown earth. They run for a mile as a striped river. Stalls on the banks serve fish – you can order clear or muddy. Above the gorge of their meeting is a vast, crenellated Mogul fort. Every invader with an eye on the plains of India has had to pass under its shadow. It marks the end of the Punjab and the beginning of the North-West Frontier Province, created by the British as a bulwark against the invasion of the Russians and the raid of the Pathans. For any bookish boy from our wet, green island, this hot, ochre-coloured mountainous place is marinated in the spice of romance. This is where the Great Game was played. It has inspired more rumpty-tumpty poetry than all the globe's pink bits put together.

The frontier scouts that as lead soldiers marched over so many nursery carpets are still here, based in another bastion that towers over Peshawar, no longer manned by C. Aubrey Smith and David Niven with topees and lances, but by tough, moustachioed Punjabis in camouflage with AK-47s. The romance of the frontier tugs at your sleeve at every turn. The city is everything a grandson of the Empire could wish for: dark, odorous and bubbling with intrigue and righteous revenge.

The old town has overgrown its red walls and seeped into broad suburbs, but at its heart it is still dense; an overladen collection of shops, barrows and stalls selling everything from doughnuts and pomegranates to plucked sparrows and broad-spectrum antibiotics. Here there's gold, precious stones and pistols. In the coagulating, slithery streets, donkeys, horse carts, lorries, motorbike taxis, nicked sedans, haughty camels and Korean Land Cruisers play an endless, slow game of chicken with the cyclists, everyone jabbing frantic bursts on their horns. The cyclists boast loud chimes that play tinny tunes, so you're continually shooed aside with a quick stanza of 'Happy Birthday'.

The crowds are dense and varied, and pressed here by the two great movers of mankind: war and trade. The men are all dressed in kurtas. The women sway in various tribal, religious and cultural costumes. There are Punjabis and Afghans, Hazaras (descendents of Genghis Khan's Mongols), Uzbeks, Tamerlane's Tajiks, Persians, Sikhs and the shifting, vengeful tribes of the frontier Waziris, Orakzais, Afridis, Yusufzai, Marwats, Mohmands, Khattaks and

Powindahs, the nomadic herdsmen and traders who follow an ancient and circular migration regardless of borders.

In the smoky bazaar I found a tray of coins left behind by Alexander's satraps and Akbar's warriors rubbing their verdigris against the medals of the Queen Empress, given for the forgotten Waziristan campaign that in its day tied up more of Victoria's troops than all the rest of India.

On the outskirts of the old town is the British cemetery. No spick-and-span war-graves committee tends these sentries, who never left their post. There's just an old man in a grubby shirt, sitting on a rickety rope bed outside the English village-style gatehouse. The bleached crosses have tumbled into the dust; parched weeds draw faint life from the graves' sagging earth and form curling wreaths of fading remembrance. You can still make out the avenue of palms, down which the coffins must have been hefted at the slow march, almost hear in the insect hum the dead march played by some red-faced cornetist.

The inscriptions are poignant. One corner is dedicated to children: 'Our little Mavis,' born 6 September 1903, died 1 May 1904. And there are the lines of soldiers at eternal ease: 'Edward Henry Le Marchant, Lieutenant Colonel First Battalion the Hampshire Regiment, shot dead by a fanatic 1889, aged forty-five.' 'Bandsman Charles Leighton' also of the Hampshires, aged twenty, assassinated by a ghazi. At the end of their tours, battalions put up stones to the memories that would stay here, on the ragged edge of empire. One poor chap died in an explosion in the soda-water factory, many more of enteric cholera, typhus and nameless fever. I walk round sucking the shire names like dry pebbles and try to explain the bosky characters of Yorkshire and Dorset and Durham to my Pathan guide; he nods politely, feigning interest. It's a salutary reminder, a nudge in the ribs that this sad, sweet wallowing in pink nostalgia goes all one way. I'm carrying around the white man's burden of Kipling and Newbolt and Gunga Din.

Afghanistan and the border tribes have suffered more than anyone on Earth from the imposed reputations of Empire. They have become Johnny Pathan, your archetypal guerrilla superman, impervious to fear and hardship; dignified chaps who can plug the eye of a butterfly at 1,000 yards with a home-made muzzle loader using their teeth as bullets.

This mythology of multipurpose warrior/trader/bandit with ethics of iron and hospitality of milk and honey creeps as fact into hard-nosed journalism and po-faced military briefing, and it must be said that the Pathans themselves like to talk up their martial CV. Across the border, though, partly through neighbourly fear and respect, Pakistanis like to add the footnote that all Pathans are screaming queens and quote that line of poetry: 'Over the lake there's a shepherd boy with a bum like a peach and he's waiting for me.'

The Pathans stalking the streets of Peshawar all make sure they look the part. Tall and wiry, they move with the loose-limbed grace of mountain men. They're chiselled, handsome people, often with faded blue or green eyes and reddish-blond hair, all swagged in their dusty brown shawls and familiar rolled woollen hats.

They don't look like anyone's victims. But the legends diminish a pitiful truth: Afghans make up the largest displaced population in the world. Daily they arrive in Peshawar starving and sick, with only a few worn-out pots and clothes and their despair. This city had 40,000 inhabitants ten years ago; now there are perhaps 3 million – and the plumbing wasn't great to begin with. Most of these families huddle in the already crowded slums.

To look for refugee camps, though there are plenty, is to misunderstand. The whole city is one vast, squalid, crawling mass of shantytown camps. Most new, fear-forced immigrants already have extended family here. I visited some who just made it across the closed frontier. They had spent the last of their money renting tiny sties built by speculating Pakistani landlords in a warren-like compound. Mohammed is a mechanic from Kabul. His wife and ten children sit together in a little concrete courtyard staring at brick. She peels a few potatoes for the minute charcoal fire.

They don't have the demeanour of a proud warrior people; they have that faraway, defeated, listless look of the universal brotherhood of refugees, people tossed out by events. The children stare with round, fly-blown eyes and pick their scabby faces, the older girls neurotically twist the ends of their shawls; they don't say much.

Mohammed recounts the litany of his troubles: house blown up, son killed, daughter beaten by the Taliban for extending a naked hand while reaching for fruit, the decision to go, the week-long walk, the hunger, the cold, the children's diarrhoea, his wife's tears, the absent husbands for his daughters, no work, no money, no . . .

His voice trails off; the appalling, undeserved unfairness of his lot has been worried over until it's ragged. It won't even keep his anger warm. There's just the crushing impotence and guilt and his ten hungry children. The future doesn't look good for Mohammed and his family. He says he wants to go home but that doesn't even have the brightness of a dream. He's only been here a week, but many of the boys running round the market trying to cadge a couple of rupees have been here all their lives, and some of the refugee camps have grown into permanent baked-earth suburbs.

I walk round one right on the northern outskirts of the city, a semi-deserted, desperate place where the sewerage ran in thick canals and children formed mud bricks in the street. I sit in the shade of a little stall that sells mould and corruption: the stock is a suppurating mass of decomposing vegetables, the smell as thick as the cloud of flies. The shopkeeper and his sons squat and watch their lives slowly compost.

'This is not a good place,' says my guide. 'These aren't good people.' He is from Kabul, a Dari speaker; these are Pashtu-speaking Pathans from the south. He doesn't trust them, so we make our salaams and go and have lunch in a rooftop restaurant in the Smugglers' Market: kebabs of sweet lamb, skewered alternately with fat, and a salad of radish and lumpy, sour yogurt and flat bread. On the wall is an old tourist poster – 'Come to Sunny Kabul' – turned green and yellow with age and longing.

He stares at it, a city built round a curve in a river cradled by mountains. 'Here's the university where I studied engineering. This is the great mosque. My family lived up here.' What was it like before the Russians? 'It was one of the great cities, all shaded with fruit trees. Kabul, you know, was famous for its fruit trees: apples, oranges, mulberries, grapes, pomegranates, guavas.' He pauses, searching for the right word for home. 'It was beautiful.' He left four years ago: his house was hit by a rocket, his uncle was killed, his brother died on the trek south, and his cousins are still up there somewhere or perhaps dead.

How many people do you know who died in the wars? He thinks thirty, forty, perhaps more. That's an awful lot; it that typical? 'Oh yes, everyone has lost dozens of family and friends. You eat very slowly. Do all English eat slowly?' I tell him that we don't really eat because we're hungry, that meals are social, and that we sit and talk, often for a couple of hours. He laughs at the weird extravagance of the idea.

In Afghanistan's cumulative wars, 1.5 million people have been killed. That's from a population of 25 million, half as many again as the US lost in the whole of the Second World War, but taken from, say, the residents of California. There are 1 million orphans, 1.5 million crippled and limbless, and perhaps 5 million dispossessed refugees scattered around an unsympathetic, distrustful world, most of them here in Pakistan. It says much for the indigenous population and the collegiate charity of Islam that they have, by and large, taken in and accepted this swamp of population with good grace. Refugees will work for starvation wages, and it beggars our own mean-minded, mealy-mouthed immigration policies.

Beyond fruit-growing, banditry and fighting, what the Afghans do best is trade. It's been their business for thousands of years, moving goods at the crossroads of Asia. It was the British who originally allowed them to open the Smugglers' Market at the mouth of the Khyber Pass because Afghanistan is landlocked. This taxless, lawless, no-questions-asked place of buying and selling has over the years crept south until now it lurks on the edge of Peshawar, burgeoning under an official blind eye.

This is the furthest you can legally travel north; lorries wait at the guard post to take relief in and bring goodness knows what back. Between here and the Khyber there is a rough fifty miles of tribal area where Pakistani law only reaches fifteen feet on each side of the road. Here, a foreign traveller in peacetime needs a company of frontier scouts as guards, and the goodwill of the ceaselessly feuding tribesmen. Up there somewhere is the home-made gun market, the hashish exchange and the heroin dealers. Here in the Smugglers' Market the Afghan and Pakistani junkies veg out in alleys and on rubbish wasteland.

A shopkeeper stumbles bellowing into the street, holding a ragged, rubber-limbed addict by the throat. He's been caught stealing a bicycle pump. The shopkeeper offers three or four haymaker punches to the lad's head, but he's feeling no pain and the shopkeeper isn't getting his just satisfaction. The boy is kicked into the gutter. He picks himself up with an exaggerated sloth, and blows his nose between finger and thumb. Heroin is one of Afghanistan's abiding mysteries. If, as we're told, 75 per cent of the world's supply is grown here, how come nobody local has made money out of it? Most Glasgow shooting-gallery tenements are better appointed than an Afghan heroin dealer.

The market's having a bad time at the moment. The shops selling Turkish air-conditioners, Chinese tea sets, Korean micro-waves and Taiwanese televisions are virtually empty. In the serried ranks of haberdashery stores, the salesmen squat among their gaudy rolls of bright fabric. Even the fabulously fake M&S, which sells St Michael knickers, shirts and twinsets cheaper than you could find them in Preston, is empty. Likely lads lounge beside their trays of Russian watches and Thai-cloned Disney DVDs, listening to knocked-off Egyptian pop songs and complaining about the war, which has made Peshawar too unstable for the streams of Pakistani brides-to-be and their clucking mothers, who trek up here to stock up on trousseaux.

Back in the centre of the old town, the muezzins compete through loud-hailers for the Friday faithful. The distinctive wail for Allah eddies through the dappled yellow fog of exhaust fumes and charcoal smoke. Outside one of the most fundamentalist mosques, lines of frontier-force policemen lean on their bamboo lathis and iron shields, checking the canisters of their tear-gas guns. In the bright midday street, young zealots stapled to Bin Laden posters try to scream up the zeal, waving Taliban flags and banners helpfully translated into English. 'Oh, sons of Saladin, crusaders fear death as you cherish martyrdom.' Perhaps, but not today. The riot is all air-punching and wind.

The chief of police, a marvellously urbane man, stands in the shade, elegantly smoking and talking cricket with his officers. In a drawling sahib accent he apologises for there not being much of a story yet, but I tell him that I have to dash, I'm late. Bizarrely, I've been asked as a visiting journalist from the vaunted *Sunday Times* – ark of the language of power and success and riches – to judge a junior school's spoken-English competition. I arrive five minutes late, filthy and hot, to be met by a line of governors as still and sombre as Odeon managers at a royal premiere. Inside, an audience of mothers sits willing smooth diphthongs on their neat little children. I'm led to the podium, where I offer my hand to the headmistress, remembering too late that Muslim women don't shake hands. Redder and sweating, I sit with pad and pencil and watch a huge fly drown in my honoured-guest water jug. The children are as bright as children everywhere. I get a stab of missing – they remind me of my own pair, about the same age; a shade or two blonder, but really no different. But then again, how very different.

One by one they stand up, craning for the microphone, flash shy grins at their mothers and gabble in that sing-song rote rhythm you hear in every classroom in the world. The subject they have to speak on for just a minute is 'volunteerism', a word my ignorant dictionary has failed to collate. But then English doesn't belong to me, or books or even *The Times*; it's a gift for anyone who takes the trouble to learn it. So it's not the children's fault I can't understand a word they say, except 'I tunk a-u'. I hand out the prizes and say a few words, which in turn they don't understand. They give me a present of a mujaheddin hat. 'I tunk a-u.' No, *I* tunk a-*u*.

In all the time I was in Peshawar I was never frightened. I walked everywhere and people argued with me, stopped me in the street and put me right, marvelled with anger and concern at my country's misdeeds, misconceptions, ignorance and wickedness. Their concern, sorrow and anger were heartfelt, but never anything other than respectful and polite. Islam's law of hospitality to strangers was automatic and absolute. I tried to imagine the reverse situation. If Afghan B-52s were dropping cluster bombs and daisycutters on Edinburgh and Glasgow, and I were an Afghan journalist in, say, Newcastle, how would I have been treated?

It's not entirely true that I was never frightened. I was once scared witless. Walking through a dark, crowded bazaar alley, I came upon a Pathan of fearsome aspect. He blocked my path and, as I stepped into the gutter to let him pass, he lunged at me. Grasping my shoulders, he pitched me up against a wall. For a horrifying moment I saw myself lying next to Bandsman Leighton, 'assassinated by a fanatic'. Then, out of the corner of my eye, I glimpsed the iron boss of a heavily bucking cartwheel spinning in the air just where my head had been. The Pathan grinned and then hugged me. Touching his heart with his hand, he said: 'Inshallah.'

East is East and West is West, and 'never the twain shall meet'. Kipling's most famous line was written about these people and this place. But nobody ever quotes the full stanza, which inverts, or at least qualifies, its received meaning. 'Till Earth and Sky stand presently at God's great Judgment Seat; But there is neither East nor West, Border, nor Breed nor Birth. When two strong men stand face to face, though they come from the ends of the earth!'

INDIA

The ghat, the landing place on a river, boasts a dumpy, municipally grand classical entrance, the sort of thing you might see on a Victorian northern railway station. It's sweat-stained and weedy, chipped at the edges, polished black by a million wet bodies. A grimy inscription in English is now barely legible. Through its arches jostle hundreds of pilgrims, shimmering gaggles of girls in bright saris with painted faces and hennaed fingers; hawkers selling deep-fried parcels, men in dhotis and turbans with corded whip-thin arms beating drums into a frantic rhythm. Trumpets howl, bus horns bellow like lost cattle, a murder of furious crows creak from a banyan tree, a slow tin train clanks past; commuters hang from open doors to catch the sticky, fetid breeze. The air eddies with charcoal smoke and incense. The ground is claggy with trodden blossom, boiled rice and chilli. Children wail, holy men chant, socially invisible widows and lepers implore.

Steps lead down to the river, the Hugli, the final leg of the sacred Ganges that frays into the Bay of Bengal. These people are all Biharis: poor migrant agricultural workers of low caste. They come to the river to celebrate a religious festival, they worship the sun, and in thanks they dunk great bunches of bananas like digestive biscuits into the muddy water that carries rafts of wild lilies, scattered foaming ashes, bloated, spinning corpses and the world's largest, longest continuous cache of prayers and incantations, all drifting in a slick of liquid toffee. The sun likes bananas – maybe it's their colour.

Men and women ritually wash, some lather up till they are bubbly ghosts, and rinse themselves like speedy otters. Youngsters pose and splash, a fat man floats past, spouting water like a small whale with a head cold. Women anoint their shaven babies from tin cups, swaying and suggestive in clinging saris, and in the throng, surrounded by taunting boys who are fascinated but fearful, there is a gaudy, grand, dramatic transvestite eunuch. These strange creatures are allowed special licence at festivals. They have the power to bless and curse from beyond the pale. Kohl-rimmed eyes flash, carmine lips pout and he/she lifts his/her sari to flash them a hirsute, confused and darkly fascinating pudendum.

It's 10.30 in the morning, 90° F, 97 per cent humidity. Eleven dull hours ago I was in London; my underpants still think they're in Fulham. This is India; it could only be India. Nowhere offers you more awe for your air miles, more rapture for your rupee, than the subcontinent. Nowhere fascinates in such depths and variety, with such horror and beauty, enchantment and frustration. Nowhere is so approachable and so utterly other.

I've come to compare two cities – Calcutta and Bombay, or Kolkata and Mumbai, east coast and west, ancient and modern. They epitomise the preconception of India. Bombay moves and shakes, has a mobile phone permanently clasped to its middle-class ear. Calcutta is communist, argumentative and still a universal parable for ultimate poverty. The there-but-for-the-grace-of-God place all uneaten greens have to think about before they are allowed to leave the table.

But Calcutta is also the fulcrum of modern India's culture, the home of Tagore and Satyajit Ray, Indian theatre and poetry. It's heavy with internationally respected universities, colleges and medical schools. And Bengalis live to argue. They are intensely literate and endlessly loquacious. Calcutta has some of the highest unemployment rates of any city in India – and one of the lowest crime rates. You never feel threatened and there are fewer beggars than in New York. Begging is a measure of opportunity, not poverty. Calcutta also has fewer tourists.

The city has a birthday: 4 August. We know its precise origin. In

1690, Job Charnock, a reckless adventurer for the East India Company, built a trading post and warehouses on the banks of the Ganges to deal with the huge, wealthy state of Bengal. This was a foolish and unhealthy place for an Englishman. The city's first graveyard was filled to bursting within thirty years. Few of its residents ever got to see forty. They were carried off by malaria, cholera, typhus, heat stroke, agues and tropical distempers, and drink, lots of drink. Kipling called Calcutta 'the city of dreadful night' and wrote a verse: 'Chance-directed, chance-erected, laid and built / On the silt – Palace, byre, hovel – poverty and pride – Side by side'. That's still a pretty apt description. Calcutta is by common consent the most polluted city on Earth. The air hangs thick and yellow with the charcoal smoke, petrol fumes and humidity. The constant sound of Calcutta is the cacophony of horns and the descant of millions of crows.

Our initial reason for visiting was the colonial architecture. Calcutta was the grandest of all Empire cities. The viceroy's house, now the governor's, is a titanic white imitation of an English-county ducal palace. It stands in municipally planted gardens, and is decorated by photographs of paintings that once might have hung here. It's resplendent with ghosts; modern Bengal rattles around like a squatter.

There's been a communist government here since the 1970s, but you can still see the room that was the original seat of colonial government. It's like a golf-club committee room, just big enough for a billiard table, without grandeur or pomp, that seems so very English; at the heart of the Empire is this little sitting-room whence were directed the lives of 1 million people in a land that stretched from the teak forests of Burma to the paddies of Ceylon for over a hundred years.

Outside in a corridor is an old gent in white uniform and a cockaded turban who has spent thirty-seven years in a gilded cage slowly shuddering up and down a narrow stairwell. He is the keeper of the first lift ever to be installed in India and he really doesn't like giving me a go.

Calcutta's colonial buildings are impressive; they have a faded, cockeyed grandeur. The central post office with the outline of the notorious black hole picked out in brass rods on its steps; the Writers' Building, the heart of the East India Company, where hundreds of underwriters dealt in billions of pounds. It's now the seat of state government. There are the bizarrely familiar churches. St Paul's, which looks like Westminster Abbey, and St James's, where I sat in on a Sunday service with just seven parishioners in its Victorian pews warbling out familiar hymns. And the Wren-like St Andrew's, the Scottish church. They are all clustered with the memorials of untimely death, native duplicity and bastard fate.

The grandest of all the memorials is the one for Victoria herself. Far mightier than anything England built for the old Queen Empress, it's a mausoleum without a body, on the blueprint of the Taj Mahal; this too is supposed to be a marble poem to the great love of a subject people for the white mother who never bothered to visit them. Around it is the great park that was left as a field of fire for the British fort and is now known without irony as the lungs of Calcutta.

Indians come to play and relax. It's full of cricket matches, the wickets laid out side by side so the fielders all mingle. Girls in their finest *shalwar kameez* sit on benches hoping to meet jeans-clad boys. Families spread out elaborate picnics and play blind man's buff; everywhere there are people arguing, gesticulating and shouting over each other. The Victoria Memorial might have been dropped in from Mars for all the relevance it has for the people here today.

Calcutta had another adoptive mother: Mother Teresa. She built her hospice right beside the Kalighat, the most venerable temple in the city. This was no accident. A gaudy plaster Christ rises over the rooftops. The sign under him says simply 'I thirst'. Inside, it looks like a hospital designed for a David Lean film set in 1947. Camp beds are laid out in rows, the rescued destitute lie supine, spindly and silent, but grateful. Nuns in their blue-and-white wimples glide smiling to and fro, and there are dozens of foreign helpers, the seriously spiritually committed young who wash sheets and fetch water. This might be God's gap-year scheme.

There is precious little sign of medicine. This is not a place for rescuing people for this life but easing them into the next, and it's difficult not to be monumentally cynical about the hand-holding, head-dabbing, salvation-mongering, morbid tourists. Most young people come to India to discover some spirituality; these have come to convert it. No doubt they're good and caring folk, and those departing have small comfort and rare attention, but the one thing India really doesn't need is any more religion.

If Bengalis are ambivalent about their debt to Queen Victoria, then they're deeply torn about Mother Teresa. 'This is the new black hole; our purpose was to make this woman a saint. Calcutta is internationally seen as a measure of misery by which good westerners can come and practise their charity and save us,' I was told, more in sorrow than anger, by a businessman.

There is a third queen of Calcutta. Hard by the Missionaries of Charity hospice is the most important temple in Calcutta. Barefoot, you walk into a complex that smells of incense and rotting flowers and butchery. Around the marble walls in the shadows, the white-dressed widows squat and beg, and in the sunny courtyard, skin-and-bone sadhus, holy men with white dreadlocks and faces painted with bliss and ashes, mutter for humanity.

In an enclosure there is a V-shaped post for the daily sacrificing of goats. The floor is sticky with blood. Pye-dogs lick the spattered walls. Women tiptoe in and abase themselves by placing their heads on the gory block. A rough queue shoves and squirms to get into the central holy marble chamber that holds the most famous image of the goddess Kali. The push is claustrophobic and faintingly hot. Underfoot is slippery and cool; as you get to the cramped chamber the noise grows piercing. Hundreds of devotees chant at me and gesticulate, 'Look, look, look at her,' and there she is, black as night, three ferocious red eyes with piercing furious pupils, a long golden tongue of blood, hunger and shame.

Kali thirsts too. Four golden hands are smeared thick with the vermilion paste of blessing. She's covered in crimson hibiscus garlands. It's an image of fathomless, shocking power, like lifting a trap door and glimpsing something beautiful and noisome, fascinating and unknowable. 'See, see, look, look.'

The other two pretenders to the throne of Calcutta – the plump English lady who never bothered to visit and the little wrinkled Albanian on a mission – are no match for this divine woman. Kali the destroyer and the creator, the patron protector who gave her name to this brilliant, benighted, argumentative, inspiring city.

I love Bombay. It's one of the great cities of the world, built on a dent in the Indian Ocean. It was the first and last glimpse of the subcontinent for millions of colonial servants, and it changes utterly every time I come here. The skyline sprouts new towers and the sense of it spins on, getting more like an international city, less and less like an Indian one. It's a generation and a continent away from Calcutta. The tiffin carriers still ply their trade but it also now has a McDonald's, selling lamb-and-cottage-cheese burgers.

I've always thought one of the reasons the British got away with so much in India for so long was because the English and the Indians share one huge, defining character flaw: they are both untiring, untreatable snobs, and Bombay, with its flash and wealth, its new, insecure middle class and the glitz of the movie business, makes Cheshire and Surrey look like Brussels. Bombay is a city of aspirations, of wanting, and I've come to go shopping, helped by a professional shopper. I end up with three: Monica, Tanya and Payal.

Bombay is one of those rare places where not only does your money go further than you can see, but there are also more things than you could ever possibly buy. That's not to say it's cheap: you could drop a million on jewellery in a blink, but you can spend 50p on bangles and look a million.

There is a lot of jewellery in Bombay, markets devoted to gold and silver, with little specialist shops. There's wedding jewellery and antique regal jewellery. Personally I yearn for table-cut diamonds, serious stones sawn in half so they have no facets; they don't sparkle or shine, just glow with a restrained, secret cool ardour. There's plenty of silk and cashmere, of course. An hour in a sari shop can turn you functionally blind, not able to register any more saturated colour. And the cashmere: you can buy pashmina by the yard and near-shahtoosh – that is, shahtoosh that isn't – but not even an antelope can tell the difference.

I bought some rare and unbleached raw silk for a jacket. The tailoring here is good but I'm told you must bring something to copy. And jewellery can be copied in the same way. Eating is fantastic. Bombay is now in the world's top ten destinations for food. Almost my favourite purchase was a rope of dried and pressed figs: elegant, beautiful, delicious and wearable. There are some eye-poppingly *Hello!*-like bars and restaurants that go on all night with Indo-European fusion menus, and the most pampered, polished, coiffed people you've ever seen outside a Miss World contest. Bombay society is small, shrill and energetic. Apparently, there's an enormous amount of infidelity but very little sex before marriage, which seems like getting it the wrong way round.

There was one thing I'd always wanted to see, something I could only get in Bombay – the men who hand-paint those huge film posters. Monica laughed and said nobody did that any more, but she made some calls and discovered the very last one. Behind a fantastic old cinema with metal seats was a great hangar, like a film set. Light shafted through holes in the ceiling, pigeons flapped in the rafters, the walls were stacked with enormous canvases and an old man with a pencil moustache came out and shook my hand. The last master of the bespoke Bollywood poster. He worked, squaring up magazine snaps and painting them twenty feet high with a mesmerising dexterity. It was as close as you get to watching Titian work, rendering the modern gods and heroes into glorious, gaudy popular escapism.

For a meagre price he agreed to do one of me, so we dashed to a roadside photo booth with a painted backdrop of a Swiss landscape with Swiss peacocks, and three days later my painted poster was delivered. If you needed one thing to convince you India is worth visiting, then having yourself Bollywood-immortalised ought to be it.

Bombay is a place that is going places. You can smell the

ambition and insecurity. It's all smiles and earrings and elbows. Calcutta is a place come to rest. Its grand future is all in the past. It doesn't need to prove anything. Its aspirations are basic.

For many, India is a destination too far – the poverty, the dirt, the toilets. But it's one place you shouldn't end up regretting you've never seen. It's the most gorgeously complex country on Earth. Go now while stocks of silk, diamonds, dried figs, film posters, charity, argument and gods last.

VIETNAM

All countries are two places, the country in the atlas and the place in your head. Vietnam suffers from the cartography of the collective imagination. We know Vietnam from dozens of movies and from shelves of books. Anyone over forty knows it as the leitmotif of their youth, the rhythm section for the middle-aged. What we know of it, though, is its reflection in the mirror of America's angst. A country that lost two syllables became atrophied simply as Nam.

The first thing you realise on arriving is that it doesn't look like Nam at all. And the reason is simple: Nam movies aren't shot here; they're filmed in the Philippines and Thailand and California, which is a bit like making a film about the English civil war and setting it in Spain.

Saigon is now officially named Ho Chi Minh City but universally still called Saigon. A bustling modern haphazard Asian town, its centre is a couple of broad French boulevards, a cathedral and an opera house. Most of what we associate it with is gone or never existed. The gum-chewing prostitutes in pedal-pushers and wrap-around shades that so inflamed the western imagination; and white-mice military policemen, the palls of smoke on the horizon, the sound of helicopters and Texan accents: none of it's here.

What's most conspicuous by its absence is the soundtrack. Saigon should be set to music. The Doors, Jimi Hendrix, Country Joe and the Fish, at the very least Jonathan Pryce. Real-time Saigon's signature tune is the hysterical whinny of thousands of two-stroke engines. Saigon has got on its bike and gone to work. Here they drive on the right, and on the left, and on the pavement. In the morning the boulevards are a torrent of little engines going this way, and in the evenings they go that way. There's no point waiting for a gap to cross: you have to trust, take a deep breath and step into what seems like certain death. But the river eddies dexterously round you. It's as close as I'm ever going to get to being Moses.

The other thing movies don't prepare you for is how elegant and poised the Vietnamese are. Women ride their bikes wearing long, pastel-coloured opera gloves. The national costume, the *ao dai*, is a high-necked silk dress worn to the calf but slit up both sides over baggy silk trousers, revealing a tantalising triangle of skin at the waist. Vietnamese men never weary of pointing out that it reveals nothing and hides nothing. A crocodile of Vietnamese schoolgirls can seriously make you reconsider all your St Trinian's fantasies.

I've come here to find the war, what's left of it, what's made of it. War tourism sounds ghoulish, a sort of panoramic rubbernecking, but then millions of people visit Flanders Fields, and when you dig a bit, it's difficult to be a tourist in any city that's innocent of battle. Venice is sunk in plunder, as is London. Istanbul, Athens, Paris, Florence and Siena are all places where yesterday's *bellum* becomes today's brochure. So perhaps it's just a matter of time, and Vietnam has reached the moment when current affairs drift into the nostalgia that is history's waiting-room. And as new wars are queuing up, champing to get started, it seemed a good time to look at what happened to this one.

Well, there's precious little to tell you there was ever a battle for Saigon. Uniquely for a communist country, there are hardly any monumental memorials; generally, they'll put up statues to heroic postmen and martyred librarians, but not here. The landmarks of war have been obliterated or papered over. The Caravelle Hotel, famous for a million dispatches, is just another comfy, hideous international bed-and-continental-breakfast. The American embassy, the fulcrum of such despair and ignominy, has been flattened for more prosaic offices and apartments. The corner where the Buddhist monk poured petrol over himself, assumed the lotus position and combusted, has a bright little shrine, and with fine inscrutable irony they've built a much larger gas station opposite. The president's palace is now a half-hearted museum, kept as it was left – a perfect example not just of the banality of despotism but of the political law that military dictators have taste in inverse proportion to their power.

The one stop all war tourists make is the War Remnants Museum, known colloquially as 'the babies-in-the-bottles museum'. Here the clunky tat of murder and mayhem is lined up. Bits of defunct ordnance detumesce in a junkyard of impotence. It's strange how old-fashioned the rusting kit looks; the accessories of war date just as fast as handbags and hats. The babies in the bottles are a pair of distressing infants, stillborn with defects caused by Agent Orange, the carcinogenic defoliant sprayed over half of Vietnam. It doesn't figure large in American war movies. Nobody says: 'I love the smell of Agent Orange in the morning; it smells like babies born without faces or genitals.'

And there's an army-surplus market, an unloved warren of drab, mouldering stalls. Most of the stuff here is modern or fake. There are enough Zippo lighters with obscene exclamations of proud despair stamped on them to make you imagine the entire army dropped them down the back of the sofa before running home; and thousands of dog tags – little tin labels written in the truncated language of the lonely-hearts ad. Who'd want to buy one of these things? If it's real, how could you live with it, and if it's fake, why would you want the notice of the pretend death of a fabricated life?

A couple of hours outside Saigon are the Cu Chi tunnels, one of the great engineering feats of the twentieth century built with the equipment of the tenth. An entire underground city on three floors that stretched for miles, with hospitals, dormitories, operating theatres, magazines, armouries, factories, canteens, kitchens and booby traps – much of it underneath a US Army base. The hellish ingenuity is staggering. Throughout the war, 16,000 people went through these tunnels, and 12,000 were casualties. Only a few hundred yards are still open; the rest have been closed like a dangerous pit. Even though they've widened them to accommodate round-eyes, they're still not for the claustrophobic or those with dark nightmares. You're shown around by old North Vietnamese Army officers in their green uniforms, who giggle when you trip the home-made landmines with a childish pop, and show you with relish the groin-tightening ingenuity of the spiked deadfall traps. In a clearing in the wood, my little guerrilla asked me to find the door; it is, he says, three yards from where I'm standing. I search fruitlessly; he's happy and pulls up a trap the size of a laptop from under the leaves. I can just drop through if I curl my shoulders. The Vietcong used their size against the Americans: a well-fed Midwestern boy would stick like a cork. My guide scuttles as I crawl along the slimy, dank burrow, which smells of the Earth's knickers. The torchlight makes the shadows dance; it's like an oven; I drop sweat, panic simmers. We drop to another level and he flicks his torch. 'Hats,' he whispers. Hats? He points. There, above my head – *bats*.

At the end of the tour, I'm asked what sort of gun I'd like. There's a range. You can have your own little firefight at a dollar a bullet, which is probably a lot less than they cost the Americans, all things considered. The cut-out target GIs have been replaced with tourist-friendly animals. I nail a badly drawn elephant with an M-16 and, just to be impartial, a Kalashnikov. It is a strangely unevocative experience. Beside me is a Vietnamese sporting a Vietcong bush hat. 'Hi there,' he says in a broad American accent. 'I just love a gun.' I ask where he's from. 'Here – well, actually, from Atlanta, Georgia.' A child of the thousands of South Vietnamese who became wrong-side rich refugees. He theatrically mounts his M-16, empties a clip and misses a tiger. He's too fat to get down the tunnels.

Going north, we travel to the old heart of the war. The names hark back to copies of *Life* and *Time* and the six o'clock news; Da Nang, Hué, the Perfume River and Khe Sanh. We stop briefly at My Son, the ancient towers built by the Cham people, who were Hindus and ruled parts of central and southern Vietnam for a while. Stuck in the jungle like the temples of doom. This should be the Vietnamese Angkor Wat, about seventy intricately decorated, astonishing, vast and beautiful tombs. They got B-52'd, and only a fraction remain, surrounded by sodden craters; they're eerie, a collateral civilisation. Hué, on the Perfume River, was once the imperial capital of Vietnam. Its forbidden city rivalled Peking's, an enclosed royal town of thirty-two palaces that's down to four now. The rest are pulverised, rubble. Here I meet a group of American military padres, middle-aged men with their wives who have come to relive their boy-scout war. They're open and instantly warm in the way Americans are, but also infuriatingly closed to insight or profundity. It's nice, all of it. They've had a nice time, the food's nice, the people are nice. The war wasn't nice but what can you say? Back home, these vicars counsel other veterans caught in a loop. The repeat play of horror. When diplomatic relations between the two countries were reinstated, old soldiers began to trickle back to lay ghosts, search for themselves, find a closure. What they found was more shocking than anything they'd imagined. A universal, heartfelt kindness. The Vietnamese were honestly touched that they'd bothered to come back in peace to share the memory and the mourning.

The infamous Route 9 points toward Laos through the demilitarised zone (DMZ) and the beginning of the Ho Chi Minh trail, the secret supply route that led to the delta in the south. At the beginning of the war it took six months to walk with mortar rounds on your back. By the end it was a motorway with service stations and barracks. At a strategic position overlooking the trail is Khe Sanh, the airstrip and fortress that saw the bloodiest battle of the war. Billed in the press as President Johnson's Dien Bien Phu, the surrounding precipitous hills and gorges have more familiar names, like Hamburger. Only now are they growing a first layer of spindly scrub and eucalyptus to replace the three-tiered rainforest that once lived here. More ordnance and chemicals were dropped on these mountains than in the whole of the Second World War.

A damp, hot fog has descended, stifling even the coffee plantation that grows here over the landmines, and it raises a question: 'What did I expect to find on this battlefield?' By their nature, battles go. There's only ever what you bring to them, a later personal history. The clipped Sunday magazine photograph for my school dormitory wall, the marches in Grosvenor Square to pick up girls, the late-night arguments with grown-ups, and the music that was the ambience for my youth. Still, there's an atmosphere: a deadened, mordant, sad echo. I find a verdigrised bullet and yearn for the hectic jazz of scooters going somewhere.

Hanoi is a beautiful city, a Frenchified place of lakes and an ancient warren of hawkers and food stalls. You can visit the Hanoi Hilton, the PoW jail, though the Vietnamese naturally remember it as where they were interned, tortured and guillotined by the French. But I've lost my appetite for memorabilia. I've been cured of what I came to indulge. There's a new Hanoi Hilton, a real one with room service. The Vietnamese economy is booming, as fast as 10 per cent a year over the last ten years. If the opposite of love isn't hate but indifference, the opposite of war isn't peace: it's prosperity. Vietnam hasn't turned its back on Nam, but it's moved on. It's America that still picks at the scab that needs the catharsis of celluloid and paper, and looks for other people and places in which to dump its frustration and vengeance.

There's a great war cemetery in the DMZ. A silent, empty place, over 10,000 graves laid neatly in the jungle. Incense smoke curls in the evening light. The guardian holds his squirming daughter and tells me that 50,000 Vietnamese visit every year. They must come secretly, like guerrillas. An underground remembrance. Three million Vietnamese died in the war, 4 million were wounded, children are yet born victims. In one of the museums is a case of medals donated by an American sergeant. Embossed in plastic is the stark message: 'I was wrong, I am sorry.'

OMAN

The relationship between Christian western Europe and the Arabs has been one of the most complex and pyrotechnically hysterical international love affairs. It's been marked by both avid adoration and cringing distaste. The communities that have sifted a hard, elegant living from the undulating sand have fascinated and repelled the West. Arabs live on the edge of our world in an older one.

They inhabit the edge of our imaginations and are the antithesis of the secure Europe of mud-and-brick road signs, wet weather, wool, sausages and a grand, decadent, fleshy culture. Out of the Arabian desert rode a ferocious aestheticism, the whirlwind of Islam, the fury of prophets, a cruel absolutism and the implacable belief in a religion of iron practicality and brass nerve. They made a civilisation of infinite, hard-edged abstracts. But there is also immense hospitality and the highest forms of moral masculine etiquette: bravery, loyalty, self-respect, self-restraint and harsh fatalism. Images of Arabs and the desert salt western art. In the nineteenth century, pictures of palm trees and belly dancers outnumbered thatched cottages and milkmaids on the walls of the Royal Academy. There were burgeoning schools of Arabists. And in the chilly foreign offices of dark Europe, young men would look out of lachrymose windows and imagine the keening, shadowless sands with a desperate yearning – from Richard Burton, the translator of *The Perfumed Garden* and one of the first westerners to travel to Mecca, and Edward FitzGerald, whose translation of Omar

Khayyam's *Rubaiyat* is still one of the most reprinted and recited poems in English, to T.E. Lawrence and his *Seven Pillars*, Wilfred Thesiger wandering in the empty quarter, and the multitude of overheated young remittance men who escaped the social strait-jacket of home to relax in souks and marbled halls. The desert nomad has seemed the paragon of manliness. He represents what we must once have been: lawless, a wanderer following his flocks, responsible only to his family, governed by an unwritten law of steely formality guarded by a spring-loaded temper, never forgiving, never forgetting, bowing to nothing less than God and the crescent moon.

We are going through one of our periodical rows with the Arab world. So it seems like a good time to go and visit Arabia and take the kids. I don't mean that facetiously. The more I travel, the more I am convinced that the search for sybaritic indulgence is morally prolapsed. It's a demi-sinful waste of privilege and opportunity. Travel should question, not confirm. It should excite, not relax. So I took Flora, fourteen, and Ali, twelve, to Oman for half-term. Half-terms are a bore break, too short for a serious trip and too long to be given over to cinemas, interactive museums, Pizza Express and Legoland. I wanted somewhere that was a doable travel time, but that when we arrived would be radical, different and exciting without being dangerous. There needed to be lots of things to do but, most importantly, I wanted the children to see something worth seeing and to question our society's growing fear of foreigners, particularly Muslims and Arabs. Family holidays are precious: the opportunities between toddling bucket and spade and the gap year are numbered. I probably only have a couple of years left when Flora will want to be seen out with me. I want my kids to travel well when they travel on their own. I want them to go with optimism and purpose.

Oman isn't one of those hasty, exit-strategy nations made up of colonial patches and desperation. Neither is it just a collection of oil wells with a hankering to look like Singapore on the Gulf, whose highest aspiration is to be a holiday resort for footballers, drunk expats and *Hello!* shoots. Oman is an ancient kingdom that was once an empire that included Zanzibar and the Swahili coast of Africa as well as ports in Persia. The Omanis were famous sailors and traders who imported ivory, gold, precious stones and traded slaves from Africa.

At home in the Arabian Sea they had the beds for the finest natural pearls. For a century and a half they have had a particularly close relationship with the British. First as a stabilising force in the Arabian Sea when the protection of trade with India was vital, then with a stream of idealistic young men who wanted to go outward bound, and finally, thirty-odd years ago, the British covertly facilitated a coup that put the present incumbent on the throne at the expense of his father. The capital, Muscat, is a modern and attractive city when compared with the neighbouring metropolises of Dubai and Abu Dhabi. But the ancient capital is Nizwah, a market with a fort and a winding souk. We arrived there in the middle of a cattle market in Ramadan.

Markets are a worldwide fundamental. All societies have organised somewhere to trade in public. They all have that comforting bartering, capitalist familiarity, but they are also an unfakable indicator of the style and emotion of a country. The cattle market at Nizwah was crowded, loud and hand-waving, but fundamentally considerate. All the men wear dishdashes and characteristic embroidered caps which are carefully creased and dimpled. The women wear a selection of billowing abbayas that are all-enveloping; most, but not all, are veiled.

Their burqas are open and see-through, not the ferocious, medieval structures or shrouds of some cultures. The Bedouin are believers but they're not political fanatics. There's a lot of bargaining but nobody loses their temper – it's too hot and everyone's thirsty and hungry, not least the sagging animals. Small boys drag reluctant sheep and truculent goats into the back of Toyota pick-ups. They'll be fattened for the great feast of the new moon. Toyotas are the real iron workhorses of the developing world. We pass a camel that's been folded into the back of a pick-up. Its haughty face is held high, eyes closed as if pretending not to notice the ignominy of being bussed in the back of a metal box.

In the shade of fruit trees, traders sell bottles of desert honey that ranges from straw-coloured to mahogany, depending on which tiny, hardy flower the wild bees have made their garden. In the souk, kiosks sell dusty metal jewellery, the silver ankle bracelets and earrings of Bedouin brides. I pick up a necklace of trade beads that has in it Venetian glass, Baltic amber and Chinese jade along with the thick imperial Hapsburg silver coins that were the international currency of herdsmen who had no knowledge of banks. Their silver content is the same as their face value. There are also racks of the curved knives that are the masculine motif for Omani men. Their handles are carved from horn, a depressing amount of which originally graced rhinos.

The great forts that dot the trade routes and wadis of Oman are thick-walled, mud-bricked organic edifices that were the basis of clan thuggery and dynastic intrigue. I particularly like one where the comfortable guest quarters were stuffed with concealed holes for hiding eavesdroppers and where the treads of stairs could be removed at night to break the ankles of anyone who decided to go visiting. It's very Arab to welcome all and trust none. In the basement were the stores for dates. The walls stained black, the sugar syrup would run out of long channels and be bottled as a preservative, and boiled to pour from the battlements on enemies.

Oman is a devoutly observant country and travelling through Ramadan, the children had to learn to be particularly considerate of other people's effort and to be careful not to eat or drink conspicuously in front of those who can't. Not that they would ever be denied or confronted. Fasting is to make Muslims strong; the fact that we eat and drink shows that we're weak. Without exception everyone we meet is polite, helpful and courteous. There is no undercurrent of the anger or resentment that has infected so much of the Middle East. I want the children to see that this is what's normal for Muslims, not the daily horror of the news.

The other more prosaic reason I chose to come to Oman is the surprising variety of environments that you can travel through in a couple of days. It's not like the Gulf states, where it's either air-conditioned tinted glass or wind-blown baked scrub. Here the oasis wadis have a miraculous beauty. Fresh, cold water frets down from high mountains through beautiful waterfalls into narrow canyons, and causes dense emerald patches of intense coolness. From a distance in the desert they look unbelievably inviting. Farmers dig intricate waterways and little canals that are full of self-important frogs. On the banks, herons stand regarding their reflections with insouciantly cocked heads. I caught sight of the flashing iridescent turquoise of an Egyptian roller.

Normally it's difficult to get the kids to walk anywhere, but these wadis are so entrancing that they dash on ahead. There's magic here like the drawings in bedtime stories; these are places of enchantment, the secret homes of djinns and genies, flying carpets and three wishes. We swam in the still water through the green shadows while small fish nibbled our toes.

Oman's mountains are stark and impressive. New roads double and redouble up their precipitous heights. On the very roof of Oman there is an astonishing and ancient market garden stepped over what they say is the second deepest canyon in the world, after Colorado's grand one. Up here they grow fruit and roses; there are thousands of rose bushes for perfume. Arabs like their smells deep, rich and opulent. Flowers have been planted here for thousands of years. Beneath us in the dead fall of the valley, huge eagles twist and hang.

Back down at sea level the coast is an empty strip of clean, white sand that stretches for five kilometres, a beach on which we see nobody. The Indian Ocean lunges at the shore and behind us mountains shiver in the heat haze. It's as fine a beach as you'll find six hours from Slough. Further down the coast, towering with gantries and spires and spinning, curling ducts steaming with a raw purpose is a natural-gas station. Oman, like the rest of Arabia, has harvested the bounty of combustible prehistoric shrimps. But it doesn't seem to have turned into one of those warped, repressive and decadent countries of the petroleum age. The money, it's true, supports an absolute royal family and a top-down largesse and philanthropy, but the dividend seems to have been used to build an infrastructure that fits the character of the nation. It hasn't made Omanis into the spoilt, graft-phobic whingers with an inflated sense of entitlement that have so softened the rest of the Gulf. Oman still feels like a country rooted in its geography, history and heritage that has a purpose beyond petrol, Ferraris and air-conditioned Starbucks.

One of the things that have all but vanished in Oman is its great sea power. The dhows that sailed the length of Africa are now only made in one shipyard. Their curved prows and elaborate fo'c'sles lean in lazy decrepitude on the shore. And the last artisans who still know how to sew planks together labour slowly in boat sheds. This was the fleet that rode the high watermark of Arab achievement, taking Islam round the ancient world – along with mathematics, astrology, applied arts, geometric craft, soldiers, pirates and holy men. This is the place from where Ali Baba set sail.

That night I had a surprise for the children. After dinner we drove back to the dark shore and waited for twenty minutes listening to the crashing surf. There was a flash of headlights and out of the dark people began to emerge. We all huddled round a small excitable Omani with a torch who led us out onto the sand. The ocean thudded and the shore hissed as we stumbled in the silver light, and all of a sudden there she was; one of the reasons I'd come all this way. A great greenback turtle heaved ungainly on land to dig a damp, gritty cradle for her eggs. Twenty of us crowded round while the expert lectured in fractured English, lifting her flippers and intruding his torch like a gynaecologist instructing first-year medical students. We were invited to pass round one of the heavy ping-pong eggs.

It was all both intrusively voyeuristic and inexplicably tender and moving. It's difficult to empathise with a turtle, we have so little in common – but the enormous power that has dragged this creature back to this beach from across the world after five years at sea to thrust the investment of her future into the cool darkness is really memorable.

We stumble and fall into the holes left by other mothers on the beach in a stream of exhaled expletives in half a dozen languages. In the torch light I can pick out the eyes of desert foxes hungry for a meal of turtle eggs, keeping their distance from the clumsy humans. Tourists have probably done more to turn round the fortunes of turtles than anything else. On the shining tide line where phosphorescent krill sparkles like fairy rhinestones, there are half a dozen little clockwork hatchlings manically working their way to the relative safety of the surf. Next morning at breakfast, beside the cornflakes is a bowl of orphan turtles who have walked towards the wrong light.

Oman is a desert kingdom and the Sahara is the point here. It's the beginning and the end. If you think deserts are big, dusty spaces with nothing in them, then there's still plenty to see and do in Oman but it's a bit like going to Aspen without the snow. On the other hand, if you think that deserts are wonders full of awe-defining emptiness, then this is the desert's desert.

We drove out into the red sand to spend a night with the Bedouin and their absolute hospitality. There is a ritual exchange of greeting, praising God and then asking for news: the reply is always good news. The rule is that it is either good news or no news. To be the bringer of bad news would be unlucky and make you a very bad guest.

People will tell you that the best thing to do in deserts is to scramble across them on quad bikes and 4x4 trucks, or to slide down them on sandboards or tea trays. Don't listen. This is not being in the desert, it is simply being all over it. The best way to see the Sahara is from a camel. Children love camels; grown-ups can abide camels; camels hate everyone. And better than a camel is your own feet. The best thing is to climb a dune at sunset, sit and watch the colours change and hear the wind play the curves of the limpid dunes and be aware of that still, small voice of calm. The song of the desert. The Bedouin share dinner and sing and dance, and we dance back and giggle and clap in the skittering firelight. They have lived much like this, tending their sheep and goats, breeding camels, pigeons and chickens and searching for water for thousands of years. In the darkness the handsome faces are lit up by the ghostly light of their mobile phones. We make our beds out on the desert, lying side by side on the cooling sand. We all stare up at the unsullied, pristine sky, the milky way, our solar system, the distant stars. You have no idea how much is hidden from you by progress. How much hides behind a veil of our own reflective glory. Lying in the Sahara with your children, watching for shooting stars, is one of the great unexpected and unadvertised pleasures of a half-term break.

IRAQ

It wasn't a rocket-propelled grenade, a Sam missile or a mortar; it wasn't a bullet or even an infidel Coke bottle full of petrol that did for the helicopter. It was a bird. The aircrew showed us the splat that broke its nose. Welcome to Baghdad, where even the pigeons are suicidal.

The Americans didn't have a Black Hawk to spare for the five-minute hop into the Green Zone, so we were going to have to drive it. This is the bit Jeremy swore he'd never do. When you're asked where you draw the line, this is the place to start drawing. Nobody drives into Baghdad if they've not been given a direct order. Even our minder, Wing Co. Willox, has never done it.

We're definitely not up for this, so we go and have coffee in the Green Bean, the American army's version of Starbucks in a Portakabin that hunkers down behind prefab black walls, 'proud to serve' skinny macchiatos in Iraq, Afghanistan, Uzbekistan and any other stan that needs shock, awe and caffeine. A pair of skinny Iraqis work their way through the fast of Ramadan, serving homesick grunts airlifted blueberry muffins.

An officer from the Irish Fusiliers tips up, all perky green hackle and steely Ulster confidence. 'There's absolutely nothing to worry about,' he says, and instantly you know there's nothing to worry about because worry is too weedy and snivelly a civvy word for what we ought to be feeling. He doesn't mention that they've just shot their way in here or that they sent an unmanned drone down the route to check it out first.

We wear body armour and helmets in the car. This doesn't make you feel safer, just an oven-ready prat. Our folksy briefing boils down to: if by the merest chance anything worrying occurs, close your eyes, put your fingers in your ears and pretend to be a prayer mat.

We travel in a small convoy. Two armour-plated Range Rovers with what they call top cover; Land Rover snatch vehicles in front and behind with a pair of soldiers sticking out the top. Being a human turret is a bad job. 'We do this a bit faster than the Americans,' a lance corporal tells me as we gingerly pull out of the airport perimeter. That's because the Americans do it in tanks. This road is code-named Route Irish. Guinness World Records has just authoritatively announced that Baghdad is the worst place in the world. Presumably in a photo finish with Stow-on-the-Wold. This twenty-five-minute stretch of blasted tarmac from the airport to the Green Zone is, as Jeremy might say, the most dangerous drive – in the world.

Unsurprisingly, there's not much traffic. Surprisingly, there is some. 'It's relative,' says the corporal. 'The worst road in the world is the one the bus runs you over on. The rest are a doddle.'

The fusiliers drive with a practised authority, zigzagging, never contravening each other's line of fire. The top-cover soldiers swivel with their rifles to their shoulders, eyes pressed to the sights. There is a purposeful tension, a tunnel-visioned concentration. Going under bridges and flyovers is the worst: they traverse the parapets with a gaunt expectation and I begin to see everything in hyper-real detail. Every pile of rubbish and burnt-out car waits to jump out at us screaming 'God is great' in a flash of hot light.

The convoy slows down; not a good thing. A car ahead crawls to a stop. The soldiers emphatically signal to it to move on. Maybe it's someone taking a moment to tell God to put the kettle on; maybe it's just a clapped-out motor that's stalled. Army convoys, particularly the American and private-contractor ones, are really dangerous for Iraqis. Lethal force is everyone's first and last option. On a slip road, lopsided purposeful Toyotas packed with grim men seem to race to catch us. Perhaps they just want to get home to break their fast. Perhaps not.

Baghdad looks like it's been beaten senseless, stamped on, bitten, battered and clawed; ugly and dirty, its gouged and grated walls ripped off, windows flapping, ceilings propped on floors. The thudded buildings look like rotten teeth in the receding gums of streets full of twisted flotsam, bent lampposts, tangled railings and pools of slime, all of it coated in ground concrete dust. But it also seems surprisingly familiar, like a hot estate from a suburb of Detroit or Dundee. The journey takes longer than *War and Peace*. So I try and think about other stuff – like what's in it for female suicide bombers? The promise of seventy adolescent virgin blokes all sniggering to give you a premature seeing-to in heaven doesn't seem like much of an incentive. And then I'm back thinking about the increasing sophistication of roadside bombs. The Land Rovers carry secret wizardry that foils radio triggers made from phones or electric car keys, but now the locals are using infrared trips and the bombs are shaped chargers, a cone lined with copper or a metal with a low melting point covered in explosives. When detonated it forms a directed stream of molten shrapnel that'll go through a battle tank. There's no armour that will protect you from being kebabbed.

And then I think about the fact that the biggest helmet available fits on Jeremy's head like a little blue office-party joke hat, and that now he's facing his deepest fear (that he will cry like a girl when they video him having his head cut off with a bread knife to the soundtrack of 'Stairway to Heaven') looking like an unnatural cross between Obelix and the Elephant Man.

The convoy gets to the first of the Green Zone's many checkpoints and the Wing Co. sighs with heartfelt relief. I realise we haven't spoken a word. In the other car, apparently, Jeremy hasn't drawn breath. We deal with fear in different ways. Silently I believe that if I see everything it'll be all right. He has to say everything.

The Green Zone is possibly the most bizarrely peaceful place anywhere, like the eye of a storm. Its peace is a long way from being safe. There are on average twenty-five serious incidents in Baghdad a day. This is when someone gets killed or their future radically reorganised – involving ramps, handrails and incontinence pads. It's an area the size of a small market town drawn around Saddam's nouveau Babylon of palaces and monuments. It has a heads-down hush, on the banks of the Tigris, amid date palms and a maze of concrete blast walls that hide government buildings, embassies, command centres, commissariat canteens, car parks and all that the gorgon's head of civil service and ordinance needed to maintain itself. The gauze of normality gives it a hallucinatory atmosphere of science fiction cut with the surreal banality of the suburbs. It's *Desperate Housewives* with guns.

There are a lot of very neatly clipped hedges. Who's tending the privet? The strangest job in the current-affairs world must be apocalypse topiary. We turn into the British military headquarters. A garden cropped like a formation of green guardsmen, with a goat. An Abyssinian goat with droopy ears and a malevolent mien that's called either Dog or Jar Jar Binks. Where would the army be without a Sunday-roast mascot? It can only be a matter of weeks before the *Mirror* and the *Mail* are vying to save it. Maud House is named after a defunct general who passed this way in the previous century. It's instant camping English. There's tea and informality and old copies of *Country Life*. An air of prefect's common-room. Nobody salutes or stands to attention. It's all first names, but the hierarchy is as keen as a pack of hounds. The lieutenant general who is second-in-command of this whole damn shooting match seems to spend a lot of his time half-naked, or perhaps that's half-dressed. He sports no rank badge but then he doesn't need one. Only a lieutenant general would be walking around headquarters bare to the waist. Apart from the naturism, Birns has more charm than I'd have thought possible to get into a single human being. I imagine the army has a special course for everyone over the rank of colonel that makes them devastatingly good in a room. The polite version of cone-shaped chargers. There is no defence against a blast of molten English niceness.

Maud House is all shiny megalomaniac's marble, mostly bedrooms and bathrooms. It was one of Saddam's private brothels. The army, bless it, always resolutely unaware of its own symbolism, turns a politely blind eye to the fact that the Americans live in Saddam's palaces and the Brits in his knocking shop. So who's the daddy and who's the Yankie bitch?

Saddam's nuclear bunker is the heart of the Green Zone. The first thud of shock and awe, dropped from 15,000 feet, were bunker-busters that crashed through the palace's domed roof and burrowed underground and exploded with maximum prejudice. They barely chipped the corner off the two-billion-dollar safe box. It was built by the Germans and Swiss, who know a thing or two about vaults. One hundred and fifty people could live down here in reinforced concrete catacombs that are sprung on shock-absorbers like a Posturepedic mattress. The air scrubbers and generators, the fixtures and fittings, are all looted and smashed. It smells of damp carpet and panic. There are bullet holes in the airlock doors and bloody handprints picked out on the walls by our leaping flashlights. They look like cave paintings. For something so postmodern, this place is ultimately primitive. A cave, a shaman's secret hole in the ground. Of all the grandiose monuments that Saddam built for himself, this bunker is the most telling, with its flock wallpaper in the dining-room, the gold-tapped bidets and the grim 1970s hotel lighting. It is the most complete skin-crawling, silently screaming evocation of hell; the reinforced concrete transubstantiation of sleepless megalomania and hysterical fear. Upstairs, sunlight streams through the two holes in the dome imitating Hadrian's Pantheon.

Saddam had a Tourette's need to graffiti his initials over everything. He was a dreadful size queen. Everything's huge and pantomime-clumsy. It's always the telltale taste of the monomaniac to evoke size without any understanding of scale.

The bunker is guarded by Georgians from the Caucasus. The international nature of the force is crucial to the Americans, who shriek and swoon like the bride's mother trying to do a *placement* when some distant guest sends excuses, mucking up their arrangement of flags and the walls showing the clocks of coalition time.

The vast majority of the soldiers spend the vast majority of their time guarding each other. The truth about the army here in the Green Zone is that their biggest job is protecting themselves. The American soldiers spend a year opening and closing barriers. It's an excoriating cocktail of weeping boredom and gnawing fear. Checkpoints are magnets for suicide bombers, but the work is so repetitively stultifying that the Americans move like zombies, pressing their faces to the car windows with the uncomprehending glazed stare of guppies in an aquarium. We go to Three Head car park, named after the trio of oversized Saddam busts parked next to the tanks. Sweetly, the Americans give Jeremy and me an Abrams battle tank each. We race them between the monumental crossed scimitars at each end of the avenue commemorating the Iran–Iraq war next to the tomb of the unknown soldier, or 'the who-gives-a-shit towel-head' as one of the grunts mutters. I ask my commander what he likes best about his tank. 'Ooh,' he sighs. 'I suppose it's the ability to reach out and touch people.'

Whatever Jeremy says, in the tank I beat him by a barrel. I always beat him. In the bright dusty sunshine we can hear the rockets and mortars land, reaching out and touching people, making someone's day. We chopper back to the airport in the mended helicopter, chugging low over the city. Baghdad is pestilent with rubbish, open streams of sewage and corruption. It's vital and virulent. From the ground someone fires at us. The old helicopter, feeling the heat, launches magnesium flares that splutter and shine like dying suns and fall to Earth in trails of white smoke.

At the camp in Basra, the night air glows an ethereal orange from the gas-burning of desert rigs. Until recently the British have had a quietly smug time compared with the Yanks in Baghdad. They've had only half an incident a day, but after we got there things went a bit Rorke's Drift.

Most of my hawkeyed reporting was reduced to watching Jeremy have his photograph taken with groups of gurning, up-thumbing crack-fighting units. It's like a military Disney World. He stands in huddles of camouflage like a big blue extra from Wallace and Gromit with a Plasticine beam and a teacup on his head.

You can't help liking British servicemen. It's the humour and the banter, the air of gawky competence, the legs-apart, four-square confidence. Our boys do a six-month tour and are trusted to have a couple of beers a day. The Yanks are drier than a desert sandbag. For many of the Brits this is the most exciting posting for years. The best thing they've ever done in their short lives. Many of them catch the old English disease of Arabism. There was a lot of optimism based, it must be said, on very little but wishful thinking and best-case scenarios, but then a war is really no place for a pessimist.

Iraqi policemen are training with Kalashnikovs – at fifty yards most of them have trouble hitting desert, let alone the targets that resemble charging Americans. I ask an instructor what they're like. He gives me a long, measured look. 'Good lads, most of them, but there are cultural differences.' I'm sorry, but firing a gun is the least culturally differentiated activity in the world. 'It's Arab confetti, sir.' And he looked at his beaming students with something short of pride. And then there are the berets. The Brits spend an obsessive and some might say risibly gay amount of time shaping and positioning their hats. The Iraqis wear them unaware. Plopped like failed souffleś.

We talk to another general, this one surprisingly overdressed, who briefs us off the record. The situation sounds winningly tickety-boo given that I only understand one sentence in fifty. The well-honed military mind runs on TLAs – three-letter abbreviations. These are opaque at the best of times. If you're dyslexic, they are like alphabet spaghetti. He refers to IEDs for improvised explosive devices. I keep calling them IUDs and asking with steely, inquisitive authority why the Shi'ites are attempting to shove contraceptive devices up our warriors. And then there was the lavatory, reserved it said, for D & V, with the warning: 'If you don't want it, don't use it.' I imagine this was military transposition for 'diseases venereal'; Jeremy works out it's diarrhoea and vomiting.

We hitch a lift in a Lynx, the sports car of military helicopters: small, agile and nippy. My feet poke out into the void. We're only held in place by a beefed-up car seat-belt. Jeremy wraps the spare webbing round his hand. Here is another difference in the way we deal with fear. He likes to know hardware stuff, facts, figures, statistics. He wants muzzle velocity and metal thickness. His world is a series of engineering problems, probabilities and solutions. Nuts and bolts are his security bunny. There isn't a metaphysical cloud on his horizon. It's like being strapped in next to a why-ing four-year-old who's taken over the body of old man Steptoe.

On the other hand, I don't care a jot for any of that. It's boring and bogus. The world isn't spun by cogs, it's turned by people. I make my judgement by sizing up the pilot, the driver, the guide. If you decide to trust him, then keep up and shut up. I'd have followed the Lynx's captain any way they fancied. The chap in charge of helicopters was a marvellously urbane floppy blond Sloane from the army air corps. A bod who was a drawling master of the military mixed metaphor 'When the wheels come off you need a big punch.' The soldiers called him Flasheart after the character in *Blackadder*. We're off to deliver a parcel to the lifeguards based in Basra.

The Lynx hurtles low, hurdling power lines, sidestepping flocks of suicide pigeons. Basra is another blasted, ugly, sewage-stained city. Every back yard a pile of rotted rubbish. Every car a cannibalised pick'n'mix. And yet most buildings boast a satellite dish pointing expectantly up at the western sky hoping to catch some good news. There isn't any. Neither is there any electricity. We fly down the canal where Saddam's yacht lies on its side, pathetically clogging the waterways. Why do dead boats look sad, but dead cars look like junk?

Then we jink off to see the Marsh Arabs. The one small, really good news story of the war on terrorism. They were persecuted to the point of extinction and their marshes drained. Now the water's back and buffalo splash through the thick reeds that are used to make delicately beautiful huts. Arabs wave from their spindly boats.

The pilot and I talk about Wilfred Thesiger and Jeremy keeps interrupting: 'Who? Who?' Then we turn again to the desert and fly over the battlefield of the Iran–Iraq war. Huge areas of baked tank emplacements and trenches. From 500 feet they are indistinguishable from bronze-age archaeology. The wreckage of ancient wars is the dusty vernacular of this, the oldest country in the world.

As we are turning back to camp, the missile snakes out at us. The Lynx spits its glowing rockets and the pilot lurches into a dive. I hang in space, watching the Earth tumble and sprint up to grab me; '300, 200, 100'; the staccato voice comes over the headset as we plummet. Thirty seconds later we're flat and level. A dot in the sky.

The machine-gunner in the door says he saw the puff and the flash and the smoke chase after us. Back on the tarmac, we don't mention the missile. Jeremy does, though. For him it's personal. 'I was told the Shi'ites watch *Top Gear*,' he says in a quavering, girly voice. Well, now you know – they obviously do. Back in camp we are mortared and shot at with unnerving regularity. Mortars land with a crump, like a severed head hitting a Persian carpet.

Sitting in a darkened Tristar in full body armour in the middle of the night, waiting to be flown back to Brize Norton, knowing that outside, in the oil-flared dark, helicopters quarter the desert for Sam emplacements – and that the RAF regiment are manning the flight paths for fifty miles but it will take a chest-thudding eight minutes before this ancient airliner is out of missile range – I try and think about something else. I realise that during our time in Iraq I've only spoken to one Iraqi, and that was to say: 'Four mocha frappuccinos, please.'

AFRICA

This is a true story. The man who picks up the towels and mops the floors in the gents' changing-room of my gym is an African – a diligent, friendly man. An American banker came in the other day with his bag of air-soled good intentions to work off a little personal surplus, and while he changed he engaged the janitor with that easy chat that seems to come with an American accent. 'So, you're from Africa, an African. Well, there's a lot about Africa in the news at the moment. It's complicated, isn't it?' He said all this in capital letters with a slow patronage. 'You must be really happy to be out of it. You know, to be here.' The African's eyes flicked round the changing-room. He smiled. 'Which country you from?'

'Liberia.'

'Oh, that was a colony, right? Whose? Which country ruled it?'

The African waited a beat before replying: 'America.' The American's face was a picture, the African's a carving. 'Really? The United States of America? You're kidding me.' The janitor went on folding towels. The banker went to jog off his newly acquired colonial guilt.

Africa is not what most of us think. To the northern world it's still a dark continent as impenetrable as it was 200 years ago. Full of unspeakable horror and unfathomable fear. The news reports, those two-minute trailers, drip blood and bathos. The myths and misconceptions about Africa may have changed emphasis over the years, but the sense of its otherness hasn't. The *sotto voce* developed consensus is that Africa's woes and suffering are of a separate order from those of the rest of the world. Africans have buckets of sympathy but thimbles of empathy. Because the lion's share of starvation, disease, corruption, ignorance, hardship, premature mortality and sheer heartbreaking loss rains on Africa, then by implication, and because they bear the unbearable, Africans can't be like the rest of us. Their suffering must be muscled by familiarity, their feelings deadened by repetition. In the arguments about the rights and wrongs of debt aid, trade, political reform and charity, Africans slip through the cracks between good intentions. They become merely ciphers, slices of pie chart and exclamations in an argument that turns out, surprise surprise, as ever, to be about us, our money and our conscience, our fine words.

One of the world's great experiences for an affluent westerner is to wake up in an African village – the sinuous smell of wood smoke, fat, sweat and dust, the crowing of cockerels in the chilly silver dawn, the long shadows of thorn trees, the twittering of weaver birds, the stretching dogs, the first buckets of water pulled from a wheezing pump, blowing on charcoal fires and, as the air warms, fat babies washed in enamel basins, men shaving in little mirrors, the scratching and nose-blowing, the hawking and pissing, toothbrushing and greeting, the treble rackets of tinny radios, the winding and wrapping of babies to backs and scarves round heads, a handful of mealie meal, a mango. A bicycle loaded with tools or onions, or a bed, or a grandmother, or a flock of hens that wiggles down the dusty red road to meet the day. Nowhere I've ever been starts each morning with such optimism as Africa.

So here, to set beside the catalogue of competing woes and misdemeanours for which Africa is pitied and accused, are a few other truths. Most Africans are not dying of Aids or starvation, don't want to kill their neighbours, neither are they venal or corrupt. Most Africans work hard, are multilingual, are spiritual, kind, and love a joke with a passion, even a bad joke. Most are poor only in cash. Most seem to be very happy most of the time. Happier about less than we are. In fact, I don't know anywhere where you will hear so much laughter spread so thickly, and so few tears. You rarely hear African babies cry. Experts study African babies to discover the secret of their frankly perverse contentment. Perhaps they could sell a book about it to guilty, fretful western mothers. And most Africans have a huge respect for old people. Of course, you meet age halfway in Africa, but when you get there you're a person to be revered, because though most Africans have so little stuff, they have each other. They have their families, their villages, their tribes, their religions. I've been to a lot of hospitals in Africa and I've yet to see a patient who had to eat hospital food. Everyone is looked after by family or neighbours. We think of Africa as the great wishing well of charity, but they are creditors when it comes to giving.

I don't want to claim that all the other stuff, the pitiful stuff, is exaggerated. It isn't, but what makes it worse is that it happens to be a continent of such ragged joy and simple brilliance. The quantity of the problems obscures the quality of the lives they fall upon. One of the great poverties of our lives is that so few of us go to visit Africa. The constant news commercials of misery and death elicit pity, not tourism, but you should go. It is the most astonishingly engaging and addictive place and it's less frightening than the south of France in August.

This is another true story. I was once in the Serengeti and I came across a minibus-load of Japanese tourists. They were wearing disposable paper anti-contamination suits with face masks and booties. They brought their own dried food and the water to cook it in. They stayed in the bus as it was driven past animals and they'd spent four days in Africa never having touched it, tasted it, smelt it or shaken its hand. The average Japanese girl born today can expect to live forty years longer than her sub-Saharan sister.

This is the one place where travellers come and actively avoid meeting the locals. An African market, an African street, is far more exciting than any pride of manky old lions. You should visit Africans at home for all the usual touristic and economic reasons, because it's good for them and good for you, but you should also visit them because familiarity doesn't breed contempt. It is the antidote to contempt. Familiarity breeds greater familiarity. Africa and Africans deserve to be included not just in the big stuff of the world – trade, medicine, politics – but also in the small, intimate, one-to-one stuff. They've had a lot of sympathy. What they deserve, what we all need, is empathy.

My first trip to sub-Saharan Africa was to write about big-game hunting in the Transvaal. The Boer white hunter drove me in surly silence, bouncing and grinding through a land that looked like God's rubbish bin for six hours. Finally we stopped and I got out, throbbing and furious, and he looked over the scrub and said: 'Welcome home. This is where you come from.'

We should all go home more often. Africans aren't some other benighted, desensitised 'them' from the darkness. They're us. They're family.

SUDAN

There are rumours of war, of genocide, of ethnic cleansing; they are whispered on the gritty, boiling wind that blows across the border from Sudan. In ones and twos and tens and hundreds, refugees struggle into Chad with stories of systematic murder, rape, slavery and scorched earth. I've been down this mine-sown track before: five years ago I covered the man-made famine that was an attrition against the Dinka in the south. That twenty-year conflict has finally been settled with a peace deal brokered by the Americans and paid for by oil; now the murderous bullying has moved up into the large western province of Darfur, where the irregular bandit cavalry, the Janjaweed, are wiping out black farming communities. The Arab-Islamic government of Khartoum denies any culpability and says with a shrug that this is a little local conflict between farmers and nomadic herdsmen.

Meanwhile, the UN steeples its fingers, sucks its teeth and equivocates, hinting that perhaps maybe this might be the worst humanitarian crisis in the world at the moment. Maybe perhaps 100,000 people are dead, and perhaps maybe a million more are on the pending list, waiting to get across the border before the rains come.

Our own US security council and the G8 have decided they don't have any immediate plans to intervene in Darfur, so the voiceless and unheeded continue to stagger through the desert into Chad, a diplomatically dumb country spectacularly unprepared for guests. The accusations of ethnic cleansing and genocide hang in the air, but few with the power to do anything about them want to say the words on record. It's like casting a spell to summon the apocalypse. Once said out loud, the world is a step closer to having to confront another Rwanda, another Kosovo. But there is a selective deafness abroad brought about by conflict in the Middle East, Iraq and the constant sirens of global terrorism, and unstated but ever present is the real-world wisdom that this, after all, is just another Africa story from the continent that brought you all the defining examples of horror; where the usual calibrations of misery don't apply.

I have no doubt there are dozens of marvellous and edifying things about Chad: being here is not one of them. Chad, or Tchad as they call it locally, as if named by some passing Yorkshireman, is really no more than a cartographer's patch. The French left it here as somewhere to keep the bottom of the Sahara in, and for those platoons of foreign-legionnaires who had the most to forget. It's about the size of Germany, with a population of just 9 million. I remember it from my school atlas – it had the lowest per-capita income in the world. It isn't quite the poorest country on Earth any more, but it is way, way down there: 80 per cent of the population live below the poverty line, 80 per cent work the sand. Its primary exports are a handkerchief of cotton, a few cattle and a near-monopoly of the world's gum arabic needs. Gum arabic is essential in the manufacture of good-quality watercolours. Not a lot of people know that; in fact not a lot of people know anything about landlocked Chad. It has no airline, no railways; it has 33,400 kilometres of road, but only 267 kilometres of them are tarmacked. Life expectancy is 48 years, and only if you don't expect much. It does, though, have a glut of human diversity: 200 ethnic groups. In the north, the Goran Zaghawa, Kanembou, Ouaddai, Baguirmi, Hadjerai, Fulbe, Kotoko, Hausa, Boulala and Maba; all Arab and Muslim. In the south are the Moundang, Moussei and Massa, who are for the most part Christian, which in Africa always comes hyphenated with animist, and they're black. They are the blackest black, blue-black, matt-black black you've ever seen.

Chad, along with Sudan, is hung across one of the least reported, potentially most volatile cultural fault lines in the world: the border between black and Arab Africa. Before the Europeans ever arrived there was a history of exploitation, slavery and massacre. Here, the appellation Muslim or Christian comes with baggage and chains. Chad isn't one of those failed states we hear so much about from smug, overachieving nations: rather it's a stalled state, one that never really made it off the starting blocks of independence. It goes through the stately motions, and boasts plenty of initials after its name from international organisations.

It has ambassadors and a billion dollars of debt, it signs international treaties (though I notice it hasn't ratified the international law of the sea yet), but it isn't defined by the niceties of statesmanship. Like Sudan, Chad is a slave to the land on which it precariously squats, earth blasted and dominated by the sun. This is the hottest place I've ever been. Temperatures are regularly in the fifties; they have climbed the thirties before sunrise. This isn't just weather, something mundane to be endured: it's a godlike thing, a shimmering, psychotic, physical presence. It's like living with a bright murderer. Achievement is not measured here, as it is in the damp, green First World, by invention and energy, but by the ability to do as little as possible, for as long as possible, in as much shade as possible.

Chad has three pressing problems. It has the black curse of Africa: unexploited oil. It has the same flag as Romania, and it has between 100,000 and 200,000 refugees. It has gone to the UN to protest about the flag business. To get about, you either hitch a lift on a lorry, hire a four-wheel-drive and stutter across the desert, or beg a seat on one of the small humanitarian flights that sustain a skeletal relief effort. After a couple of days hanging out in the two-storey breeze-block and barbed-wire boredom of Ndjamena, we managed to get a flight into the east. At the airport the top-secret French Mirage fighters screamed secretly into the shimmering morning air to spy on North Africa. The French can never actually leave their old colonies. They hang around like gun-toting divorced husbands. We fly to Abéché, which puts up with another French base; legionnaires lounging in the shadow of their jeeps, sporting nut-hugging camouflage shorts and coquettish little berets. For all their surly élan, they always look like the backing group for the Village People.

We drive on to Iriba, a town made of mud that rises out of the desert like geometric worm casts. The deafening silence is broken only by the morning throb of the baker's generator and the occasional call of a lovesick donkey. There is nothing to see here, nothing to play at, nothing to talk about, nothing to do, except squat in the shade and throw stones at meagre chickens. You can't help but wonder at the terrifying boredom threshold you'd need to call this place home.

Iriba has the only hospital for the thousands of refugees stretched across hundreds of miles of border. It's a brick building of three or four little wards and a room that makes do as an operating theatre. In the compound are some sagging, dusty tents for the therapeutic feeding of malnourished children, and there is some shade for their mothers and those who have no bed. The hospital is run by Médecins Sans Frontières – Chad has few doctors, and they all work in the capital or for the UN.

There is only one doctor-surgeon, a Belgian girl who looks like she has stepped from a Frans Hals painting; bosomy and blonde, she's like a ghost among her black patients. She dreams Belgium dreams, of dairy products, yoghurt, cheese, fountains of milk. She makes her rounds with professional cheerfulness. The sick regard her with that stoic fatalism that is the small dignity of African hospitals. Just having made it here is staggering good fortune.

She stops at the bed of a woman who has given birth to tiny twin boys. They lie like little plucked birds, their bodies flickering with breath. Their mother arranges her shawl to give them shade, gently flicks away the flies – but she won't feed them. She is lactating but she won't feed them. And the hospital won't give them powdered milk because they can't guarantee its supply for the whole of their infancy. It's a stand-off. The mother won't or can't say why, one remorseless hour at a time, she can starve her sons to death. She lies apart with an impassive, locked-away beauty, like an odalisque, watching her boys eke out their tiny reserves of existence. The doctor is frustrated. The mother stares, speechlessly daring judgement. The universal blessing of children is for the refugee a curse. How could a lonely girl without a husband or family welcome another pair of mouths, two widow's mites, into this stark, hopeless life? I can only guess at the monstrous ill fortune and misery that led her to this hopeless impasse. She can't kill her babies, as women sometimes do out here *in extremis*, but she can't help them into her world either, so she lies here silently jammed between the intolerable and the unbearable.

Outside, a thirteen-year-old boy takes painful little steps, helped by an orderly. His brother stepped on the mine that killed him and took this boy's foot, and doctors had to remove one of his testicles. A group of men sitting in the shade give him a little clap. They may be guerrillas: they have bullet and shrapnel wounds; one is paralysed. Nobody asks.

I stand in on an operation in the little theatre. It's hardly sterile. There are sheets over the windows to keep out the desert, but it becomes stifling. Flies hopscotch over the sixteen-year-old girl lying on the table. She has been hit by a truck. They use ketamine as an anaesthetic. In the West it is only used as a veterinary drug; here it's a godsend. But while the bone-deep lacerations in the leg are being disinfected, the girl comes round. Her eyes roll with terror, hands jerk, a soft mewing grows to wails, then screams. The nurse reaches for another hypodermic cosh. 'I think she'll probably lose this leg,' says the doctor.

In the therapeutic feeding centre, children are given high-protein porridge; mothers and grandmothers finger-feed tiny mouthfuls into slowly ruminating mouths. These children, with their stretched-parchment faces, sparse hair and huge, sorrowful eyes, are always shocking, and I am aware of the irony of how ancient, wise and calm starving children always look. A woman rocks a spindly, floppy toddler. He is dying, she says. And closes his eyes. 'No,' explains a nurse through an interpreter. 'He's very dehydrated. He will die if they don't get fluids into him.' She adds that the mother shouldn't have taken out the saline drip they put into his arm. She tries to fit another, but the mother pushes it away; no, she insists, her child is dead. The nurses, though compassionate in a matter-of-fact way, get grittily frustrated at the lack of understanding in these mothers. Medicine is so second-nature to us, yet so mythical to them.

There is a little albino lad about two years old who is everyone's favourite. They call him Petit Blanc. He is responding well to the therapeutic feeding, the wrinkled skin filling out and dimpling. 'He won't last long,' she says. 'They never do, albinos. Skin cancer.' Does his mother know? 'She does now. I told her.' Can't she do anything? The doctor shrugs: 'Keep him out of the sun.' But all this woman has between her and the blistering, baby-murderous sky is a thin veil. 'You see, already he has the melanomas.'

About an hour away from the hospital, past dead tanks, relics of a defunct civil war, is the desert refugee camp of Iridimi. Built for 6,000, it sags under the needs of 14,000 souls who live beneath plastic sheets and rags stretched over thorn trees. Each day brings more lorries laden with Sudanese blacks and their bright bundles of belongings. They trundle in from the border, herding skeletal donkeys and matted goats, moving further inland as the Sudanese Arab militia cross the border to rob the last vestiges of property and livestock. The gunships that make up the Sudanese air force drop handmade bombs on border towns. The war in Darfur is being pursued by the last irregular cavalry still plying their trade: the Janjaweed. On horses and camels, they surround black villages. They are supported by regular army troops. The Sudanese government denies involvement, claiming they are local groups. The Janjaweed live by looting cattle, grain, small amounts of cash and slaves.

The government's reason for not intervening is clear: it's ethnic cleansing and genocide. There is meant to be a UN-monitored ceasefire, but the casualties, terrified women and starving children still stream across the border. The refugees' stories have a metronomic repetition: their villages are shelled or bombed, the Janjaweed surround them and kill all the men and boys old enough to be remotely threatening. They systematically rape the women, taking some as slaves; they then burn the villages and the crops they can't steal, and ride off the livestock. And still the government claims the Janjaweed have nothing to do with them.

Khartoum offers access to the international community to check these calumnies, these accusations. Anyone can come to see that really Sudan is lovely – a hot Switzerland with mosques – but invariably the promised visas for observers and NGOs never materialise. If they do manage to get one, access to the worst area is limited. There are 500 applications from humanitarian agencies alone gathering diplomatic dust. This pattern of denial and opaque promises of transparency is familiar after twenty years of war in the south. Who is going to do anything about it? Who will stand up to the Janjaweed? They are among the most feared, sadistically ruthless, irregular thugs in a continent glutted with military horror. The refugees joke about them with terrified black humour; they all wear leather necklaces of little bound spells that are meant to protect them from bullets or knives, landmines and violent death. Little dark-age incantations against the ordnance of modern war.

Anyone who doubts that this conflict is either genocidal or ethnically motivated only has to visit these camps. All the refugees are black; there are no Arabs here. And even more shocking, 90 per cent of them are women and children. The children up to the age of five are about 50-50 girls and boys, as you'd expect. From five to fifteen they are 70 per cent girls. Some of the men would have stayed to fight or hide with their livestock but, as Sherlock Holmes used to say, 'when you have eliminated the impossible, whatever remains . . . must be the truth'. It is impossible to imagine any other explanation for this disappeared generation of men than systematic murder. The women tell of deaths, terrified flight, lost children, missing husbands. 'We will never go back,' says one. 'Unless the UN have soldiers, and only if they are white soldiers,' adds another.

The refugees are related linguistically and tribally to the Chadians on this side of the border; they have moved and traded together for hundreds of years, and are now welcomed. It is humbling to see with what good grace the people with the least offer shelter and succour to those with nothing. The majority of refugees are not in the rich First World, but in the poorest bits of the Third World, where they and their hosts grow poorer.

The greatest problem after safety is water. From sunrise to sunset in the camp, a long line of women wait under the deathly sun to fill containers from a couple of standpipes that are fed by large plastic bladders, which in turn are filled by lorries. I have to drink at least six litres of soupy water a day to stop my tongue cracking and my throat closing up. But I never see these women drink. Their bright cotton shawls flap in the wind, revealing a little arm or resting head tied to a back. In the white light, the rivers of cloth look like spinnakers of saturated colour, printed with the repeated pictures of other people's good fortune. You see Mercedes badges and BMW signs, footballs, mobile phones, aeroplanes, the faces of politicians who've promised prosperity, cities of skyscrapers – the ragged incantations for an unavailable life, and the shaming irony of a desperate African version of designer labels. Here is a picture of a house you would be happy in, a diploma you could get if there was a school, a car, a comfy chair. Impossible, ridiculous cotton dreams of a fantasy luxury.

A mile or so outside the camp, in a stand of knotted acacias, is an ancient stone-lined well, one of the Sahara's fabled oases. It doesn't look like the painting. A dirty, shit-strewn muddy quag, where herdsmen sweat and slither at the heavy job of tending their xylophone-ribbed flocks. They perch precariously on the edge of the well; the thick water at the bottom is only a few feet deep. In the bed of the wadi there is a stinking half-burnt pyre of donkey and goat corpses. The desert is littered with animal cadavers; elsewhere, parched livestock stand in little bits of filigreed shade and wait to die. The sun desiccates their bodies to tough bags, leather and bones that grin at the sky. For some reason there are no carrion-eaters, no vultures, so the dead lie around like old teabags. When the rains do come, they'll become slimy and get washed into the wells and wadis, and leach into the water table. The risk of a cholera epidemic is just one runny, squatting child away.

The desert and the water won't support the Chadians and the

Sudanese refugees, and there are signs that the welcome is growing thin. Charities drilling in search of new wells for permanent camps have been angrily stopped by farmers.

We drive on a spine-fusing, hip-dislocating, brain-poaching journey to Tiné, a market town that crosses the border. It sits on one of the skeletal lines of trade and communication that bleach into the Sahara. The route down from Libya meets a crossroads from Sudan into Central Africa here. The border itself is no more than a dry wadi and some trees, under which sit a squad of Chadian soldiers. There are a couple of impressive mosques and a large covered market. Prices are astronomic for the bits and boxes of white goods that made the Homeric saga through the desert to end up here.

Across the dry river and the shade trees you see the other half of town, the Sudanese half, a mirror image of mud brick and minaret, utterly deserted, where not a soul, not a donkey exists. It's a town that's suffered a stroke: one half paralysed, the other bereft and staggering. The Janjaweed came, murdered and expelled the left-hand population. People ask, how could the Sudanese do this to their own people? I've heard Sudanese spokesmen with honey voices rhetorically ask the same thing. 'Why would we do these things to our own people?' The answer would seem to be that the Arab-Muslim regime in Khartoum doesn't consider the black inhabitants of their southern and eastern regions as their people, their kin, at all.

With its rigid, prescriptive interpretation of sharia, Khartoum attempted to develop chemical and nuclear weapons. It was Khartoum that sheltered Osama Bin Laden and Al-Qaeda while they planned the embassy bombing in Nairobi and Dar es Salaam. Khartoum pursued a civil war in the south for twenty years, engineering famine as a weapon of mass murder. And it still accepts the oldest, most inhuman of mass crimes: slavery. Blacks are captured, kept, bred and ransomed as slaves. This is a blatantly racist, genocidal regime. The UN has called the catastrophe in Darfur the worst humanitarian disaster in the world, but that's a euphemism. It describes a consequence, not the cause. This is a calculated crime. The greatest inhumanitarian disaster in the world.

In another refugee camp, at Touloum, a boy, perhaps twenty, approaches me. He is wearing a once-smart sports jacket and trousers and – a rare thing – spectacles. 'You speak English?' he asks. 'I was a student of English in Darfur at the university. I was in my second year.' He looks round the ragged shelters. 'This is a bad place, very bad. We need two things: water and an English department.'

I think he means it as a joke; it's a bleakly funny line. But he is absolutely serious. He is close to tears and I understand what a struggle it must have been to get to university at all, what a monumental investment, not just for him but his family, his village; this slightly bookish boy in his western charity clothes and wise glasses, already approaching statistical middle age, cast out as homeless, begging flotsam among a diaspora of grieving women. It is such a pitiful waste. A damnable squandering of this heroic spark.

On the long, dry road home, I stop off at the hospital in Iriba. The woman who had pronounced her son dead has had her prophecy fulfilled. The war-wounded men come and bury the little bundle in the graveyard behind the latrines. She sits hunched, facing the wall. She doesn't cry. I haven't seen one of these women cry. Inside, the mother has begun feeding her twin boys, her reasons for offering them life as secretly implacable as had been her decision to withhold it.

SOUTH AFRICA

I

Nobody ever forgets their first night in the bush. It's among the precious, meagre handful of life firsts that remain indelible. I was a sure thing, a pushover.

We first-time holiday trippers fresh from the concrete-and-neon north world sat around a leaping hardwood fire, picking over our plates of warthog and mealie meal. Above us the blue-black sky flashed, a vast bowl, the southern constellation as unfamiliar as everything else. We were newborn into the oldest landscape on Earth.

At the centre of our tight semicircle lounged a sandy-haired boy with his legs akimbo. He wore a threadbare khaki shirt and shorts that were way too tight. Beside him rested a bolt-action rifle. The rest of us were bulgy and creased, Velcro'd and fleeced in the finest tropical gear Outward Bound shops could provide. We hung on him with rapt attention – you didn't have to be Desmond Morris to work out who the alpha male in this herd was.

What was odd was that by every economic, social and cultural hierarchy, the boy should have been at the bottom of the pecking order. Third World poor are remedially educated, semi-skilled, socially inept, with the style sense of a gay municipal gardener, but here were swinging-dick bankers, captains of industry, commercial goliaths, top predators in other jungles, ogling him with hero worship, fighting like school kids to sit next to him. Here was the most exciting creature in all of wild Africa, an endangered species, one of the world's last properly romantic boyhood heroes: the game ranger.

The next day, the boy took us out into the bush. We came across a young male elephant. When I say young, he cast a shadow big enough to play golf under and he was in musth, a sort of pachyderm's male PMT. Hormones leaked down his face.

Elephants in musth are best left alone. In fact, elephants on Valium doing yoga are best left alone. He was just walking, ripping up trees the size of rugby goalposts. The hero scout suggested we wait behind a termite mound. 'He's going to scent us in a minute,' our hero whispered. 'Do exactly what I say and don't, under any circumstances, run.'

The elephant appeared and smelt me. I know it was me, because at this point I was smelling a lot stronger than anything else in the garden. It was as if he'd stumbled on a convention of ivory-carvers. With a speed and dexterity that would have been fascinating on television, he spun to face us. The ears came out (elephants are the only animals that have really frightening ears), he put his foot down and came at us like a big grey post-office van. I'm not good at distances, but he started over there and within no time he was blocking out the sky. At which point the hero jumped up, waved his arms and said: 'Boo.' The elephant turned on his back feet and stomped off. I asked the hero how certain he'd been it would behave like that. 'Pretty certain. Nine out of ten times, that's what'll happen.'

I've thought about this a lot since. Nine out of ten was supposed to reassure me, but would you get on a nine-out-of-ten plane? Eat a nine-out-of-ten oyster? Have nine-out-of-ten unprotected sex? So why didn't I run? In those extruded seconds I'd understood Darwin's herbivore question: you don't have to run faster than the thing chasing you, you just have to run faster than the slowest thing being chased. I think the reason I didn't was because I'd rather die than look a fool in front of a schoolboy hero.

I've been back to the African bush pretty much every year for the decade since and seen a lot of game rangers, and here's the thing:

they're like marriage-guidance counsellors, aromatherapists and mercenaries – anyone can call themselves one. They are a breed, a type, the shorts don't vary much and they're the only men on Earth still fighting to make ankle socks sexy. But they vary greatly in ability and knowledge. A man who can handle himself in the bush isn't necessarily a man who can handle a hysterical honeymoon couple from Dundee and a surprised hippo.

In retrospect, I realised I'd gone walkies behind lots of people I really shouldn't have trusted to baby-sit exotic house plants. And they lie. They lie for the same reason lions kill each other's children: because they can. Game rangers prove a truth about jungles everywhere: an expert is simply someone you think knows more than you do. If I didn't do what I do and I could do anything else, I'd be a game ranger. And so I went to discover the secrets of the last real boy scouts, to see if I had one in me. There are no agreed standards for guides. To be a lifeguard on a beach in Cornwall you need a certificate of proficiency. To take a dozen Japanese tourists who think they're on the Discovery Channel into the most dangerous environment on Earth, all you need is a pair of shorts.

One of the few companies running a properly structured comprehensive training course is Conservation Corporation Africa, which offers some of the most environmentally, socially sensitive, high-end tourist lodges in Africa. I went to Phinda in KwaZulu-Natal in South Africa. It has various habitats, including the rare and exceedingly delicate sand forest. The guide in charge of training was Alastair Kilpin, whose family had been fruit farmers in the Cape for umpteen generations. As a rule, guides tend to be lads who grew up in the bush and/or served in post-colonial armies. Their style is part Just William adventure, part military reconnaissance.

But the emphasis is moving away from the white hunter to the ecological conservationist. I'd boasted to Alastair about my elephant encounter. He wasn't impressed. 'We don't do that sort of thing here – we don't like to stress the animals.'

The course takes six weeks and has a dropout rate that would make an SAS sergeant smile. It's physically and mentally tough – this isn't about being an Outward Bound redcoat with added aloe vera. It's a head-bulging amount of information and skill, and I've got to try to do it all in a week. I said I would do anything they do except wear the shorts. I'd had my kit made by Gieves & Hawkes, who did Livingstone and Stanley.

To start I have to learn a new language: Zulu. Now, if your mouth comes fitted with a European tongue, then speaking Zulu is like trying to gargle and whistle at the same time mellifluously.

Every guide comes with a tracker. The trackers are Zulu, the guide drives the Land Rover, the tracker sits on a little jump seat over the radiator, catching flies like a hood ornament. We go for our first game drive. 'Right,' says Alastair. 'What's the most dangerous animal in Africa?' I already know this. It's not lion or buffalo or hippo. It's the mosquito. Malaria kills a million Africans a year. He shakes his head. 'They're behind you.' He nods at the empty bench seats. 'It's us, it's humans. Never forget that.'

The tracker reads the road at thirty miles per hour. 'Leopard,' he says. We stop. He points at the red dirt. There's nothing.

'Look closely.' A slight indent, a mere shadow here and there. 'This morning, a big male.'

If you are looking for a hobby, I can't recommend tracking enough. Once you get into it you can't stop. It's like learning a magic trick or discovering X-ray vision. Slowly, dust reveals the hieroglyphs of a secret code. As you decipher it, it becomes ever more subtle. Nuanced, specific, every track has a plot, tells a story.

This is a hyena with its toes turned slightly inwards. This is the amazingly dainty warthog, and the bizarre trail that looks like a miniature unicycle driven by a drunk elf turns out to be a scarab beetle pushing his sarcophagus of dung. Before you know it, you're plunging your arm into elephant shit, and mentioning en passant: 'This leopard's got a tummy upset because it hasn't killed and is eating rotten meat.'

Nothing makes you feel more sure-footed, part of a place, than reading earth and turds, and nothing makes you feel blinder and stupider than being with someone who does it well.

Bush tourism has moved on from just showing busloads of Americans the big five: lion, leopard, elephant, rhino, cape buffalo – or 'the big hairies', as the guides dismissively call them.

Next we do birds. Now, I would no more be a twitcher in East Anglia than I would grow a beard, but doing it in Africa is extraordinary. The variety is as engrossing as a Las Vegas chorus line. To make it more interesting, they all have common names, Afrikaans names, Zulu names and scientific names. Apart from the essential standard work, Newman's *Birds of Southern Africa*, there's another invaluable tome, LBJs, which stands for little brown jobs, and I need to identify them all, not just by sight, season and range but by nest and call.

Having done live birds, Alastair makes me dissect a juvenile tawny eagle that has been brought in as roadkill. Just for your information, you can tell this one apart from other brown eagles – steppe, lesser-spotted, brown snake, etc. – by its gape; in layman's terms, that is the corner of its mouth, which never, ever, extends past the centre of its eye.

We could move on to trees and bush medicine and spiders and beetles and ants. But time presses and I have to learn driving over rough terrain without making the passengers sick, then driving over rough terrain while talking over my shoulder without sending them to sleep.

Then Alastair tells me it's the big one, the difficult bit: I have to cook breakfast. He makes it sound unbelievably tricky. 'Are you sure you're up to it? Coffee, eggs, sausage. Are you sure?' I suppose that, being South African, he thinks the idea of a man cooking is innately transsexual.

To compensate, the next day we do guns. Rifle training takes up a whole week of the course; guns are central to the romance of guides – it's their link to their romantic ancestors, the white hunters. Tourists like to see a man holding a rifle, partly because it makes them feel safe, but mostly because it emphasises the danger.

Alastair is ambivalent about the rifle. Out on his own he never carries one – it gives you a false sense of security and subconsciously makes you a predator and potentially aggressive. The greatest asset our species has in the bush is the same as it was 15,000 years ago: the ability to think ahead. Carrying a gun impedes the cognitive process – you think like metal. If one of his guides ever fired a shot, he says, it's 90 per cent certain he'd be sacked immediately afterwards. 'I can only think of a very narrow set of circumstances that would make it acceptable. Virtually every time a gun is used, it's because of a mistake made earlier.'

The rifle is a no-frills bolt-action with open sights. The bullets are hard- and soft-nosed, and have huge charges. The first thing is safety, the second is no warning shot. 'Warning shots are for movies.' If you shoot, you shoot to kill. The third thing is speed and accuracy. I have to put four bullets into a plate-sized target at twenty-five yards. That's not too hard, but I have to do it in under fifteen seconds. I do it, just. Then three shots at targets set at twenty-five, fifteen and ten yards, rapid fire. That's much more difficult. I jam the bolt, I panic, I miss a target. 'Your shooting's probably okay, but your safety isn't. Too many fingers in the wrong place.'

I'm getting the feeling that the gun is academic, mostly symbolic. A lioness that means business will cover twenty-five yards in about three seconds. She'll come low and she'll zigzag. Chances are, even if you manage to get off a shot, you'll fire over her head. Far better to understand her behaviour. She'll give you one warning, a single coughing growl. If you do the right thing – move away without showing panic or your back – then nine out of ten times (that statistic again) she'll let you go.

Forget about lionesses only attacking to protect their cubs: they've all got cubs all the time, that's what lionesses are for. And forget dummy charges: the lion and the elephant haven't decided if this is the real thing until they see how you react. And buffalo and rhino don't tease when they start coming: they're coming right for you.

With buffalo, you aim up the nose before they lower their heads. With rhino, you have to avoid hitting the horn, so you must wait until they lower their heads in the last few yards, then do some complex trigonometry to work out the spot between ears and eyes that contains their walnut-sized, prehistoric brains. See how ridiculously academic all this is? 'What do you do about a leopard?' I ask. 'Forget it,' says Alastair, drily. 'You'll never see the leopard that gets you.'

'So what have you learnt? In an emergency what would you do?' Me? I'd stick as close to the tracker as possible and do exactly what he does. Alastair beams: 'Good, you're getting the idea.'

This raises a question I'd been putting off, and over dinner, with a covey of guides, I ask it: 'Look, all of you are white; all the trackers are black. With due respect, the trackers are in a different league when it comes to bushcraft. You all rely on them completely. So why aren't any of them driving?'

'We're very aware of this; we're trying hard to promote trackers to be guides. Sometimes there's a problem with language but mostly, you know, they just don't want the responsibility. It takes time. It's about changing the culture, but it must change.'

CC Africa has built its reputation and its profit on being sensitive to indigenous people. It tries to treat its staff well, sets up schools, funds medical facilities and wants to be part of the community. But those innate and fundamental double standards in the African bush, the way we see wildness and animals, are specifically colonial. The taxonomy, the names and biological relationships, the ecology are all white, a western overview. Most black Africans living in townships and cities have only ever seen a giraffe on their banknotes. And those who live in the bush view game as competition for cattle and goats as opportunistic food supplements. Poaching isn't done by quasi-military gangs financed by erection-obsessed Chinese, but by desperate subsistence farmers for a few shillings.

But more important than that, the Black African connection with the bush – spiritual, medical, historical and familial – is quite as complex and exciting as western zoology and ecology. But tourists never see it. Wild Africa is an experience divorced from black Africa except for quaint tribal handcrafts and photo-opportunity natives. And it's a terrible loss for Africa and for us.

Conservation must also mean preserving and encouraging

diversity in ways of seeing. And, it must be said, there is still an unspoken racism here. It's not from the white rangers or keepers of game reserves: it's from us, the visitors. Our experience feels more authentically Isak Dinesen, Happy Valley Hemingway with white officers and black servants; we're happier and feel safer seeing a white man carry the gun and a black man out front.

When they say they don't want to take responsibility, it's a euphemism. There's a historical reticence about telling rich, powerful white folk what to do. If it doesn't change, the guides, the trackers and the game will be swept away by a tide of subsistence farming and erosion and jealousy.

On the last day, it's time for my final test. I'd been shown the rudiments; now I must do it for real. I have to take a group of 'tourists' – made up of guides, hotel staff and Nicola, my girlfriend – on a game walk. I'll be in charge without a tracker.

The principle of walking in the bush is that you see as much as you can but avoid confronting animals. Alastair has told me something will happen. I have a gun but no bullets. And a decent pair of Savile Row trousers. I lay down the rules: we'll walk in close, silent, single file; if you want to ask a question or draw my attention, make an organic noise, like clicking your fingers or clucking; I'll use hand signals – this means stop, this means move back, this means you, you wanker. And so we set off. After ten minutes I'm relaxed, feeling a bit like David Attenborough with just a dab of Stewart Granger.

We walk around a stand of thorns, and there in the clearing, thirty yards away, are four South Africans in very tight shorts, lying in the shade, pretending to be lions. I know they're lions because their body language is so good. I can even tell which one is the lioness and which are the year-old cubs. It's sort of spooky. The adrenalin pumps. I make the signal to stop. There are some trees behind us and an acacia to our left. The lion with the thick, pink thighs and baseball cap sits up and gives the characteristic warning growl. She's nervous: we're too close. I give the signal to move back.

At this point a cook from the hotel grabs my gun arm and starts shouting: 'Do something, do something, we're all going to die.' 'Look here,' I say. 'Calm down, get off and move over there.'

The lion with the short socks has got to her feet. This is not good. Out of the corner of my eye I notice something move. It's Nicola running around the acacia tree. Nicola is an African, she knows how to behave in the bush, but she's waving her hands like she's drying nail varnish, and doing 'I've seen a mouse' shrieking.

The lioness charges like a prop forward in injury time. The hysterical cook's got his arms round my neck. I consider clubbing him with the gun. The short, bow-legged, roaring South African leaps on my girlfriend and they roll in the grass. He can't make up his mind whether to eat her or mate. His ruddy-faced cubs look on expectantly. The exercise has finished in confusion.

Alastair strides over. 'Why are you laughing?' Well, because it's sort of funny, I feel like a naughty schoolboy. He's not amused. 'You just got a guest killed. Why didn't you shoot the lion?' The truth is, I was stunned. I've never seen Nicola run before, I didn't know she could. 'Well, I hope you've learnt something,' he says without conviction. Yup, that the most dangerous animal in Africa is an anthropomorphic, ruddy-faced boor with no dress sense and double buttocks, and that nine out of ten times you can predict the behaviour of women, but it's that one time that stitches you up.

High above us, a bateleur eagle rocks in lazy circles, thinking, I suspect, how much he hates these teasing mock charges.

II

Above the Kloof mine, a white man sits all alone in a hut. The hut is hidden in a two-storey hangar and the hangar is built over some heavy-duty muscle machinery. Engineered in England when engineers weren't just youths who mended radiators, it's caged in and hung with clanging stairways. The man sits in front of a console of buttons and switches; he stares out of a window at a large calibrated circle with a moving pointer like the wheel of fortune. Nobody's allowed to enter the hut. There must be no distractions. He notices me out of the corner of his eye and cups a surreptitious fag. Another man hangs around the landing; perhaps he's here in case his mate needs a pee; perhaps he's here to kill him if he goes *tonto*.

The lives of thousands of men hang on this bloke's attention span and his reactions to a complex series of Morse whistles that come from deep underground. He is the winch man, the winder. He plummets the double-decker wire cages packed with men down into the earth, so that they can mine gold.

The lift doors clang shut. Daylight slides up the cage; we start to fall. It feels like someone losing their grip over a cliff. The lift vibrates and judders, down, down, gathering speed. After mere seconds we're in the Cenozoic era, past the Holocene epoch; instantly past the time of the first whites in South Africa; past the first black tribes to migrate from the north's steamy forests; past the Pleistocene, Pliocene, Oligocene, Eocene and Paleocene epochs. Down, down past the time of the super-mammals; down past the first hominoid; down past the Sahara as a jungle; into the Mesozoic era, past the Cretaceous, Jurassic and Triassic periods. Down past the first dinosaurs, the reptiles and amphibians, the land plants, down past the continental separation; down into the Palaeozoic era, the Permian period, past the Carboniferous epoch, past the Devonian and Silurian periods; down to Protoerozoic rock that is $2\frac{3}{4}$ billion years old, two kilometres beneath today's sunlight.

High above, the man in the hut watching fortune's needle fall pulls a switch. The lift jars to a halt. The door shudders open, and I step out into the hot, damp air that doesn't belong down here any more than I do.

South African gold mines are not at all what I expected. I was looking for some approximation of a northern English pit village with better weather. But they sit alone in the beautiful country of the rolling high veld. Their headgear stands like castle keeps or *campanili*. The mines look a bit like futuristic Tuscan hill towns; there are no shanties, no bustling camps of shebeens, markets and brothels, just suburban back roads with municipal flowerbeds and alleys of trees punctuating miles of discreet razor-wire fence.

The gold mines might almost be deserted; only the arc lights and complex security at the gate betray their importance in the land. Gold mines, like icebergs, hide their power beneath the surface. The reason for South Africa is the cold comfort of gold. This reef of ore was discovered in the 1880s on farmland in the Boer homeland of the Transvaal. The area, Witwatersrand, gave its name to the currency. The discovery started a rush of prospectors, first from the Cape and then from all over the globe. Out of the mining camp grew Johannesburg – a city the Zulus call Egoli, the place of gold. And out of the ground came money. Inconceivable amounts of cash, to pay for the most successful country in the world's most unsuccessful continent. The gold was formed by a great inland sea, washed up on its tide line. As the sea dried up, the gold was covered by new formations of sediment and rock, and then the old sea bed was tilted sideways – one edge touching the surface, the rest falling away in a great arc underground. It was, and is, by far and away the largest deposit of gold ever discovered.

But gold has its curse. It paid for the apartheid regime. It brought injustice and torture, it paid for clandestine wars in at least three neighbouring countries, and it financed the southern hemisphere's first and only nuclear bomb (in 1993, South Africa abandoned its secret nuclear-weapons programme). This gold should now be making amends and helping pay for a new rainbow South Africa, but just when it's needed the most, mining gold has faltered. It is, they say, a sunset industry. It may only last another fifteen years, perhaps another fifty.

Having once accounted for half of South Africa's economy, it's now down to 12 per cent. And the mines are prone to strikes. Their history and ownership make them unpopular with the ruling ANC government. Gold Fields, which owns the Kloof mine I'm going down, is at the moment resisting tooth and nail an asset-lipo-sucking, hostile bid from the ironically named Harmony Gold Mining Company – a smaller, loss-making outfit. It's an expensive and desperate raid to dig the deepest grave in Africa for one or other of them. Troubled Harmony needs a rich seam of gold to mine, or else its future looks bleak; Gold Fields would be devalued by association.

The high value of the rand against the weaker dollar makes deep mining an unprofitable business at the moment. Gold stands at 2,633 rand ($427.70) an ounce, but only needs to go to 2,643.80 rand for it to be very profitable; at 2,799.31 rand, they are drowning in money. Mining is cyclical, but the cycle is emotional, not economic. There's nothing rational about the value of gold – a war, a disaster, a dramatic shift in geopolitics, a frisson of unease and the world runs to the security of gold as it always has. They're planning even deeper mines, perhaps six or seven kilometres deep. The technical problem is the lift rope. It becomes too heavy to support its own weight. But they're working on it. No, it's not what I'm thinking about as I start to walk down the tunnel towards the stope, the gold face. What I'm thinking of are earthquakes. This part of Africa is low-risk for tremors, but the constant blasting deep underground slaps the face of Hades; it teases and irritates the silent, blind rock, which twitches and shudders. Two days ago a quake that broke windows on the surface trapped forty-two miners. The last I heard, they were still down there in the fetid blackness. Do you worry about quakes, I ask the guy next to me. 'Ach, they happen most days.' Aren't you frightened? He looks at me sideways. 'Yes, very, but what can you do? Where can you go?'

And I'm thinking about my outfit. A one-piece cotton overall that was laid out in the VIP changing-room, along with a pair of woolly socks and wellington boots. Rubber knee and elbow pads (made by crippled miners), a white plastic hard hat, a pair of rubber gloves – one red, one green – and some second-hand red pants. I draw the line at the pants. If I'm going to be buried for ever, or brought back up in a bag, I'm not meeting my maker, or the surgeon, in a pair of someone else's puce Y-fronts.

At the mine head I'm given a belt with a heavy battery pack, a lamp that clips to the helmet, and a silver box with breathing apparatus in case we hit methane or CO_2. 'It'll give you half an hour's breathable air, as long as you stroll and don't panic,' says the cheery miner who offers the unnervingly sketchy health-and-safety talk, which mostly boils down to: 'No worries, trust us and look where you're going.' Smilingly, they make me sign in triplicate fifteen pages of medical legalese that indemnifies them from having to have the remotest concern for my well-being.

To all intents and purposes, I'm now the mine bitch – don't panic, stroll. Up above, everywhere you look there are safety posters, imploring care and attention the way communists used to demand sacrifice and patriotism. One billboard points out that there have been almost a million shifts without a fatality, which sounds encouraging until you realise that each miner counts as a shift, so it's only about four months. Nine people die down the Kloof mine most years, usually from what they literally and amusingly call 'ground falls'. That's the mine ceiling hitting you on the head, crushing your organs, snapping your spine and mushing your pelvis to dog food. Occasionally they just get hit by a train.

The mine tunnel starts off high and broad, like an underpass or a Tube platform. There are lights bolted to the roof, and along the walls run tubes and hoses carrying water and compressed air. The ground is flat and even; there are narrow-gauge rails set into the rock. Every so often a right angle of timber is placed across them; if one of the locos goes loco, then this is meant to derail it. The trains pull the rocks and, as the tunnels get narrower and the ceiling lower, when they pass you have to push yourself against a wall. There are holes in the floor that drop down to other levels, the engines dump their rock down them, and from there they are humped to the surface. The railway line stops and the tunnels become rougher, bored-out holes in the rock. The floor falls away, we have to scrabble in single file down hastily hacked stairs, in corners there are piles of pit props, and metal jacks. The air smells acrid and mineral; it seems to rise and fall. Pumped in, it gusts through defiles like the breath of a sleeping dragon. Slick with sweat, I stumble and reach for a guardrail. Something brown darts over my hand. A cockroach. Astonishing, this little creature, our most faithful companion, like a loathed ex, stalked us here to the centre of the Earth. This brazen, admirable, wavy-feelered meaty pebble skitters through the hot dark, feeding on sweat and skin flakes, and drill grease.

The tunnel loses coherence and direction. We stumble and graze on the rock. The ceiling crawls down the walls, the floor crawls up to meet it and I stoop in between. Up and down and around, I lose all track. The path is like a slow, sharp, awkward switchback. I've no idea where I've come from, or which direction is back. The lights have run out. There is only the lamp on my head to keep back the darkest, matt-blackest blackness on Earth. It's an absence of seeing. I'm bent double, my hard hat jarring the jutting cliff, my belt catching and battery jamming on the shale. Now I'm wriggling, scuttling and crabbing in the loose, sharp gravel. I feel so soft and squidgy and alien, blind and maggoty in this emphatic mineral world.

Up over a trench wall of rock and I'm there, dripping, panting. This is the end of the tunnel, where there is no light. Here is what it was all for, a slanting reef of gold-bearing rock. It's a yard of pebble dash that is dun and coarse. There is no gleam, no vein of bright fire: that's just Old Testament stone that hasn't felt air or seen light, undisturbed for more than two billion years. This is as close to the centre of the Earth as we can get. The rocks down here can reach forty degrees. The piles of wood buttressing the ceiling stuffed with metal bags, inflated with water to jam them tight, lean and strain at mad angles. The stout, wound jacks, their metal elbows aching, strain against the ceiling. Within a day the earth's pressure will compress them, inch by solid inch.

This face is blasted new every morning, the supports are ad hoc, the mine chases the shoreline of this ancient beach. The miners work along the slanting stope of ore, the lights on their helmets make the shadows dance and stutter, eyes and teeth and black sweat gleam. It's a scene of theatrical chaos, medieval illustration, biblical, mythical. It's a devil's cathedral. If the root of all evil is the love of money, then this hole is where they planted the taproot. This is the bargain basement of sin, the adoration of all lucre, the well of avarice; this anaerobic blackness harbours the metallic seeds of progress and civilisation and the wide-eyed yearning that still sends men billions of years back underground.

I'm in a space that's a metre high and drops or climbs out of sight after about thirty feet. I look up and the oven rock touches my nose. A black miner, naked to the waist except for a string of good-luck charms, taps my shoulder and I take up a drill like a Lewis gun with a ten-foot bit attached to the barrel. It's driven by compressed air and cooled by water. A man behind me supports the snaking power lines. I push the trigger; it howls and spits with a horrific torment. The noise careers around this slit in the rock, looking for somewhere to escape. Slowly it spins a hole in the reef. We drill a hole every yard; I ask the gang boss what they put in them. He throws a foot of plastic-bagged grey sausage of sticky putty at me. This is the explosive. Is it fired electrically? 'No, we have a half-hour fuse.' Do you use a warning whistle or horn? 'No, it's done at a specific time.' So you make sure everyone has a watch? 'No, the team leaders make sure everyone's out.'

Although all I can see around us is a team of ten or twenty miners, actually down here, above us and below, in front and behind, burrowing along a myriad of wynds, there are 10,300 souls, working on faces stretching miles from the main shaft. Every day they blast new faces; every afternoon the next shift collects the rubble. There is an unmappable filigree of years of tunnel, blocked and collapsed, healed and gaping underground.

An engineer back in London described deep mining to me as being like that game where you stretch a tissue over a glass and place a coin in the centre, and then burn the tissue with a cigarette, trying not to make the coin fall. Every blast alters the geophysics of every bit of the mine. The tensions holding the ground up are constantly readjusted in a way that is impossible to measure or predict. Down here you think that perhaps the only thing that keeps it from crushing out the light and the air is the vanity, the sheer naked desire of the mystical power of gold.

We walk back to the main tunnel and wait for the lift. The miners are mostly black, but not necessarily South African: they're drawn here from Mozambique, Botswana, Zimbabwe, Lesotho and

Swaziland. There are eleven official languages in South Africa, and underground they speak a twelfth: Fanagalo, a made-up tongue broadly based on Zulu. The white mine executives are shifty about it – embarrassed. Fanagalo is old South Africa, the racist sound of apartheid. It's the voice of orders, masters and servants. Officially the miners speak English, but Fanagalo is what they call out down here in the dark. The white miners are mostly specialists and officers: big Afrikaners with unconsciously gay moustaches. They tower over the small black Africans. The relationship between them is both touching and strained. The body language of each group is defensive; there is an exaggerated courtesy and patronising smiles, but little eye contact. Even their handshakes are different. The Afrikaners squeeze your knuckles so you'll never play rugby again; the black Africans shake your hand and then grip your thumb, a gesture of welcome and solidarity.

The lift has got lost, so I sit and talk to some of the miners. Crespo, forty-four, from Mozambique, starts teaching me Fanagalo. *Molo* (hello), *sphoku sphoku* (stupid), *hamba kahle* (go well). He speaks good English as well as Portuguese, Afrikaans, Sesotho, Shangaan, Tswana, Inhambane, Ndau, Swazi, Zulu and Xhosa. 'You say you speak twelve languages?' a white miner interrupts. Crespo looks away and shrugs. 'Really?' The white man raises his eyebrows, juts his chin. His look says: 'You can lie to this soft, liberal English journalist, but don't think I don't know you.' Have you ever been abroad, I ask him, to cut the atmosphere. 'Oh yeah,' he says, misunderstanding. 'I've travelled all over this country. I've been everywhere.'

The friction wasn't just between whites and blacks in the mines: there were vicious, bloody inter-tribal wars. The men's dormitories were segregated by allegiance and there were battles underground, gangs waving crowbars like assegais, chasing each other like moles.

The lift finally arrives and there are a hundred or so miners waiting to go up. A delicate, smiling black man in the huddle says he's a trained geologist, but he can't tell anyone here, because they're only hiring unskilled miners. 'It's no good in this country, no good with my skin,' he whispers. But then everyone in South

Africa with a skin could say that. The wire door clangs open and I'm pushed by helpful hands into the back of the cage. And silently, as if by convention and ancient habit, all the white miners rise to the front of the crowd and squeeze in. As the door closes, one black chap in a hurry pushes in; a fat, aggressive Boer shoves his sweaty-bearded face up close and screams questions and abuse. It's pointless and unprovoked bullying, perhaps for my benefit, probably just for fun. It gets no response, so he turns to teasing a mate who is phobic about the lift. Finally we step out into the bright, clear, warm sunlight of the high veld in autumn, and the world seethes with colour. I hadn't realised how muted and monotone Hades below is, nor noticed how gloriously blue and domed the sky is. The miners stream past as I look up and slowly spin like Julie Andrews.

At Kloof mine they get nine grams of gold per tonne of rock, and they extract 34,000 kilos of gold a year. That's a lot of rock. Much of refining is about reducing that volume. The ore-bearing reef is brought up from the face and tipped onto a conveyor and fed into huge silos. From the silos, it's moved to spinning drums like tumble-dryers the size of Bovis homes. Inside these are rods or steel balls; water is pumped in and slides out as a thin slurry, which is then treated in great vats with cyanide and carbolic. This is filthy and dangerous. I walked on a gantry round the top of one of these vats at night. It was ten storeys up. A soup of rock and poisonous water was bubbled with compressed air. It was very scary.

The gold is then transferred to carbon, in the shape of burnt coconut husks from Sri Lanka, and baked in ovens. The resulting grey ash is taken to a hangar that's half-demolished, with ecclesiastical light streaming through the holes in its ceiling. In the middle of this huge room is a smelting pan, and dropped into it are three white-hot elements that turn the metal to liquid. The pan steams and glows white. This is the central mystery of gold. Very few miners ever see this, the final act, the consummation of the drama. The heating elements withdraw, and slowly the pot is tipped sideways. Over its pouting lip trickles the neon-white-and-yellow ore. It smokes and bubbles and moves like live eels. It slips into moulds on steps; the molten metal falls from one to the next. This is the dance of gold, and it's as mesmerising as it's been for 7,000 years.

Gold-mining was the first industrial job. Men were watching the magic of the bright, molten gold before they'd learnt to write. Gold is bewitched and murderous and exciting – it's the antidote of divinity and holiness and selflessness – but gold gets things done. It's the measure of achievement, it's the spur and the reward, and it's been the answer to the meaning of existence since men first asked the question.

The ore cools in the brick mould, then is tipped out with a dull thud. A miner in rubber gloves picks it up, puts it in an incongruous kitchen sink and starts to scrub. A shell of base dross falls away; the bar shines, yellow, golden. It's fascinating. Out of that black, hard rock emerges this stuff that never tarnishes, never rots, never rusts, that glows for ever. All the gold ever dug still exists, except for a couple of ounces burnt off the nose of the space shuttle. It's all still here, the riches of Troy and Egypt and Babylon, the jewellery of Rome, the vast treasure of the Andes and Central America; pirates; doubloons and empires' sovereigns; wedding rings, the regalia of kings and the teeth of pimps; the wealth of nations and the confidence of currencies.

It's in vaults, in mouths, on fingers, in ears, in gardens, in secret crevices, under the mattress or the floorboards. We dig it up and polish it and hide it again. And if that's not madness, then it's golden. And of all the gold that was ever mined, 40 per cent of it has come from here, out of the Rand on the high veld. Since the 1880s, South Africa has smelted 1.6 billion ounces of gold, and you know what? There's the same again still down there, underground, in the blackness, waiting.

Nobody told me I'd need a sarong. The girl at the desk with the open-heart-surgery scar down her impressively toned chest never mentioned it. She just looked at me with a touch too much wide-eyed surprise and said, 'So you're going to do the African-dance class?' and then paused a beat too long before adding an open-heartfelt 'Well, *good* for you'.

The others have all got sarongs. We're standing in the basement of a Crunch gym in downtown Manhattan watching some strange and extreme form of callisthenics reach its epileptic climax through the picture window. It looks like an exercise in existential drowning. When three fat, dripping girls waddle out, we terpsichorean Africans traipse in barefoot, because that's how Africans are.

What makes African dance special, I'm told, is the live music. Turns out to be an unmatched pair of bongo players: one an old hippy who smells so strongly of marijuana he could be an air-freshener in a glaucoma outpatient clinic, and the other looks like Scooby-Doo's less bright friend. Neither has any discernible or indeed compatible sense of rhythm.

The teacher is a spry, bouncy lady whose enthusiasm is two feet taller than she is. She's about as African as matzo balls. We all find our personal space. I'm the only man if you don't count the androgynous, hip-swinging little minx making like an Egyptian up front. If you tied any two class members together, I'd still be the eldest by a decade.

We start with some 'simple warm-up moves'. 'And *step*, and *step*, and hands together and *dip*, and *shimmy* . . . Got that? This is the dance they do in Africa when they're sowing the fields.' The rhythm boys chase a beat that's way ahead of them, and we neophyte Nubians undulate across the room.

All my shimmies and dips get tipped into the field in a confused heap, and I consider, not for the first time, how strange it is that we so often connive in our own humiliations. I'm British, divorced, and I went to boarding-school, so there's not much you can tell me about humiliation. But African dance as exercise is on another level of humbling altogether. I feel light-headed with humility, and I keep thinking that it'll get better, that I will sort of rise above it and see myself dispassionately. But what I see are the lumpy, cropped boys outside doing repetitive things with their man-breasts and smirking through the window as I attempt to dance 'as the women going to fetch water – and *glide*, and *glide*, shoulders back, and *glide*'.

I can unequivocally say that this is one of the top five most abysmally, hyperventilatingly, throbbingly appalling experiences of my life. The only small ray of consolation was that I wasn't alone. It's not just me being humiliated, it's the culture and inhabitants of an entire continent.

Why are we doing this? Why are these dumpy little girls spending their Friday evenings gliding and dipping through an open audition for *Springtime for Idi Amin*? It's not that they're all African-Americans doing some *Roots* thing. Most of them appear to have Central European and Middle American genes that have shortchanged them in the leg department but been generous with the buttocks.

New York takes gyms more seriously than any place I've ever been. Everywhere has them, of course. People all over the world work out, but it's not the same. The closest is Rio, the vainest city on Earth, but there it's all about the beach and being or pulling the girl from Ipanema. But not in New York, where everyone dresses four sizes too big in one of the city's two colour options – black or basketball.

Drive down the canyons of Manhattan, look up at the plate glass, and see the serried ranks of treadmill runners, roadless cyclists, snowless skiers and riverless rowers. Like animated, sweaty shop dummies advertising something. Not fitness. Not health. But more a Marcel Marceau mime of getting on. Personal progress.

I spent a weekend in New York gyms trying to discover, uncover, exorcise what on earth New Yorkers thought they were doing. All glossy-magazine day-in-the-life profiles of plutocrats and role models start with exercise. It seems that if you want to move and shake you must first move and shake, run and pedal, play tennis with a rented opponent, or swim hither and thither like a hungry guppy. And it's the received wisdom that you must do this earlier than everyone else. In Get-Up-and-Go-Ville, being up first is vital. So I imagined that at six-thirty on a rain-razoring, howling grey morning what I'd find at Chelsea Piers – the huge sports complex on the site of the docks the great transatlantic liners used to call home – would be wave upon wave of ravenous, clear-eyed, square-jawed CEOs of tomorrow. Actually, what I found was not so much the worm-ravenous early birds but fugitives from the cuckoo's nest. People in a gym this early are obviously too disturbed for sleep. They have pedalled and run here, driven not by dreams of power and lucre but by demons and powerful prescriptions.

Near the spot where Einstein first set foot in America, I jogged in line watching the banks of silent screens beaming breakfast mayhem and MTV, while on both sides of me barbed-wire-skinny women sprinted along having animated conversations with the weather forecast. On the running track a gasping man in black socks scampered around the inside lane constantly looking over his shoulder for pursuers who were never there. This is not an exhilarating start to a focused day, but the compulsive repetitive behaviour and self-medication of the lost and the losing. Not people you want to find yourself naked with in a confined space.

And I must admit that I have mild locker-room phobia. I can't do collective displays of smug penises. I can't manage that lolling stroll to the showers – a chap wearing nothing but flip-flops and clutching a plastic man-purse looks absurd whatever the state of his pecs or the girth of his schlong.

I do secretly envy men who can unselfconsciously sit cupping their testicles while discussing hedge-fund management or some awesome new stretches for avoiding groin strain. But I have a rule: never talk to a damp man without underpants on. The eye contact gets way too intense. I don't think this is the whisper of a gay thing, but rather the loud 'Yo'-ing, backslappy, hairy-buttocked, yellow-toenailed, hetero thing. Like most Europeans, I feel effete in extreme male-bonding situations. For gay men the changing-room is a stage hallowed by familiarity. It has a wealth of literary and video association. It's a theatre set. The changing-room is homo-Stratford-on-Avon, and a lot of the ones I visit, intended or not, play up to the dropped-soap, towel-biting-décor theme. And in a nation famously devoted to comfort and excess, why are the towels always too small?

Fitness is a class indicator. Slimness is a measure of power and prestige. We know that rich people live longer than poor people. There is also research indicating that conspicuous consumption and achievement are linked to longevity. Survival is the only true measure of success and, statistically, a man with a four-bedroom house is likely to get a longer stay above ground than a man with three. An actor with an Oscar enjoys more encores than one without, so it may seem that simply having a membership to the right gym can lengthen your mortal coil before you've even straddled a Swiss ball.

The type of exercise you choose to do indicates the type of person you'd like to be taken for and the style of life you aspire to. Hefting weights is for movie actors, waiters and those who miss prison. Martial arts are for men with ponytails and silver-tipped cowboy boots, and women who grow their own food and apply their make-up with chopsticks. Old-fashioned boxing is cool, but only if you promise never ever to actually box anyone. Now it's done almost exclusively by women and is particularly popular among six-foot-two-inch models. I watched a trainer with hand pads bellow, 'Come on, hurt me, hurt me – *harder, hurt me,*' at a beautiful spindly girl who grunted and swung haymakers. 'Come on, hurt me. You're not hurting me, *hurt me.*' Exhausted and dripping, she shrieked back, 'I'm not going to sleep with you *ever again.*'

Competitive balls – golf, tennis or squash – are so blatantly bankery and businessy. Competitiveness is so Bush, so Texan, and the clothes and accessories are embarrassing. Yoga's good. It gets you lithe and firm without looking like you're on parole. And it has a touch of spirituality without the inconvenience or embarrassment of having to believe in anything. But it's like playing bridge – everybody who does it has been at it for years. It's difficult to just jump in, and in modern gym terms it has one fundamental flaw: you can't fake it. And gyms are all about cheating. Cheating age, cheating death. But you can't pretend to be standing on your head. You can fake Pilates, though, which is why it has the metropolitan edge. So I went to Equinox in the West Village to do Power Pilates.

The man at the door with the wifebeater tank top and multiple piercings, and a demeanour that implied a boxed set of *Will & Grace* on the bedside table, was marvellously rude. It's an indicator of the social standing of gyms. I bet when they were all cauliflower ears instead of avocado conditioner, when they were for boxers who actually hit one another and Catholic boys' clubs and men with anger-management problems, the guy at the door was a sweetheart played by Walter Brennan. Now it's like getting a table at Da Silvano on a Saturday during Fashion Week.

Power Pilates is a fashionable workout with intellectual pretensions. I get down to it under the supervision of a nice lady who minutely corrects my posture on a lot of machines that look like they were bought from the Berlin State Circus and originally involved poodles and doves. We talk about Italy, travel and food, and generally sound like we're reciting the box ads from the back of *The New Yorker*.

The thing about Pilates is that you have to have someone standing over you because a millimetre's deviation from the prescribed position means it's all utterly wasted effort. And another reason is that, if there wasn't someone fit holding you down, wittering on about the dear little honey shop and San Gimignano, you'd run screaming into the street.

Pilates is without a doubt the single most boring thing you can do lying down. It is the physical embodiment of reading Henry James in Spanish on a kitchen table in your underwear. Apart from that, if you do Pilates correctly three or four times a week for a mere couple of years, you'll never need to suffer lower-back pain again.

After Pilates, I had a couple of hours before the horror of African dance, so I went to Nickel (pronounced Nih-*kell*) – an all-male spa and grooming salon. On the face of it there's no reason men shouldn't clean up as nicely as women. There's no rational argument against male cosmetics that doesn't rely on sexism, fundamentalism or homophobia. And they've made Nickel as gravely-voiced and reassuringly masculine as possible – but then, when you see a line of blokes waiting for a manicure next to the waxing price list, you know that, irrationally, this isn't comfortable. They're all in their twenties and thirties and nonchalantly flicking through copies of *Aviation Monthly*, *Monster Catfish* and *Off-Road Driving and Shrieking*. But they ain't fooling no one. They're more self-conscious than patients in the waiting-room of a genito-urinary specialist in Salt Lake City.

I realised while walking around the cosmetics shop, willing myself to want nurturing post-shave balm, eye-bag revitaliser or even a back, sack and crack wax, that we're not evolved enough to do this yet. For women, it's part of who they are. They can have their nails done in a shop window. They bond over this stuff. No man wants some other guy to say, 'Hey, where do you get your chest waxed, dude?' or '*Nice* matte foundation, bro.' A woman is happy if you notice her manicure – a man would be mortified. Nickel is a secret vice. It's a cross-dressing porn shop.

First thing next morning I'm back at Crunch for a spinning class. It's Saturday. Most normal people are having a second cappuccino, doing some window-shopping, thinking about lunch. Here in a basement that looks like an underground car park, forty of us perch on cycles nailed to the floor. Our invigilator is an enthusiastic (of course) woman who's short and round and, to be perfectly honest, not a great physical advertisement for pedalling on the spot. 'Are there any virgins here?' she shouts into her fast-food-drive-through head mike. I put my hand up and so does a blond boy next to me. We smile at each other feebly. For a moment I think that maybe this is a joke and she's going to say, Hey, but you can ride a bike, can't you? But she comes over. 'Boy, are you in the wrong place – this is the toughest spinning class in the city. These guys are *mad* . . . really out of control. They bring their own saddles and pedals. Whatever you do, don't try and keep up. Take it easy. And if you feel like you're going to pass out or be sick, stop, drink water.'

I'm afraid to ask how you keep up or indeed get ahead on a bicycle that's screwed to the ground. But off we go. *One, two, three*, and Gloria Gaynor is still surviving at maximum decibels. The teacher screams encouragement and threats. We pedal for our cardiovascular lives. Too late, I discover that the flyweight wheel will snap your ankle if you try to stop. For the next hour the class is transported by '70s and '80s disco and heavy metal. The 'mad for it' section whoop and scream and stick their Lycra bottoms in the air. This is as close as most of us non-Hindus will ever get to knowing what it's like to be a hamster. It's a mechanical chorus line, and if they ever make a musical of the Tour de France, this is what it will look like. If you could hear yourself think, you'd probably be saying, 'After 10,000 years, how did civilisation arrive at synchronised cycling in the basement to disco music?'

As we finish, I ask the blond virgin what he thought of it all. 'Well, it's OK, but it's a bit hyperactive. I'm going back to aerobics. You should come.'

Upstairs, amid the resistance machines and weights and little juice bar, I sit and watch. One of the mysteries of gyms is why the customers don't look fit. Why aren't they handsome and beautiful and well made? Collectively, people in gyms look no different from people who never go to gyms. They're just more extreme around the edges. In here, you'll come across more anorexics with furry faces, more lopsided blokes with un-ironic tattoos who look like tights stuffed with ground beef and snails. You won't see any elegance or poise or style – just a lot of women with sloping shoulders, sagging breasts, puffy red cheeks, wobbly buttocks, pinched faces, bony chests, sinewy arms, dead eyes, gritted teeth and breath like an open grave.

The great misconception about gyms is that they're palaces of vanity, theatres of self-love, where the shallow preen and pump in front of ten-foot mirrors with devoted narcissism. Actually, it's precisely the opposite. Gyms vibrate with self-loathing and doubt. The mirrors mock. People come because they're disgusted by or frightened of their bodies. Going to a gym is an admission of failure. It's the realisation that you're not forever youthfully regenerating. Your body isn't a temple to fun and fornication any more; it's a decrepit, leaky, condemned shell that is decomposing faster than you can shore it up.

No one is more dissatisfied with their corporeal cover than the gym junkie. The faltering esteem and masochistic self-criticism get ever more myopically lacerating. There is no end to it. No rest. Because age inexorably creeps on. Death is still the safe bet. The gym is a confessional, where they take their weakness and guilt. The hangovers and doughnuts, the sad middle-of-the-night icebox raids, the black, incoherent fears of cancer and stroke and ending up like Dad. The average age of people in gyms appears to be between the late twenties and mid-forties – the years of maximum torque and worry and the realisation that your career was a mistake, your marriage was a mistake, the kids are a mistake, and from now on it's all a sliding scale of compromise and disappointment. Gyms aren't happy, adoring places; they're hard religious metaphors and symbols. The panting grunts are the prayers and pleading of penitential flagellation.

My last class was by far the weirdest. Up a flight of stairs in a knocked-through room in Midtown they do Bikram yoga. This is an extreme form done in an oven. Industrial heaters are slung from the ceiling, belting out a temperature way into the hundreds. For an hour and a half a dozen of us sweat gallons. The smell is fearsome, the pain almost intolerable. If you've ever wanted to know what being in a Japanese prisoner-of-war camp was like, or how it feels to be a self-basting chicken, well, I imagine this is pretty close.

I found out what leaning forward and hooking both big toes with your index fingers felt like – surprising, but not amusing and not worth repeating. The point is that the heat loosens your joints so that you can achieve poses and positions you've previously only seen on the walls of Indian temples performed by clusters of priapic demigods.

I was told afterwards that this slipper hubris is more foolishly dangerous than being a quarterback in a tutu. The chances of unhinging a connection are excellent, but I'm transfixed by our guru. He stands on a little plinth and encourages with brittle queenie irritation. He looks utterly extraordinary. The hair is neatly coiffed and quaffed. Sort of late Everly Brothers or early Gotti. His face – entirely innocent of wrinkles or blemishes – is the colour of sunbleached terracotta. He could be any age between thirty and sixty. It has a spooky blandness, as if all his experiences had been non-stick, but what's truly weird is that it's attached to a hairless, supple body wearing minute satin shorts that you would swear belonged to a fifteen-year-old-boy – except for the telltale varicose veins. He is the Puck of the gym.

If you worked out assiduously and looked after yourself to the exclusion of all others for decades, then this bizarre, hairless, ageless ethereal beige creature is what you might aspire to. This was the body at the end of all the gyms in the world.

Afterwards, I'm so desiccated and shaky I can barely dress myself. I have to sit on the kerb for half an hour. That evening I weigh myself. I've shed seven pounds in two days.

Sunny Saturday afternoon and the gyms are packed with youngish, hip-ish workers in their sloppy weekend kit. There's a palpable atmosphere in here. It's not exertion or pheromone or flirtation or relaxation. It takes me a bit too long to realise it's familiar. It's loneliness. It's the terrible subdued, self-contained, endured loneliness. Most of the customers aren't working out in a focused or deliberate sense. They do bits of this and that, lose themselves on the treadmill, push a bit of machinery, wander about, suck water bottles, watch and wait.

The great thing about exercise, its real blessing, is that it's not physical at all, it's mental. It demands just enough concentration to stop you from thinking about anything else – about yourself. It's white noise. If you live in Manhattan and you're under forty, chances are your apartment costs you two-thirds of your income. You work every hour the boss sends and then some because you've got to get on, earn more, live better. You didn't come here to lig and loaf. The one thing you give yourself as a perk, a treat, a lifeline, is this ridiculously expensive gym membership.

So you come and do some classes, spin a bit, jog on the spot, aerobicise while plugged into your iPod. There is the whale song of social interaction, little recognitions: 'How ya doin'?' 'Lookin' good.' It almost feels like a virtual party or a cool club – almost.

New York is the loneliest city. It doesn't smoke any more, it doesn't drink much any more, it doesn't do drugs, it's too rich and too expensive. The people who made the fun for the people who made the money have moved out. It's safe. But the city that doesn't sleep can now barely stay awake for dessert – if it ever ate dessert. Music's gone from something you shared in a dark room to a white box that hangs round your neck. Dance is no longer the vertical promise of horizontal desire; it's self-improvement. In a generation, New York swapped Studio 54 for an African-dance class. We don't just connive in our own humiliation, but in our own loneliness, too.

LAS VEGAS

There's one of those plastic laminated non-biodegradable notes in my hotel bathroom. It's headed, PRESERVE OUR FUTURE: 'Preserving the Earth's vital resources is something we can all take part in. In an effort to save water and energy and to minimise the release of harsh biodegradable [*sic*] detergents . . . please leave this card on your pillow and we will remake your bed with existing linens.'

I read it twice.

I'm in a hotel that has built a replica of Venice's Grand Canal – on the second floor, so that it won't wash away the crap tables downstairs. This is a city that blows up the hotels when they're slightly soiled, that sweats neon, that sprays ice water from the lampposts and puts dancing fountains in the desert. This is a place that when they started nuclear testing next door sold picnics for those who wanted to get a closer look – and held Miss Atomic Bomb contests with bikinis shaped like mushroom clouds. These are the people who are wagging a finger at me and asking me to be parsimonious with the laundry.

Well, welcome to Las Vegas – where irony just curls up and dies.

There are no clocks in Las Vegas. Time is as welcome as a temperance band. And they don't like windows much, either. Sunlight is a nag. The oxygen-enhanced, mortician's chilled air pumps sprightly through the perma-dusk, rolling over acres of slot machines numberless to man. They in turn chunter and twitter, halloo and burp, with a replete mechanical joy. A syncopated cacophony that sounds like a goblins' stockyard. It goes on ceaselessly; twenty-four unmeasured hours a day, seven nameless days a week. It is the song of Vegas, a tuneless choir, a turbine, a great bulimic consuming engine.

But if you really want to see what makes Las Vegas hum, where the juice actually comes from, then you need to get into your gold stretch limo and motor into the desert, where the temperature's touching 120 and the wind's fresh-baked from Death Valley. Out here it's hot enough to melt silicone implants.

Go on until you get to Black Canyon. Stretched across it like concrete biceps is the Hoover Dam, holding back the mighty Colorado fresh from carving the Grand Canyon. It takes your breath away. In its time, the Hoover Dam was a lexicon of superlatives and a directory of statistics. Longest. Deepest. Highest. Strongest. Farthest. But now what it mostly is is beautiful. Beautiful and moving. It's a staggeringly elegant, emphatically muscular paragon of form following function. It's one of the great engineering achievements of a mightily engineered nation. Amid its restrained dabs of Deco decoration is a plaque that proudly proclaims that the Hoover Dam was built 'to make the desert bloom'.

And then you turn around and look and consider what the desert actually grew.

From here, Vegas looks like the cover of a schlock science-fiction novel – you can just make out the Great Pyramid and the Eiffel Tower, the Doge's Palace and the New York skyline, all set in a desert. It's like a parallel universe. Here's Earth's doppelgänger. It exists almost lifelike – like life, but not quite.

If you're in the market for metaphors, the Hoover Dam and Las Vegas represent the contradiction, the dichotomy, the yin and yang, the Cain and Abel of America. On the one hand its amazing can-do energy, the guts and the belief in the ability to build your way out of depression, to conquer the West, the vision to weld, blast, and rivet a modern Promised Land out of hot air and rock; and on the other, that glittering Shangri-la of cynical exploitation. A place conjured not out of hard work but from luck, whose foundation is the fortuitous fact that, given a chance, pretty much everyone's guaranteed to be a loser.

In Spanish, Las Vegas means 'the meadows'. Within living memory there was grass here. But the water table has dropped. It's all dust now. Yet this is the fastest-growing area in America – 6,000 people move here every month. It fills two new phone books and a new street map every year. Suburbs sprawl over one another and down the valley; unnaturally emerald-green golf courses and gated hacienda-style communities with orange terracotta-style roofs sit box-fresh and spookily silent.

Many of the people moving here are old – they huddle in the icy shade. But why shouldn't the American Dream end up in an air-conditioned desert with golf courses and Krispy Kreme doughnuts and Celine Dion? Celine lives here. In a high-end, lockdown community, guarded by a squad of 'men in black', who are the only visible living things. There's an Italianate-ish hotel and a shopping mall, pristine in pastel shades that vibrate with a lonely boredom. The man-made lake and the putting greens are empty; not even a shadow would venture out into this heat.

Celine Dion, the woman made mega-global by an iceberg, has famously signed the biggest, fattest contract known to belted ballads to perform at Caesars Palace: a rumoured $100 million for three years and 50 per cent of the profits. It cost another $95 million to build her the Colosseum, a 4,000-seat circular state-of-the-artless auditorium. The acoustics are so amazing you could hear a tear drop. Its pride and joy is a new sort of smart rear projection that has the clarity and brilliance of a TV screen. It's very impressive, and as we wait for Celine to come on, they project a picture of the audience back at itself. We're entranced. We can't get enough of ourselves. Waving and grinning. Applauding our own wonder, breaking out into helpless self-gratified giggles. You can tell we're going to be a hard act to follow.

However elaborate, grandiose, and monumentally tasteless Vegas becomes, it is never going to be anything as astonishingly and monumentally tasteless as the people who come to visit it. For starters, it's the sheer size of them. These are the fattest people on the planet. Vast, lardy, adipose flesh, ladled into sweatpants and sports shirts; grotesquely ripe girls add cartoon plastic breasts as a moment of firm bas-relief between their gobble-gobble triple chins and the rolling savanna of their stomachs.

As a visiting foreigner I understand that fat is a measure of class here. But, oddly and unexpectedly, so is hair. The confections of intricate macramé, the weaving, haymaking, clipping, twisting, tying, fretting, teasing, lassoing, gluing and dyeing that go into these coiffures are remarkable, and it's all apparently extempore, amateur, home-made, created with the verve of frontier embroidery and done without mirrors. Hair lives aloof and apart. And for the men, their facial hair is an equally exuberantly vernacular that bears scant regard for the formal function of the features it swags.

Anyway, Celine finally comes on, and the audience drags itself away from itself and claps as best it can, with its hands full of napkins nestling pints of sticky cocktails and boxes of snacks to ward off the ninety minutes of rumbly pangs.

My guess is that most in this audience don't get out to live shows much. Just being here seems to be a jewel in some sort of bigger experience. Certainly Dion doesn't have to work hard to win them over. They're a sure thing. Not that that stops her – she doesn't so much project songs as implore them to leave her body. Those huge, overproduced, emotionally incontinent power ballads sound like the forced exorcism of goody-goody ghosts. You half expect – half wish – her head would swivel 360 degrees as that ungodly French-Canadian glottal accent sobs, 'Could taste your sweet kisses, your arms open wide.' For all her gym-tuned, dance-coached stagecraft, Dion still manages to look like the fat kid who won Weight-Watcher of the Year. Her body is corded and knotted with self-restraint. Her movements are over-rehearsed and picky-precise – more Prussian cheerleader than Martha Graham. She looks good for an age she won't actually reach for a decade and does that Vegas thing – begs. She begs the audience to love her with a naked, generalised, 'I'm everybody's' sycophancy. There's more than a hint of bunny boiler, a manic desire to please and a smiley-implied nameless threat if we're not appreciative enough.

In fact, her stage presence is a weird hybrid of Pinocchio and Buffy the Vampire Slayer. The show finally sinks beneath the applause during an encore of Celine, alone, howling on the deck of the *Titanic*. The audience troops out, stuffed but underwhelmed. Still grazing from tubs, hungry for the next gobbet of experience.

Next door, the dedicated merchandise shop will sell you any amount of Celine-ish memorabilia – books, calendars, coffee cups. Oddly, they all seem to have someone else's picture on them. Mostly a chubby, plain, brown-haired girl. Only a forensic scientist could make the connection between this Celine and the wind-tunnel face and tortured blond hair of the woman we've just seen. Dion has succumbed to the Vegas makeover.

It happens to all acts that end up on the Strip. They lose kitsch control.

There is some style gland that goes malignant in Nevada. The most famous example is how Rock 'n' Roll Elvis morphed into Vegas Elvis. It happened to Sinatra and Noël Coward. There is a museum here dedicated to Liberace, where you can look at his wilting and dusty capes and flares, marvel at his mirrored Rolls-Royce, peek between your fingers at his bedroom and wonder how this man successfully sued a newspaper for suggesting he was gay. And then, of course, there are Siegfried and Roy. Celine, incidentally, is beginning to bear a distinct resemblance to Roy – or perhaps it's Siegfried. Siegfried and Roy put on, without hesitation, the very worst speciality show I've ever seen. They do tricks so ancient and so bad that they must think we were all born yesterday. But then, compared to them, we pretty much were.

Visitors to Vegas adore Siegfried and Roy. They're an institution. They're like folk-dancers. Or folk art. And you have to be one of the folk to get the point. What else could explain adults' watching a nonagenarian in a leather codpiece whipping a giant puppet dragon for no apparent reason.

But everyone's really here to see the white carnivores, hoping against hope that just maybe, just once, the tables will turn and Siegfried and/or Roy will get to see the inside of a big pussy. Sadly, not this time. Siegfried – or maybe Roy – stands up, his voice syrupy with that authentic Vegas-style emotion, and says that their life's work is to breed these rare species that have already become extinct in the wild. Well, without going into the whole Germanic, eugenic, white-power-subtext thing here, do you think they really believe this? These sad animals are mutants; how long would a white lion last trying to inconspicuously blend into the Technicolor Serengeti? A white python looks like nothing so much as an elephant's tampon, but then you realise . . . well, of course! Las Vegas is their natural habitat. Where else in the world would be the environment for a Liberace tiger?

Dion's show is directed by a former member of the creative team of Cirque du Soleil. At the moment, there are three Cirque du Soleil shows in Vegas, and there are plans for more. One of them is *O*, at the Bellagio. The title is enigmatic. It could mean naught, nothing, zero. It's spectacular. It cleverly steals images from surrealism and children's-book illustration and mixes them with elegant and simple acrobatics and dance that rely heavily on costume and props. It is unencumbered with plot, character or narrative. It makes absolutely no intellectual demands on the audience whatsoever. It's a perfect Vegas commodity and the ideal evolution of the big lounge act. There are no stars. All the performers are immediately replaceable. The production can be edited without anyone noticing. It's Lego theatre. You add bits, take bits away, make it taller, shorter, longer, cheaper, more elaborate. There is no end to the fun you can have with this circus.

In one of the Bellagio's fine restaurants, the dining-room is unnaturally quiet; high rollers and their bored by-the-hour dates eat in comped formal silence. You can't help but notice that gamblers have very small stacks of words – and they don't like risking them.

I'm gripped by a party at a centre table: rough-looking men in matching goatees and Hawaiian shirts; women with exuberant hair and cantilevered chests. They're all solidly drunk. The man who is apparently the host rolls in his seat and shouts over and over, 'Porterhouse and Roquefort, honey ... porterhouse and Roquefort ... That's all the words you need to know tonight, honey, only the best tonight, only the best, porterhouse and Roquefort.' The other diners shoot daggers from under their brows. These trailer-gawky hoi polloi don't belong. They have their burger bars and fist food. Waiters hover with intent. But they *do* belong. More than the rest of us. This is who Vegas is for. The glitzy, fleeting imitation of highlife and good luck for the habitually, congenitally luckless.

Outside on the steaming Strip, little Artful Dodger pimps hand out business cards for prostitutes. 'Nature of business will not be shown on credit card statement.' They offer two-for-one deals. I haven't the nerve to ask if this means you get an extra girl thrown in or you can bring a friend.

Downtown, away from the Strip, lie the low, sagging, aluminium-and-cinder-block bungalows of Vegas poor. 'Slums,' the limo driver calls them. They wouldn't count as slums anywhere else in the world, but they're a definite contrast to the imported-marble-and-fibreglass wonders of the world up the road. Here, the time that's been banished from the casinos sits heavy and ticks away slowly. Storefronts are boarded up. In a pawnbroker's window the trays of chunky, 'lucky' diamond rings sit unredeemed, and unredeeming.

The wedding chapels advertise their past nuptials – Michael Jordan and Joan Collins (not to each other, as far as I remember) – and their special deals. The runaway brides hover in their tulle or Guinevere outfits. Best men and ushers sit in air-conditioned waiting-rooms like extras from *Blue Hawaii*, *The Godfather* and *Cleopatra*. The limo drivers lounge, smoke and flick through pornography. There are stuffed white horses, chariots, thrones, slaves, coffins and sequinned, bewigged and smoky-glazed Elvises. Across the road a porn shop advertises for dancers. No experience necessary.

If you want to love Las Vegas, if you want to imagine it as an egalitarian, glittering, high-kicking good time that can be had by all, then you have to pay it off. You need protection. You need to keep feeding it from a very deep cup of irony quarters, because the moment you lose the knowing irony, it's pretty rough.

This railway stop in the desert turns everything it grasps – energy, water, civilisation, art, marriage, talent, hard work – into dross and kitsch and sad, temporary, tacky junk. And it manages to do it without any élan, sophistication or sincerity. The longer you stay here, the harder it is to keep the smile pinned to your face. This isn't quite the banality of evil; it's just the cheapness of avarice.

In a neglected corner of town, where pick-ups slump in front yards and the air is thick with sunburn, there's an empty lot which collects the shards and fragments of old hotels and casinos, bars and restaurants. It's a cemetery, a boneyard of electric signs and neon, and there's something very peaceful about it. The billboards rest in the sunlight. The extinguished cowboys, giant cocktails, lucky clovers and cartoon mice all recline with an unexpected final dignity. A man apparently short on luck, holding a bottle in a brown bag, scoots through a hole in the chain-link fence and slides into the shadow of his lean-to home. It's a name: Debbie, written in script. It rests against a wall. 'I remember that,' the limo driver says. 'That was from the Debbie Reynolds Hotel – didn't work out.'

TEXAS

Where are we, I ask the boy at the coffee counter. 'Where are we?' he said, looking round the airport as if it was some trick of the light. Yes, where precisely are we? 'Kansas City.' Kansas City, where? 'Kansas City, Missouri, sir.' Why isn't it in Kansas? 'Because of its location, sir.' Right. Kansas City sure ain't Kansas, Toto. 'What?' Never mind.

If you ever happen to find yourself in the big middle bit of America, the big blue Republican bit where the states have straight edges and too many vowels, where men wear moustaches without irony and the women have names that sound like graffiti, nothing is quite what it seems. For instance, when the sprightly, pleased-to-be-of-assistance airline girl says your flight's direct, that doesn't necessarily mean it's non-stop. Which is how come I've landed in Kansas City, Missouri, when I expected to be in Dallas, Texas. I didn't want to be in Texas either, but Jeremy wants me to be there. Jeremy doesn't want to be in Texas; he hates it. But he hates everywhere and everyone in America. He hates it all except New York and Lake Tahoe and, bizarrely, Detroit, which he really adores. He says the places he loves aren't part of the place he hates. They're somewhere else trapped in America. 'Texas really is America.' I haven't the energy to point out that Texans don't think Texas is America precisely because it's not like New York and Detroit.

Size matters in America; it really matters in Texas. Here, steaks are bigger than heads, hats are bigger than umbrellas. Boasts are bigger than credulity and anorexia is probably a tropical disease. Dallas/Fort Worth airport is the size of Monaco. Three months ago they lost an Alzheimered transit passenger. She's still missing in there somewhere.

We go to rent a car and Jeremy gets into Yank-loathing top gear. 'Look at this. I mean, this is America.' Actually, it's a Cadillac with bald tyres and suspension like an Amsterdam brothel's waterbed. We bounce and slither onto the interstate while Jeremy gives the wheel sadistic Chinese burns and makes noises like a trainee longhorn inseminator.

We drive into the grey, flat, featureless vastness that is the heart of Texas. Sagebrush and stunted mesquite. A buzzard waiting for roadkill. If this is God's own country then God moved out some time ago, taking everything of interest with him. Only the road is wonderful. There is a unique excitement about driving across the States, and this road aims straight at a distant western horizon and undulates like a sad song. Journeys don't necessarily need destinations but they must have a soundtrack. I prod the radio and there it is, the sound of big hearts and small minds.

'Oh, for Christ's sake,' huffs Jeremy. 'You have to be the only person in the world who's actually made happier by country-and-western music.'

The billboards along the way become metronomic, a sort of Kerouacky poetry, lugubrious explanations on behalf of sticky ribs, prize catfish, mufflers, cowboy boots, motels with thirty-seven channels and, oddly, a recurring refrain for 'vasectomy reversal or your money back'. And then there's the sign for Abilene. Now, if you've grown up with cowboy films, Abilene's very name can fill a ten-gallon hat with romance. But it's a terrible disappointment. An anaemic place where no building has seen its tenth birthday, and the bouncy streets are deserted by everything but the bright Texan sun. There's not a cow or swinging saloon door in sight. 'See,' says Jeremy, 'this is what America's really like.' He beams with pleasure.

On the outskirts of town we pull over at Joe Allen's, a clapboard shack advertising 'the best steaks in all Abilene'. It's a lie. They're the best steaks anywhere from the Rockies to the Pacific. Fabulously musky with mesquite smoke, cooked in a tar-pit Hades of a kitchen by gangly good old boys who do party tricks and farmyard impressions. On the walls are cowboys about to propose to horses, and secret warplanes inscribed to God and the waitress by gung-ho pilots.

There's A1 steak sauce and warm corn bread on the tables. The customers at four in the afternoon are those American families who have to eat substantially every hour to stop themselves feeling deprived. In a corner are a pair of 'bikers for God', a husband and wife who easy-ride the state on behalf of the Lord. 'On a Harley,' says Jeremy authoritatively. The lady God-biker looks sad. 'We had a Harley once,' she says. 'We loved it more than anything,' they both say. 'But the scripture says thou shalt have no graven images, so the Lord burnt it to teach us humility. Now we've got a Yamaha. God be with you.'

I went to pay and asked the bomber-beloved waitress where I should leave a tip. 'We don't accept tips, sir, but thank you kindly anyway.'

'You see, that's what I really hate about Americans,' frothed Jeremy, 'they're so friendly.' You hate them for being friendly? 'That man, he just said, "Nice knowing you"! He's only just met me, how can he say, "Nice knowing you"?' Perhaps because he doesn't. If he did, he wouldn't. I think Americans are nice because they're nice. Jeremy thinks they're nice because they've been taken over by aliens.

The sun starts to set and the sky looks like a bad cowboy painting. The grassland begins to support a strange livestock – ungainly metal dinosaurs. The nodding rigs of oil wells, first in ones and twos, then in herds. This is the sticky black heartblood of the Texas oilfield. The dipping hammerheaded behemoths rhythmically suck up the liquefied remains of prehistoric fish. Oil is what made Texas rich, but only in cash. Middle America is by far the richest and the most powerful place on Earth, but in every other measure of human existence it's desperately poor. America didn't, in the famous phrase, go from barbarism to decadence without an intervening period of civilisation: it went from physical hardship to physical comfort without a collateral thought for aesthetic quality. Down-home America is the place that poor, hard-working, God-fearing people buy when they win the lottery, and I can't hate them for that, although Jeremy can. 'And another thing,' he rolls on, 'the whole world's being taken over by McDonald's and Coca-Cola and have a nice day and high-fives, health warnings, air-punching group hugs, the American dream, child-proof caps, cinnamon flavouring, Scooby Doo, comfy-fit, pledging allegiance, precipitation and baseball caps.'

Jeremy believes in the chaos theory of cultural imperialism but he won't allow that Americans have invented anything. What about baseball caps? 'Look at the label: made in Bangladesh, see.' So, America is taking over the world with micro-mall culture but none of it's really American? 'Just think of me as French,' he explains opaquely. 'If America's for it, I'm against it.' It would take a breadth of imagination that only Leonardo, Einstein and Tolkien achieved to be able to see Jeremy Clarkson as French.

I'm always astonished at the ephemeral impact of American culture imperialism. What will be left from America's moment as global top dog? Some benign films, a lot of pop music, jeans, the memory of odd food. Americans are, in my experience, enthusiasts at home but apologists abroad. I don't see a pandemic of popcorn and safety caps, I just see the transient power that, like electricity and cash, seems to vanish without trace. America's gift to the world is ideas, impermanence, the lure of the road, the new beginning and a heroic optimistic capitalism.

As the sun sets we reach Midland. Jeremy chose it for my lesson in the horror of real America because it's utterly typical. The local newspaper proudly sports the motto: 'Midland, the middle of somewhere.' This place isn't the middle of nowhere, it is nowhere. Back in London, trying to find a way to make Midland live on the page, I can't remember a single thing about it. Not one image, smell, sensation. My job is to look at things and describe them, and this has never happened to me before. Midland, Texas, is just ( ). Midland is famous for being President Bush's home town. Spend time on its forgettable streets and you understand an enormous amount about George W.'s weird world view. Everywhere else must seem so vivid, clamorous and shocking, possibly unnatural. George W. didn't just come from here – he left and then returned to marry a local, which shows a lack of imagination of stoically asinine proportions.

There's nothing to do in Midland, or precious little that isn't solitary, embarrassing, fattening and, if not illegal, then immoral. That evening in a roadhouse rib restaurant with the obligatory sign warning you that 'hidden guns are not allowed', the achingly nice waitress, says: 'I'm sorry, I'm going to have to ID you, sir.' Me? But I'm forty-seven. 'It's a rule, sir. I've got to ID everyone who looks under thirty.' I offer my passport. She holds it gingerly, and flicks through the pages of smudged stamps as if they were runic incantations. 'Okay.' But she's not convinced. 'What'll it be?' A Coke. 'All that for a Coke?' she laughs.

Jeremy's back in the groove. 'That's what I really hate, they're so stupid.' What? Not knowing which way up a passport goes? 'No, thinking you were under thirty.' It's not stupid, it's incredibly kind and nice, and she didn't ask to see yours.

I lied. There is one thing to do in Midland: visit the petroleum museum. This is Clarkson's idea of a joke. It is also his mecca, his spiritual home, his raison d'être. The petroleum museum is huge and expensive, comprehensive and incomprehensible. After two hours we emerge. Do you know how oil is found, extracted or made into petrol? No, me neither. We're not stupid, we're over-informed to the point of stalling. The high point of the museum is the petrol hall of fame, a collection of men who all look like the same man with a slightly different wig. Outside is the world's largest collection of oil derricks. We stand in what amounts to a scrapyard, feeling less than awe. 'You see, this is what I hate about America,' says Jeremy. 'They claim the world record when no one else is competing. Who else would be stupid enough to want the world's biggest collection of oil drills and take the baseball World Series? Which world would that be? No one else plays their stupid game.' They just wear their hats. 'I hate baseball hats.' I know.

Outside Midland, I discover the real reason why Jeremy wanted to come here: the Confederate Airforce. There's a historical oxymoron for you. It's a collection of old warplanes and naked ladies painted on aeroplane noses. He skips and coos. He's in Airfix heaven. Actually, I've never seen him happier than in Midland, Texas. If he had a spiritual home then it would be here with the petroleum museum and the Confederate Airforce and the great road to nowhere. Jeremy is the very embodiment of Middle America. Denim, motorcars, stadium rock, war movies, fast food, red Marlboros, instant gratification, anti-culture and television. His hatred of America is his most precious and polished possession. It keeps him warm, it defines him and it is also very American – illogical, implacable and tireless. If America ceased to exist he'd be utterly bereft. But it's difficult to disagree with him about the great gut of America, which is a hard place to admire or visit with pleasure. It is a country ardent for freedom that is relentlessly prescriptive. It extols individuality but chooses rigid conformity. It is aesthetically bereft but venerates the merest shard of culture; it invented freedom of speech but bans books and opinions. It believes in the great optimism of the American dream but behaves as if Armageddon were pencilled in for next week. I love it because out of this head-butting argument comes some of the most inspiring, creative, thoughtful and agreeable people – not despite the contradictions but because of them.

On the long drive back to Dallas we're stopped by a state trooper, all flashing lights and Ray-Bans. 'I'm giving you this ticket for speeding. Now, it won't go on any record. It's just a warning to help you drive more safely. You have a nice day, Mr Clarkson.' Jeremy drives on and I can tell that he's unhappy. He's disappointed that he wasn't spreadeagled over the bonnet and I wasn't given the full cavity search. The easy friendliness of the cop was unnerving. 'You know,' says Jeremy sadly, 'I am driving slower.'

We stop at a cowboy shop where an old man dressed in full western fig explains the intricacies of buying a hat: 'The quality of your hat is delineated by the number of Xs it has.' So a one-X hat is Boy George, and five Xs is John Wayne? He laughs at our naivety.

'This hat I'm wearing is 200 Xs. But they have a hat here with 2,000 Xs.' Jeremy and I just stare at each other. What can you say about a country that can find 2,000 calibrations of quality in hat felt but can't create one single beautiful thing? I laugh and he starts: 'Now, you see, that's what I hate.'

GREENLAND

Two o'clock in the morning, and I can't sleep – I'm too excited. I stare out of the window at the hunkered, dozing town of Angmagssalik. Little wooden houses painted pretty, bright Scandinavian colours huddle round a natural harbour in the lee of snow-blown mountains. It's very peaceful, very still. But something's wrong. Or rather, something's not right. It takes me half an hour to work it out. It's the street lights. The street lights are on. It's the middle of the night and the sun's out. It's the middle of summer. It's not going to get dark for three months, but they put the street lights on anyway. They glow enigmatically.

Out in the bay, the ice floes glide; ghosts of sea and mist eddy across the aluminium ocean and the pale faces of the mountains – it's all quite weird. Welcome to Greenland. The cul-de-sac at the end of the world where the lights are always on but there's not always anyone at home.

For most of us, Greenland is a place to be seen from 30,000 feet. It's the big nothing on the way to America. You look out of the window and there's Greenland. You go to sleep, you wake up; it's still Greenland. It's the biggest island in the world. It looks like a bit of the atlas that we haven't got round to colouring in. A white hole at the top.

There is no map of the interior of Greenland – there's nothing here to draw, just thousands of feet of ancient ice, sculpted by wind and temperatures that defy any form of life. Nothing lives up here. The place just keens and ties itself in slow, cold knots.

Greenland has four time zones – two of them don't even contain a clock. Size matters in Greenland. The great whiteout of the interior splits the country into east and west; west is where most of the 56,000 Greenlanders live. It's where the capital, Nuuk, is. It's cheaper to fly from east Greenland (where I'm sleepless, staring at the northern street lights) to Reykjavik, then on to New York and back again, than to spin across to west Greenland. Here in the east, there are barely 3,500 people stretched along a coastline that's longer than western Europe's; 1,500 of them live here in Angmagssalik. Down on the waterfront there's a jetty and warehouses where four ships a year come from Denmark to bring everything that the Greenlanders have that isn't made of bone, fur or driftwood.

People have lived here for over 4,000 years, yet they've never got further than half an hour's shuffle from the sea. There's something temporary about this little wood-and-corrugated-iron town. It's as if it were looking over its shoulder, waiting for the chill wind that will blow it back into the sea. They get very chill winds here. The Piteraq is a dry, Arctic man-killer that huffs at 200mph – harder than a tropical hurricane, with a temperature that will freeze the eyeballs in your head and turn your tongue into a meat lolly.

A hundred thousand years ago men started walking out of East Africa and slowly, slowly, they worked their way up and across the world, adapting to each new environment and climate, on and on into every thin height, every dank, sodden jungle, every scalding desert – until, finally, at long last, they got here. This is where the long march of men stopped. This is the finishing line. The end of the road. Here on the Greenland coast is the furthest reach of mankind. It's as bitterly extreme as we can manage. I'm looking out at the beach at the end of the world.

If you look at an Eskimo you see the adapted features of central Asia. Though nobody is sure, it's likely they originally came north from the endless Steppes and settled in loose, fluctuating and affiliated clans that circled the top of the world in Russia, Canada, Alaska and Greenland. They share variations of a tongue-defying language that is loath to use the space bar and has an immodest love of 'a's. Eskimo isn't a particularly insulting name, though

Inuit is now commonly used by liberals. The Eskimos simply call themselves 'the People'. Their name for Greenland is Kalaallit Nunaat – 'Land of Human Beings'. The possibilities of life here are skinflint-meagre, the margin for survival so fine that it's honed and whittled an existence of the most pristine minimalism. Eskimos live on the thinnest end of the world's wedge.

I get into the plastic dinghy with not a little trepidation. The outboard looks like it's been rescued from a washing-machine. The boatman, whose name won't fit into my southern-European mouth, but whom I childishly called Ron because he's a seal hunter – Ronseal – smiles and indicates that everything is just dandy. But it's freezing. Really freezing. I'm inside an oil-rig-industrial, thermal boiler suit with a prat-jaunty knitted hat I bought in Reykjavik, but the cold pinches and slaps my face and searches like a dog's nose for tiny chinks in my clothes.

Eskimos are, first and last, hunters. All Eskimo men hunt – or they dream of hunting. To lose touch with the white tracks and the blood in the snow is to lose touch with your culture. Hunter and Eskimo are synonymous. They mostly hunt seals. Only women fish. The seal is the staple. He is food, heat, clothes, utensils, mythology and conversation. We putter out down the fjord to sea. All around us the ice floes slide past. There is a glacier up here that chunters between 20 and 25 billion tonnes of ice cubes a year, some as large as country houses, others the size of briefcases. The wind sculpts them into dramatic shapes; the ice refracts the light and the carvings shine bright, butterfly-wing neon blue from the inside. It is the most astonishing phenomenon. Cameras never really capture it. The blueness is spectral. The ice floes appear out of the steely, violet mist that drapes and slithers across the water, one moment blanking out everything, the next revealing crenellated ranges of mountains that glisten against the mouthwash sky and make you crane your neck. The ice looks like the inverted moulds that all the world has been made in: there is the imprint of a huge piece of machinery, there a tree, a cow, a telephone box, a dining table – they all slide by, ghostly negatives of creation, glowing ethereal azure. In all my life I have not seen anything so startlingly beautiful and awful, so terrifyingly mesmerising, so completely other, all wrapped in a vast, fast stillness and silence.

Fog and ice deaden the air. It's more than silence: it's the inversion of noise, the ghost of sound. Utter and complete, a thick aural blank. We talk in whispers, as if the voices might be snatched from our throats. The ice floes stretch for miles out into the Greenland Sea. They baffle the waves and calm the water until it's as flat and smooth as a velvet shroud.

Ahead of us pops a green head. A seal. It's like a seaside glove puppet. Ron idles the outboard, pulls up a dirty, wobbly rifle, then shoots it in the face. The head turns sideways and a spigot of blood fountains gently into the unruffled sea. We race the forty yards to grab the corpse before it sinks. The waters curdle ink. Ron throws the little sleek body into a bucket and we burble on, playing hide-and-seek with little green heads.

It's their insatiable curiosity that does for them. Even if Ron misses, they come back, all bright eyes and quivering noses, to look at the strange creatures in the plastic ice bucket. I have a go, but the motion of the boat, the bobbing of the little heads and a natural squeamishness queer my aim and I miss, with an apologetic relief.

Plastic dinghies have replaced the skin-and-driftwood kayaks; .22 rifles have replaced the harpoon. Ron and his mates are real hunters, not nostalgia-heritage sentimentalists. They're from Greenland, not Greenpeace. And they'll grab anything that makes their lives easier and more efficient. GPS (global positioning system) and mobile phones have revolutionised their lives, saved hundreds from hideous, lonely deaths.

The original kayak, though, was an amazing piece of extempore engineering. Made from sealskin, bone and driftwood, it was attached to the hunter's coat. He could capsize and still be watertight. It is the ultimate minimal expression of form following function – energy-efficient, silent. But still, the kayak was the most lethal vehicle for its occupant. No racing car or chariot claims as many souls as the kayak. A generation ago, by far and away the most common cause of death among Eskimo men was drowning. If you fall into this water, even in the height of summer, you have about two minutes before the cold grips your vitals and bludgeons your brain, and you stare up into the ethereal blue with the great ache of frozen-to-death. Up here in the still vastness there is no margin for error, no wiggle room, no leeway between getting it right and dying. There is no learning curve, just knowledge or death. No 'better luck next time'. And in the end, everybody makes a mistake; everybody's luck turns slippery.

This is the thing you notice about Eskimos – their unwavering concentration. Every skidding footfall could be the one that breaks your ankle and leaves you a frozen corpse never to be found. This is what makes men stoical with a fatalism that is so complete it allows for neither optimism nor pessimism.

Seal meat is boiled or dried. Every house has a rack of stinking, blackened fillets, and it's fed to the dogs that are chained up outside in fractious, bullying teams that find small clefts and holes to shelter against the elements; surrounding are the chewed spins and skulls of seals. The Greenland husky is the only dog in the world that can live solely on a diet of snow and frozen seal meat, and it's probably the only one that's tried to. They're not allowed inside because they're dogs and because they'd overheat. A team and a sled is the highest acquisition of an Eskimo man. When the winter sets in and the fjords freeze over, the dog teams go out in search of more seal and bears. Being able to work dogs and being good enough to afford them is to have respect.

The Greenland Eskimos never made igloos. They have the wrong sort of snow, apparently. They used to build turf huts with stone walls that were seven feet thick with sod roofs. There were tiny windows glazed with seal bladder that let in a faint uric light. The roof was held up by wooden beams. The only wood on Greenland is the stuff that drifts here; tree trunks are of immense value. The lodges were a single room the size of a container that would house extended families; as many as twenty-seven people would live together, sleeping on pallets. Through the long winter the only light would be a stone lamp of seal oil with a moss wick. The food would be 'Oh, lovely, seal . . . '; the blankets, seal. They would stay here for four months – 120-odd endless, stinking, crepuscular days. How people live on seal meat without dying of malnutrition is a mystery. The Eskimos shrug and say: 'Seals seem to live okay, so if we eat them, why shouldn't we be okay?'

It's not worth arguing – they patently are okay. They spent their time in the lodges naked because of the fug, occasionally pausing to wash their hair in the communal stone bowl of fetid urine by the door. Considering the teacup-sized Eskimo gene pool and the close family relationship of everyone to everyone and the long winters, the darkness, the nakedness, the proximity, the boredom and the endless seals, it's astonishing that Eskimos aren't all three-toed, cleft-palated, blind, dribbling dictionaries of genetic distress. But apparently they're not. They're as hale and hearty and diverse as the rest of us. It is true that any male visitor from outside the community was traditionally pressed with as many women as he could manage as a sensible collective way of increasing the available DNA.

When the spring finally came in June they would rip the roof off the huts and let out the foul air. You can still see the humpy carcasses of the old turf houses all over Angmagssalik – nobody lives in them now, nobody spends four months incarcerated with their twenty closest family members and a lot of seal. Within two or three generations, Eskimo life has moved into wood-and-glass homes, though still many of them don't have running water. There's a post office, a Danish-built school, computers, the internet and a supermarket that has everything you'd expect in a convenience store, but at four times the cost.

Greenland is the most expensive country in Europe by an icy furlong. Everything comes by helicopter or the four annual boats. In winter an apple costs £1, a cucumber £3. Eskimos are some of the poorest people in Europe, and a large proportion rely on state subsidy and benefit from Denmark. The cost that matters most is beer – £1.40 a can. Alcoholism and chronic drunkenness are endemic. It doesn't seem to take much to get them walrus-faced, and there is no shame or prohibition against public drunkenness. The mayor can pass out next to the dustman, because the purpose of drink is drunk. And a good drunk is a comatose drunk.

On Friday night when the cheques are cashed, the chilly streets become a weaving, staggering train of silently concentrating Eskimos trying to make it to the next can of beer. Around the walls of the rudimentary pub, the drunks lean on each other's shoulders like collapsed wardrobes; one or two foreign mining engineers have come in to pick up compliant, vegetative women to have blubbery semi-conscious sex with. Outside, men lie crumpled, their faces stuck to the ground, grouted with snot, vomit, blood, dribble and expressions of mild surprise. Eskimos make passive drunks for the most part. Every man seems to concentrate on some internal gyroscope. In private, though, there is a lot of family violence, and endemic depression brought on either by the twenty-first century or by the absence of sunlight, drink and boredom.

One man follows me all evening, too pissed to talk; he shakes his head occasionally and looks with baleful disbelief until finally I leave him standing in the hotel hall, swaying and regarding his feet with a wild incomprehension.

The most obvious form of Eskimo culture is carving. Eskimos have always whittled practical things with a delicate, firm beauty born out of intense observation and the need of their sparse, rarefied world. At the dark heart of Eskimo myth and belief is the Tupilac. A summoned monster, a homunculus made in secret by an individual out of bone and incantations. It is put secretly into the sea, where it will become alive as a monstrous being that silently and stealthily searches out a named enemy and waits to kill him. The missionaries asked to see the Tupilac, but the Eskimos explained with embarrassment that they were far too intensely personal and awful to be revealed. But they could make these PR-rated imitations, and that was how their fantastic carvings in bone and tusk, of seal men, fish men and fearsome bogeys came about.

But imagine that. Imagine living in that gloom of the turf house, with its stink, its seal, its stories without beginnings, endings or punch lines, its shagging relatives, its piss hair, and finally a belief, a certain knowledge, that monsters, part fish, part man, were burrowing up through the floor to come and kill you in the dark. As if life weren't hard enough, the Eskimos had to go and invent a web-footed vendetta from the deep.

The only part of Eskimo culture that is purely aesthetic is their music. We went to see one of the great Eskimo musicians. An ancient lady with big hair who lived in a neat little house full of family photographs. She spoke a bit about her life and her father's reluctance to teach her traditional music, then asked if I would like her to change into a traditional costume. Eskimo music is drumming; in all those long nights they never got round to evolving a bowed, plucked, blown or tintinnabulated instrument, only a drum made of – well, you know what it's made of – and then only one type of drum.

The lady came back in her costume. I know it's not nice to laugh at other people's cultures, but there is a line behind which even the most anthropologically sensitive liberal can't contain the tickle of xeno-sniggery. Eskimo national dress is way over that line. What conceivable thought of couture hubris, what dressing-up-box exuberance, arrived at sealskin hot pants as an appropriate uniform for the coldest place on Earth? Sealskin hot pants with a fur bomber jacket and hood and thigh-high sealskin boots. Tom, the photographer, and I were unmanned by the worst, most painful lip-chewing, fist-clenching, toe-crossing, snot-snorting, corpsish giggling I've ever known as we helplessly shook in armchairs with bulging watery eyes when she began to drum and sing. The drumming has no rhyme, rhythm or reason. The singing follows no tonic scale, no identifiable melody; it is only reedy, ethereal keening. But the most gripping part was the faces. The old lady in hot pants pulled faces with the exuberant mania of someone with a wasp up their nose. By the time she got to the third all-time Eskimo favourite, which bore no discernible difference from or improvement on the previous two, I was sincerely praying for Ron to come and shoot me in the face before my internal organs burst, my eyeballs lolled on my cheeks and I swallowed my frontal lobes.

If human civilisation began with a handprint on African rock and reached its apex in the libraries, proscenium stages and vaulted ceilings of the great metropolises, then what the Eskimos had managed to wrest from the farthest edge of their physical existence is deaf flotsam. But then, that's not the point. It's their very survival that is their greatest creation. Their existence is the performance that commands an ovation.

Kulusuk is an island where Greenland's international airport is. It also has one of the weirdest flights of postmodern archaeology. If you drive up a winding military road a mile behind the runway, up a blasted cliff to the top of the mountain, you come upon a radio mast and a generating hut hawsed to the rock. All around are the rusting, wrenched remains of a US early-warning radar station. This was one of a chain of listening posts that were supposed to give us four minutes' warning and the continental United States twenty minutes. Nowhere was the cold war colder than in Kulusuk. The wind howls and springs through the wreckage like a mad child, an Arctic fox sidles through the rocks and browning steel, and I look out at the permanent dipping nearly sunset – or perhaps sunrise – that's pricked by the dragon's teeth of the distant mountains. In the clear air I can see far, far across the pack ice. The water is mauve and violet, the floes rose-pink and azure; it is as eerily splendid, as belittlingly beautiful, as any place on Earth. My face is numb with the icy nose of the gale; just as chilly comes the remembrance, the spectral fear of nuclear war. That white light that haunted the childhood of my generation. How close, how terrifying it seemed. Above Greenland's clockless ice cap, a B-52 of Damocles carved lazy, vaporous figures-of-eight twenty-four hours a day, day after day, throughout the 1950s, '60s and '70s. It was Mutally Assured Destruction armed with the end of the world.

In the scant one hundred years, Greenland and the Eskimos went from being a closed, self-defining, self-sustaining hunting culture without even metal to being the primary target on the nuclear hit list. Anyone who wants to feel the full, farcical, pitiful, chill truth of the hubris of geo-politics should pay pilgrimage to the early-warning station at Kulusuk.

Last winter the ice around Greenland's coast failed to freeze to a thickness that was safe for the sledges, so the hunters couldn't hunt the bear, and the seal and the dogs starved. It seems that maybe this year it won't freeze again. Some say that the south of Greenland will never freeze again. This would be a catastrophe for the Eskimos.

There are three indigenous political parties here; each clamours for home rule, autonomy and Eskimo rights, but, unbelievably, not one of them has global warming or the environment as a priority on its political agenda. I asked Ron and other hunters what they thought about the sea warming. They'd noticed small changes, things happening earlier, staying later, things shrinking and dripping, and they shrugged. 'It isn't an issue because it's not in our power,' one said. 'You must understand, hunters follow the tracks that are there, not what might be. Who knows what the winter will do, what the ice will be, where the seal and bear will go? There is only ever the bird in the hand.'

It's happened before, of course, in one of the spikes of temperature a thousand years ago when Leif Erikson led the first Norse farmers here, having made this place's one joke: calling it 'green'. There were no Eskimos. Then, as year on year the temperatures dropped, they returned with their bone blades and ivory arrows, slipping through the ice floes and the white mist; with their unsmiling hunter's pragmatism, they killed the starving scurvied snow-blind Vikings.

Greenland doesn't have time or days, or the past, or a plot, or a future, just the long track of a linear present. If the sea warms, if the glacier pumping 25 billion tonnes of ice into the sea turns into a big slush puppy, then the Eskimos will hitch their dogs and follow the bears that will follow the seals that will follow the cod that will follow the krill north, into the hideous, pristine white. One way or another they have all always lived on thin ice.

CAPRI

From the moment I first saw Candida, I knew I'd made a huge mistake. She was lying in the sun with a gaggle of other girls sporting improbably double-barrelled names. She was naked, not a stitch on, and she had the most beautiful figure I have ever seen. All the others were lumpy and exaggerated, with big plastic curves.

She was so obviously built for ogling, all top shelf and jewellery. They wallowed but Candida rocked. She was the real thing. Neat, sleek, ethereally pleasing. She wasn't just there to be looked at and boasted about: she was aching to go for it. Take you on the slicing, smooth, stomach-churning ride of your life. Candida was in a class of her own, the J class. And she was all mine for a week, to come and go at my bidding. To have breakfast with and, of course, sleep with. The big mistake was that I'd left it so long. That I'd lived half my life and never got off with a yacht.

With the arrogance of negligible experience, I jettisoned a long time ago almost anything to do with water. Frozen water as in snow, and wet water as in fishing, swimming, white-water rafting and, dear God, waterskiing. Water is not my medium. My natural propensity is towards drowning. And so I've arrived at my half-century never having done anything pleasurable in a boat. I've crossed the Channel, I've chugged up the Arabian Sea in a vomitous little steamship, and once I made a raft out of a door and three oilcans but wasn't foolish enough to actually get on the thing.

And I've made a virtue of my prejudice. I don't like boats,

because ridiculous people inhabit them. Appalling people, tasteless, ocean-going bores. There can be no tedium like listening to a yachtie blow his own wind, or some office-bound plutocrat coming over all nautical two weeks a year. The Mediterranean and Caribbean flotillas of pleasure-set motorboats look to me like floating bathroom equipment showrooms. Why would you want to consign yourself to a plastic tenement, crammed into a space that would be condemned as unsanitary and cruel on land? And the money, of course, is something else. The cost of bobbing in diesel, smelling liquid filth, is astronomical. Or perhaps that should be oceanomical.

No, no, I didn't do boats, until I saw Candida from the tender as we putted across Capri harbour. Now, marine anoraks will tell you Candida is not a pure J-class yacht, because she has a stick on her nose, or some such arcane technical minutia. But to me, and I expect to her, it doesn't matter a damn. She is one of the elite. That short-lived school of boats built in the 1920s and '30s to challenge for the America's Cup. There are only a handful, mostly designed by a man called Nicholson for titanically wealthy tradesmen who had ugly wives and more money than anything except style.

The J class are the biggest ever built, and by all rational terms they're ridiculous. Before mechanical winches, they took thirty crew to sail, but only slept a couple. They have masts so tall and booms so heavy that they are as delicate as china. They are fast but they take an inordinate time to pick up speed, stop or turn. In mitigation, they are utterly, beguilingly beautiful. The J class are aquatic supermodels.

On board, everything is warm wood and glowing brass. There are two well-appointed but catholic cabins. A saloon and a galley and, up in the pointy bit, a minute cupboard where the six crew and two anchors are stacked when not needed for rope-curling, brass-polishing or drink-serving. On deck, a canvas awning is stretched over the boom to shade a table and padded banquettes. But this boat's Edwardian luxury isn't gleaned from padding and pampering but from the confidence of performance. It just feels right. As Katharine Hepburn put it in *The Philadelphia Story*, 'She was yar alright.' Very, very yar.'

Naturally, the first thing I wanted to do was make her go. Get the canvas out, get her glad rags on. But the captain was a nautical man through and through, and he did what in my limited experience nautical men do best – he sucked his teeth, looked at the sky and said: 'Well, I don't know. The wind's here, but it might be there. The tide's doing this, but in an hour it's going to do that. The water might be too salty. The sunset's the wrong colour and I'm an Aries.' In short, we'll see. Why don't you go off and explore Capri, and perhaps we'll go later? Tomorrow, next week.

Capri is a pretty place, an island invented as a paedophile theme park by some rabid old emperor, where the main preoccupation of the maddening summer throng still seems to be looking and behaving as childish as possible. Once you've navigated the little whitewashed shopping streets, glanced at the same windows you left behind in Bond Street, eaten an ice cream in the little square, copped a snide glance at the mountains of heaving breast implants, and decided against the screechingly hideous carved coral cuff-links, you've pretty much done Capri. Anyway, my mind wasn't here, it was with Candida. This lump of hot, expensive rock was just the buoy to which she was tethered.

So, half an hour later, I was back. Please put up her shrouds. Please let's go. Having run out of teeth, the captain gave an order and the crew slithered hither and yon. The massive boom was effortlessly released from its rest, sails stuttered up the mast, we broke the cover of the harbour, and I swore I could feel her shiver like a greyhound. The curtain of sail took a tentative breath and became taut. Candida did what she was born to do.

Now, I'm not one who naturally anthropomorphises inanimate objects, but now I understand why we give boats names when we don't go baptising buses, bicycles, Tube trains or vans. Under your feet, this yacht felt as living as any born thing I had ever met. She curled through the waves, sunlight glittered on spume. The whole heavy thing heaved and became as light as a trumpet note. The island receded, and the biggest thing on the horizon was the late afternoon cumulus turning a soft pink, and I never wanted it to finish. I wanted to chase the bowl of the horizon for ever. Listen to the creak of plank and canvas and the rope slapping the mast. I wanted to live on the deck eating grilled fish and pasta with clams, drinking lemon and soda. Feeling my skin grow sticky with salt and turn the colour of mahogany. I wanted to suck my teeth with the best of them, because this was it. This was what I had been missing. This is what Ratty tried to explain to Mole. That there is nothing, simply nothing, as fine as messing about in boats. And it's depressing to realise that all your life you've thought yourself a mink but in fact you are a mole.

The next day, just after dawn, we slipped anchor from the lee of Capri and set *Candida* to patrol the rocky coast. I'd hardly slept, partly because of the rock and moan of the boat. The mast acts as a giant inverted pendulum, and it was new to me. But mostly I lay awake because I didn't want to sleep and miss any of the thrill of it.

The Amalfi coast is harsh and precipitous. It scurries into the sea as if this side of Italy had been torn out of a giant atlas. There are tiny white sandy bays only accessible from the water, and thin beaches where supine, oily Italians look like schools of noisy mermaids. Across the steep grey and amber hills, lemons and wild thyme grow, their scent wafting out to sea, along with the clamour of a dozen campaniles. We stopped where we liked, to swim or take the tender to eat lunch in little harbour restaurants, where I just watched *Candida* snooze from a distance. Or we went in the morning to buy fruit and have coffee and clotted-custard cakes in little town squares like the one in Amalfi, as perfect as a sentimental film set.

This quite conservative little town was once a great maritime nation. There's a statue to a local lad who may or may not have invented a set compass. The town's cross adorns the Italian naval flag along with those of Venice, Genoa and Pisa. We did all these things, but mostly we just sat and stared out at the distant ocean. On land, your horizon is rarely further than you can throw. One night as we went to bed, the thunderous clouds that had been gathering broke into a storm directly overhead. Through the portholes, the cabin strobed with lightning and *Candida* tugged and keened against her anchor chains, yearning to run with the wind. The rain careened across her deck and the sailors ran through the night securing rope and shutters. Over the gale the captain explained that, for some properly physical reason, lightning was unlikely to strike the inviting mast, which looked as if it were playing tag with the bolts. The chain that held us to the sea bed jerked and clanked with the strain. If once it had skipped free, we would have been smashed on the rocky shore in minutes. It was frightening and I wouldn't have missed it for anything. 'Awe' is an overused word, but in its old sense of catching a howling glimpse of the face of God, this night was properly awesome.

In the morning it was as if nothing had happened. Clear and warm and sparkling as before. Coffee and sweet rolls on the table. The thing I'd always thought about boats and the sea, why I never wanted to go out in them, was the assumed claustrophobia, the sense of being trapped. Marooned on this uppity, sick-inducing bit of wood. But the truth is, the sensation is quite the opposite: I felt released. Free to wander. Two-thirds of the globe is water, and in a boat it's all your garden.

Finally, of course, I did have to leave *Candida*. We said our goodbyes, shook horny hands, sucked our teeth and got into this suddenly airless, constricting smelly contraption: a car. What a horrid way to get about. It burped and growled along the coast road, and at every hairpin bend for miles I caught a brief glimpse of *Candida*. Splendid and free, basking beneath us. And for a week after planes and trains had returned me to the brick embrace of the city, I could still feel the soft undulation under my feet. And I knew that somewhere out there, with a magic synchronicity on the sparkling blue-green sea, *Candida* was swaying in time to the waves and the wind.

MYKONOS

Let's get one thing straight. Jeremy Clarkson. Clarkson is very straight. He's so straight you could grow soft fruit up him. If you put oil in his bellybutton you could use him as a spirit level. There isn't a kink, a curve or a rococo gesture about him. Clarkson likes to define himself by what he's not. And what he's principally not is bent. He's so unbent that there are those who might say he was actively homophobic.

But they'd be wrong. He's not homophobic in the way some are, say, arachnophobic. If Jeremy came across a homosexual in his bath, he wouldn't jump on the loo seat holding his nightshirt tightly at the knees and call in a desperate falsetto for his wife to come and deal with the huge, hairy thing. No, Jeremy feels about homosexuality rather what Neville Chamberlain felt about Czechoslovakia. A far and distant place of which he knows nothing; and, frankly, he doesn't care who buggers about with it, just as long as he's not expected to lend a hand. Though it must be said there is a sweaty whiff of the lower fourth about him. A touch of the schoolboy sniggers when it comes to queers.

When we first planned this article, he wanted to take me to Norway for the World Powerboat Championship. Well, you can imagine: all Heineken, herring and handbrake turns. No, I said firmly, you really don't need to get in touch with more high-octane petrol heads and their interminable back problems. You need to get in touch with some sexuality. Not yours; yours is best left sleeping under its rock. You need to reach out for someone else's. And so it was. We landed on sunny Mykonos. My own relationship with homosexuality is perhaps no less irrational than Jeremy's for a heterosexual man. I love it. Having been brought up in a theatrical family, I spoke Polari (gay slang) as soon as I could speak English. I'm drawn to camp humour, bitchiness and gay culture. I feel at home with everything except their genitals. My hard-and-fast rule has always been one willy in bed at a time. 'You know what you are?' a gay friend told me. 'You're a stray – a straight gay man. But there's still time.'

I haven't been to the Greek islands for a decade. Christ, make that two decades. But I have happy, sybaritic memories of them, and as we stepped off our little jet it all came back to me. The memories were despite the geography, rather than because of it. The Greek islands must have been made when God was going through his brief minimal, brutalist period. Mykonos is a sparse, crumbling camel-coloured lump. There are features, but none of them are interesting. The building material of choice, which the Greeks use with chaotic abandon, is concrete and breeze block. But then this is the only landscape on Earth where they look organic and harmonious.

Despite being mentioned in the *Odyssey* and Herodotus, and therefore possibly the oldest tourist destination in the world, Mykonos is principally famous for its very modern homosexuality. Since the 1960s it has been a mecca (probably not the right word) for young gays in search of a bit of the other, or rather, a bit of the same. Mykonos means 'island of wind', which you, like Jeremy, may find a sniggeringly funny joke for a gay resort.

The first surprise is that not everyone is homosexual. I don't know exactly what we were expecting. *La Cage aux Folles* meets Gay Pride week, I suppose. But as well as being slippery heaven, Mykonos is also Hellenic St Tropez. Athenian families weekend here and pay monumental sums for whitewashed Portakabins and rock gardens. They do that paternal promenading thing of getting all dressed up and strolling purposefully around town in the early evening. But whereas in Italy or Spain this would be a jolly occasion, a chance for young people to meet and possibly mate, here the families march in descending size, led by fathers who have the mien of minotaurs and glare at any male under fifty. They're followed by daughters who sulk behind thick fringes, their eyes streaming from the fumes of their moustache peroxide. Mykonos is obviously a place for dressing up. Not fashionably. This is Greece, after all. But making an effort. And plainly, oh, you can't imagine how plainly, Jeremy needs some holiday clothes.

I can't think where he thought he was going when he packed. A weekend's go-karting in Lincolnshire, perhaps? After an enormous amount of coaxing I manage to get him into a beach-front boutique run by a mere slip of a chap who immediately confirms all Clarkson's worst fears by asking him his star sign. Getting Jeremy to try anything on is more effort than getting Naomi Campbell to choose a wedding dress. Finding something he *could* try on is even harder. The small Asians who stitched this stuff can't have imagined anything his size outside of a Hindu temple. The waif-like shop boy regards his stomach the way a plumber regards a blocked septic tank. Then, with a little squeak, Clarkson dives into a corner and pulls out a pair of culottes. They fit. After a fashion. A long way after any known fashion. They are, without qualification or demur, the most appalling item of holiday clothing ever made. They can only have been designed for a bet. They're a patchwork of garish, oriental offcuts that look like a mental hospital's sewing bee's quilt turned into po'boy's clam-diggers. They come from the Waltons' cruiser-wear collection, and Clarkson adores them. He does little mewing pirouettes in front of the mirror. Out in the unforgiving sunlight, Jeremy saunters. I follow at an anonymous distance and watch as sensitive gay boys press themselves against walls to let this taste-apocalypse pass, just in case he's contagious. It's time to meet gay guys and they come out at night.

Pierro's is, they say, the oldest and most popular gay disco bar in the Aegean. It's a two-storey town house, set on a tiny square. We arrive fashionably early. I've managed to convince Jeremy to leave the Tennessee troll kecks in his room. And he's relaxed and ready for a night on the town. Except he's not. He's about as relaxed as a greyhound in the soft-toy department of Hamleys. He sits stiffly on a bar stool, clutching a beer, imagining he's insouciantly invisible in the way only a 6ft 4in pubic-headed, Spacehopper-gutted, hulking heterosexual in mail-order chinos and docksiders can.

After five minutes he hisses: 'Psst . . . I've been picked up.' Where, how, who, why? 'That man over there. Don't look.' He shrugs at a gaspingly beautiful olive-skinned, long-lashed twenty-year-old Greek boy with black curls falling over his shoulders, and a thin singlet barely covering a body that would keep a girls' school dormitory panting for a fortnight. 'He fancies me.' No, he doesn't. 'Yes, he does.' No, he's having a thing with the transvestite barman who's standing behind you. 'How do you know?' I just know. Gaydar. Gaydar is a queer sixth sense. 'But you promised, swore you were straight.' I am. I just inherited gaydar from my mother's side, and anyway I saw them kissing two minutes ago. Jeremy is not convinced. The only thing he is convinced of is that every homosexual on the planet is yearning to do the love that dare not speak its name (unless you hit your thumb with a hammer) to him. This, you will have noticed, is a common delusion among stridently heterosexual men. What makes you think gay men want to worship at the temple of your body, Jeremy? 'Well, they do. It's obvious. They're homos. I'm a man. I'm virgin meat for them. It's well known that what homos really fancy are straight, married blokes. I thought you were supposed to know about these things.'

Jeremy, let me say this with utter conviction. Trust me. Relax. Nobody here fancies you. Not on drugs, not for money, not remotely. Virginal and married as you are, you really aren't God's gift to gay men. You're not God's gift to straight women, either. In fact, you're not God's gift to anyone, except perhaps Colonel Sanders. The only thing that's remotely, attractively gay about you is your name. 'What, Jeremy?' No, Motormouth.

The bar begins to fill up. By 2 am it's a hog-throbbing, bouncy, smiley pick-up joint. Jeremy and I might as well be fire extinguishers. Apart from all the other stuff, we're just way too old. The age limit is severe – young men between eighteen and thirty who look like footballers. The street outside could be a Manchester United summer school. There are one or two overtly camp queens, but in general the desired effect is sporty and butch.

On a balcony next door, three taut Hinge and Bracket trannies strike Dietrich poses. They look as coyly old-fashioned as black-and-white movies. I get caught in a corner by a nice Spanish architect who intensely explains the gay blitzkrieg theory of culture. Apparently, all culture is trailblazed by gay men. They're followed by straight women, who in turn attract straight men, who make the scene passé and mainstream, so the gays move on and invent something else. I nod and smile and apologise for being here and messing the place up.

Jeremy has managed to find a pair of organically grown real women. They've just been married to each other in Vermont and are on their honeymoon. He gives me a wink. By four I'm exhausted by the relentless fitness and exuberance. I don't think I can stand another bump-and-grind conga in a miasma of Egoïste and Le Bleu.

We walk back to our hotel through the wide-awake town. I pass on the gay theory of culture to Jeremy. 'Well, they didn't make any Ferraris or the Mustang or the Blackbird Stealth Interceptor, did they?' No, I don't think gay culture stretches to engineering. Though they might have done the Teasmade and the trouser press.

'Have you noticed anything strange about this place, apart from all the puffs?' he asks. 'There are no drunks. No vomit in the streets, no fights, no screaming gangs. If this were northern Europe, the place would be awash with blood, piss and sirens by now.' And it's true. A recent US study found that gays were the least violent and aggressive men on Earth (beating Tibetan monks on a technical knockout). There must be more muscle and testosterone in Mykonos tonight than in a season of rugby league. But there's no trouble. In fact, gay men as a demographic are more law-abiding than the rest of us. More civic-minded, socially concerned. They vote more, earn more, clean up more. They read more. Go to more theatres. Consume more. Have better jobs. Better health. Pay more taxes. And are better educated. In fact, gay men are model citizens. On paper we should all be aspiring to be gay men. By rights, logically, we should hope all our sons were gay. There's just that one little thing. 'It's not a little thing,' splutters Jeremy. 'It's a bloody big thing. A huge, hideous, humiliating, hurting thing. And I'd rather live on a sink estate in Cardiff and ride a bike without a saddle.'

Next morning, Jeremy comes down for breakfast. So how did he enjoy his first gay nightclub? 'It was surprisingly good fun. Those two I was talking to.' The Velcro Sisters? 'Yes, the fuzz-bumpers. I was in there.' No, you weren't. 'I was, I could have pulled.' Jeremy, they were lesbians, on their honeymoon. 'Exactly. What's a girl need on her honeymoon?' Oh, good grief.

Today we're going to the beach. Now, how many beaches are advertised as being paradise? Plenty. All over the world, paradise is offered as standard. But here on Mykonos they've improved it. Here they've got Super Paradise. Super Paradise Beach is a long strand of grey gravel that swelters under an unrelenting sun. It's a bit like walking on the bottom of a goldfish bowl. At one end there's a bar that has a throbbing techno-house, garage, conservatory, granny-flat disco pumping continuously. The beach is gay-graded. It starts off as Greek hetero couples, drifts into international hetero singles, then Euro singles peeping out of the closet onto vanilla gays with fag hags, then very gay gays, and finally, up at the far end, very stern, serious, professional, alpha-male gays.

Jeremy leads the way until we're sitting pressed up against the far cliff in the middle of a seal colony of vast, oily, naked, predatory homosexuals. You'll have to imagine this. These men don't just have honed, chiselled bodies; they have the sort of bodies that no sport, exercise or lifetime with Twyla Tharp can contrive. These muscles are solely for the purpose of display, and they are staggering. Entirely hairless and greased up to shine like a motor show. Every time they move, a new bit of body pops up. These guys are human advert calendars. The comparison with Jeremy's body is as astonishing as it is hilarious. It certainly seems to astonish the rest of the beach. Only David Attenborough could swear that Jeremy and the gay men were from the same species.

Clarkson is Day-Glo white. Yorkshire white, with a tinge of blue. He looks like a collapsed wedding cake displayed in a mixed grill. The alpha gays don't do much except smoke and rearrange their muscles. Occasionally they saunter to the water until it laps their groins provocatively. Now, I haven't had the pleasure of a lot of willies all together since school. My, they've changed, and I must say I was astonished at the sheer variety.

Pubic hair is not completely depilated. It's tonsured into amusing little penile moustaches, which seen together rather resemble a group photograph of pre-1914 Austrian hussars. The penis is the one muscle that really doesn't improve with exercise or working out. I mean, there are some organs here that are frankly distressing. Bent, humpy-backed, varicosed, spavined, goitred, gimpy bits of chewed gristle. They've been so abused, they should be made wards of court and given their own social workers. The owners never leave the poor things alone, they are endlessly tweaking and arranging and straightening and fluffing up. Actually, it's quite funny. Like a lot of obsessive, surface-wiping suburban housewives rearranging the front-room cushions. All keeping up with the Joneses.

Do you know the difference between a heterosexual man on the beach and a homosexual man on the beach? Well, apart from the body and the back, sack and crack wax, obviously. A straight bloke walks into the sea and looks at the horizon. A gay man faces the beach. It's all about front. There is a constant scanning here. Everyone's staring and sizing up. Every time you look up, you make eye contact. 'I am an insecurity camera.' The gaydar is jammed with traffic. Even the gently frotting men in the surf look over each other's shoulders, sending out intense sonar messages. There's not much noise here. There's no laughter. Just a bit of low muttering. It's not remotely relaxed. It's not a holiday. This is a naked sales convention. Pure erotic capitalism.

After an hour, Jeremy's bored. He's exhausted his game of seeing how many euphemisms for back-to-front sex he can come up with. He points up a concrete hill. 'They keep going up there in ones and twos. Why?' Well, why do you think? 'Let's go and see.' This is it.

For him, this is confronting the great fear. The peek into the heart of Boy's Own darkness. This is what he came for.

So we trudge up the hill. Very separately. It's uncomfortably hot. The light is neon-bright and along the cliff there are men standing or lying. Entirely on their own, like dropped bits of gay litter, waiting to be picked up. It's Hampstead Heath without the trees and wet knees.

I get to the edge of a cliff and lie down. In the pale blue sea below, naked men swim lazily, looking perversely like they're in old Hitler Youth movies. About 20 feet away on a flat rock, a man with a body apparently made out of knotted brown pipe cleaners and bacon rind has laid out his towel. He's wearing nothing but black leather biker boots. Now who gets up and thinks: 'Nice day for the beach – towel, suntan cream, condom, biker boots'? He hasn't even got a book. He's here all alone like some Greek-myth punishment, marooned on this rock, chained by his libido. He stares at me, then slowly turns round and bends over; sporting a pendulous scrotum, he looks like a malnourished, shaved bulldog. I look away, then glance back. He's gently masturbating at me. More for effect than intent. I can't say I'm not flattered, then I can't say that I'm interested either.

Jeremy, sweaty and puffing, stumbles up. 'Have you seen . . . I mean, have you seen . . . ?' He's Bill Oddie after sighting a dodo. Yes, I've seen. You need a beer. So we go back down to a little hill-top bar above the beach where a waiter in a cerise mini-sarong, matching cut-off singlet and alice band serves lager and fried octopus. I look down at the supine, oily gravel and admit that I don't like it here. I find the constant appraisal, the naked audition, the mime propositions wearying and uncomfortable. And the pitiless eugenics of homosexual coupling are depressing and sad. There is no space here for the old, the fat, the ugly or the shy. The emphasis is on a particular style of physical beauty to the complete exclusion of imperfection, intelligence, humour, flirtation or courtship. Not that these things aren't valued by gays per se: they're just not packed, along with the condoms and biker boots, and brought here.

It's this little matter of zipless sex where gays and I part company. 'It's quite good here,' says Jeremy. 'I'm glad we came.' Well, that's him all over. The great contrarian. Never happier than when he's next to something he can tease and have a bit of a cathartic rant at. As I said, Jeremy's defined by what he's not. Here he's successfully confronted that last frontier – the pubescent boy's fear of homosexuality – and it's not that bad. He's not been gang-banged by the Village People. He hasn't caught a falsetto laugh or a burning desire to collect Lalique or an ear for show tunes. Best of all, they haven't asked for his autograph. He's finally found some butch blokes who blissfully couldn't care less about cars.

AMSTERDAM

The Dutch enjoy telling you that riding a bicycle is like having sex. Once learnt, you never forget. Well, up to a point, Wit Van Man. If you are well into middle age and haven't done it since you were sixteen, it's probably best not to hop onto a rented stranger and attempt to make the beast with two seats in public. You wobble and have to put your foot on the ground to stop falling off, changing lanes is hit and miss, and passers-by laugh at you. But when you do manage to go all the way, there is that same sense of achievement. Perhaps the biggest difference between mid-life cycling and sex is that the old girl underneath doesn't mind being called a bike.

Now, what phrase are you least likely to hear in this lifetime? Will it be George W. Bush saying *'Ich bin ein Babylonian'*, or Cherie Blair whispering: 'I'm not wearing anything underneath, your honour'? I suggest the most unlikely of all is Jeremy Clarkson bellowing: 'Let's go by bike.' Jeremy and bikes go together like chandeliers and squash courts. In fact, watching Jeremy ride a bike is rather like watching a large Greek mount a small mechanical goat. Pedalling at a respectable distance behind him over treacherous Dutch cobbles and tyre-grabbing tramlines, all I heard were little exclamations of astonishment. 'Good Lord, wasn't that Jeremy Clarkson on a bike?' 'Don't be silly, he was mounting a small mechanical goat.' You may be wondering what Jeremy was doing on a bike in Amsterdam and, more germanely, what I was doing tagging along. The truth is, he was gate-crashing my story.

I'd mentioned that I wanted to do a piece on the Dutch, who, of all our neighbours, seem to be the most like us, and I wanted to know if there was anything in their political contradiction – the struggle between egalitarian liberalism and bourgeois mercantile rectitude, that we might learn from.

'I hate the Dutch!' said Jeremy. Oh, come on, how can you, even with your capacity to gestate prejudices that is wider than a hippo's front bottom, hate the Dutch?

'I hate them more than anything in the world,' he said, with a satisfied and measured understatement. 'Have you any idea how many caravans the Dutch own? Did you know they eat sprinkles on everything? I'd better come with you – you obviously know nothing.'

And that's how we found ourselves standing on a bridge over a canal with flower-decked barges and families of ducks, in what is arguably the most humanely civilised and comforting city in the world. So I asked again, why do you hate the Dutch? 'I don't hate the Dutch,' he replied with astonishment. You said you did. 'No, I didn't.' Yes, you did. 'No, I said of all our neighbours they were the most like us and that they had an interesting political contradiction thing, what with the struggle between liberal egalitarianism and bourgeois mercantile rectitude stuff.' That's what *I* said. 'No, you didn't.' Yes, I did. 'Get your own story.' Okay, what does 'rectitude' mean? 'Get a dictionary.' You don't know. 'I do.' You don't. 'You're pathetic.' You're more pathetic.

Our free and frank exchange of ideas in the land of Erasmus and Rutger Hauer was interrupted by a group of Dutch youths who all wanted their photographs taken with Jeremy. It turns out he's more famous in the Netherlands than he is in Cheshire – perhaps because the Dutch don't have famous people of their own. There is a Madame Tussaud's in Amsterdam: its big attractions are the spitting-image figures of Rembrandt and Vermeer, and you've got to sort of love them for that. It's very un-Dutch to be famous: the idea of celebrity goes against their sense of civic collective accountability and the quiet serious business of business. But they are very happy in a liberalish way with other people's celebrities.

They are immensely impressed by Jeremy, which makes him insufferable. But then there are the prowling hordes of foul-mouthed, leery English stag-nighters to remind him of what celebrity is really all about. Amsterdam is an agreeable city. It's human-sized, and it doesn't set out to awe you or shout at you. It doesn't make you feel insignificant or out of place. It doesn't blind you with ostentation or stun you with physics. It's a nice place. It's not built for eternal glory but for commodious, comfortable, aesthetic utility. And although it isn't monumental, it is a monument of sorts to the greatest invention of human civilisation: the middle class.

There has been a sense recently that perhaps the milk of liberalism is running thin, that the Dutch are fed up with being taken advantage of, disgusted by the detritus of vice, angered at being a clearing house for drugs and, most important, being deluged – this time by foreigners, economic migrants. The Dutch understand both sides of most arguments. That doesn't mean they're confused, but that things are complicated. Having an ideology, left or right, means you set the political thermostat and never have to think about it again. The Dutch are constantly tinkering with the temperature. Dutch liberalism isn't a position, it's a process.

For northern-English youth, Amsterdam is famous for just two things: the siamese indulgences of young fun, sex'n'drugs. And in these two preoccupations you can best see the Dutch dilemma, the tug of liberty against probity. The two longest queues in Amsterdam are outside Anne Frank's house and a live-sex-act nightclub. I didn't even suggest we venture into Anne Frank's house: I couldn't have stood the embarrassment of Clarkson elbowing his way past quietly weeping New York backpackers, shouting: 'She's upstairs behind the wardrobe.' And Jeremy couldn't face the hordes of his fans at the live-sex show. Like the Motor Show but with more lubricant. It was a Dutch friend of his who pointed out that Amsterdam's humanist claim to be the shrine of Anne Frank was again a very Dutch conundrum. True, she was hidden here, but what about the neighbours who betrayed her and thousands of other Jews, stealing their homes and businesses? It was, I said, very Dutch of him to bring this up.

'Of course, nobody is more open about their shortcomings than we Dutch,' said Jeremy's friend. You mean, like the Dutch Reform Church? What on earth could it have been like before they reformed it? He smiled. 'It's a bit like being gay. We're very keen on gay rights and gay marriage. Have you been to a gay zoo?' No, and please don't mention it to Jeremy. 'But it's difficult to find a Dutchman who's actually willing to be gay.'

The red-light district is set along a canal. There is a museum of eroticism, boasting an animatronic mannequin of a girl with no knickers riding a bicycle with no saddle but just a bobbing phallus. It's very Dutch. We went into a sex shop. 'Hey, aren't you the *Top Gear* guy?' said the chap behind the counter. 'You want to drive the chicks crazy?' He produced 'the Ferrari of vibrators'. The Dutch are very Dutchly open about vice and prostitution. The girls stand in windows; gangs of hair-gelled, shirt-tailed English boys full of Dutch courage and wind window-shop. They grab each other's crotches, snigger and are generally oikish.

'What is it with you English?' asks a prostitute, whose name I've forgotten and whose number I've lost. Less of 'you English', thanks, I'm Scots. He's English. Jeremy, the prostitute and I rented three windows for an hour and sat in them looking at all those young men about to get married and become decent citizens. The prostitute was doing a master's degree in sex-industry law at Amsterdam University; her night job was as a dominatrix. That was exceedingly Dutch. 'The English have real problems with sex, don't they?' If you say so. 'They don't handle it very well. They drink too much and all want to use the same girl because they've spent all their money on beer and dope. And when they can't get it up they abuse her.'

Apart from the English, the red-light area is very well organised. There's an office where the windows and sex cubicles are let in shifts. There's a big white board with a card-index system showing who's working and who's on holiday. There are lots of Dutch rules concerning sex. For instance, you can pay to spend a penny on someone, but not tuppence (it's not a moral injunction, mind, but a municipal health one), and working girls are checked for trim fingernails. Bad manicures can lead to torn condoms. The little business rooms themselves are neat and hygienic, with bidets and plastic bags in the bins. There's a strong, comforting smell of industrial-strength disinfectant.

Sitting in a brothel window is an odd sensation. The cavalcade of men troop past staring bollock-eyed; they laugh, whistle, make obscene gestures. It doesn't exactly make you proud to be a man. We look so transparently needy, pathetic and childish. A guy leers up to my window and gesticulates at Jeremy. I open the door a little. Yes, it is him off the telly. Do you want an autograph?' *'Nein,'* he says. 'I vas wandering how much for straight doggy, no kissing.' Better phone his agent, love.

It's impossible to ignore the fact that the working girls are Asian, African and eastern European and the clients are Italian, Spanish, French, German, Scandinavian and English. Neither the Jades nor Johns are Dutch, and this hasn't escaped the indigenous population either. They are pleased to be liberal about prostitution; they just don't want to be prostitutes and don't want to visit them. On the whole, they rather wish the rest of Europe would stop being so drunkenly infantile about their bodily functions. They are realistic about soft drugs too, but they don't want to encourage it. So it's legal to smoke dope in some cafés but illegal to take drugs into cafés. How the drugs get into the cafés is a Dutch grey area.

For my generation, which associates joints with bedrooms and squats, ordering it in a café doesn't feel right. In general they're not alluring places, mostly looking like corners of university common-rooms. Thankfully, my drug-taking days are over, but for the sake of investigative journalism someone had to skin up, so I took Jeremy and Matthew, our snapping monkey, to a late-night drug den where they could go Dutch. Jeremy approached the bar with all the swagger of a sixteen-year-old carrying a fake ID. 'Hey,' said the man behind the bar. 'Hey,' said Jeremy. 'Hey, you're the *Top Gear* guy.'

For some reason, Jeremy had begun talking in a Dutchish accent, which made him sound like a bad impression of Sean Connery. 'What can I get you, motor man?' asked the barman. 'Something light, not too heavy,' replied the dumb Bond. 'Something a bit okay, but not too dry, with a touch of leather briefcase and Christmas cake. I'm thinking North African rather than New World.' 'I've just the thing, man.' The waiter weighed out a tiny amount of dope. 'A nice smoke, man, mellow, a bit of a buzz with no heaviness. A perfect de-stress, end-of-the-day executive blow.' Christ, things have changed since I was a dealer.

So Matthew skins up. After five minutes, Jeremy has come over all Basil Fawlty. 'No, it's not working. Never does. I'm impervious to hemp.' He says this with a huge, melon-slice grin on the bottom of his face and no eyes at all on the top. He then falls sideways and concentrates for ten minutes on a pair of local heads concentrating on a chessboard. Finally, one of them moves a piece and Jeremy dissolves into fits of nasal giggles. 'Did you see that move? They can't play at all. They're really stoned.' How stoned, Jeremy? 'Really, really, really, really stoned.' He goes up the register until he's squeaking, then subsides into hysterics. 'Good stuff, eh, J.C.?' says the barman, with a sommelier's pride. 'Can't feel a thing, rubbish,' gasps Clarkson.

When I was little, one of our Dutch au pairs asked my father about the war. He'd been in the RAF and had taken part in the devastating bombing of Rotterdam. 'My grandparents were killed in that air raid,' she said. 'You know, we in Holland owe you a great debt of thanks for your help in the war.' That still seems to me to be utterly, characteristically Dutch. 'I'll tell you what's typically Dutch,' Jeremy said. 'Abel Tasman. He discovered Tasmania. He went all that way but missed Australia. How can you miss Australia? That's really Dutch. I bet he had a caravan. It took a Yorkshireman to find Australia.'

INDEX